CW00810502

LIFE IN CORNWALL

LIFE IN CORNWALL

IN THE EARLY NINETEENTH CENTURY

BEING EXTRACTS FROM THE WEST BRITON NEWSPAPER

IN THE QUARTER CENTURY FROM 1810 TO 1835

SELECTED AND EDITED BY R. M. BARTON

DYLLANSOW TRURAN

Originally published by D. Bradford Barton Ltd. Truro

This reprint published by Dyllansow Truran
Croft Prince, Mount Hawke, Truro. TR4 8EE

ISBN 1 85022 112 X
Printed and bound in Cornwall by Troutbeck Press
(a subsidiary of R. Booth (Bookbinder) Ltd.)
Antron Hill, Mabe, Penryn, Cornwall

ILLUSTRATIONS

I, III, IV, V, VI, are reproduced from engravings in Thomas Allom's Cornwall Illustrated [1831]: *II, VII, VIII, are from engravings in H. Besley's* Cornwall [n.d.]

PREFACE

THE CONTENT OF THIS BOOK COMPRISES APPROXIMATELY SIX hundred extracts from *The West Briton*, selected and edited to illustrate life in Cornwall in all its aspects during the first quarter of the nineteenth century. The choice was made from leading articles, international, parliamentary and local news reports, advertisements, correspondence, mining intelligence, sailing lists, packet news, births, marriages and obituaries, as well as reports to the Cornwall Assizes and Quarter Sessions. This proved to be a more difficult task than at first may appear to be the case, since throughout the close study of over 1200 issues of the newspaper it was necessary to maintain proper balance between all facets of Cornish contemporary life whilst at the same time including as much as possible of that mass of material which has hitherto gone unrecorded by historians. Had the significance of every detail in every item been explained in full, the nature of the book would inevitably have been destroyed by the provision of lengthy footnotes at the expense of the original extracts. To prevent its becoming yet another social history book of the more usual kind, therefore, explanations [in the text and at the end of entries] have been kept to a minimum. The extracts themselves, together with their captions, a few of which are also taken from the newspaper, retain the original grammar, punctuation and spelling, however erratic, since these irregularities are part of the character of the whole. A number of the longer entries have been shortened by the omission of certain passages but in no instance has the text been altered.

As source material for this interesting period of Cornish history, early copies of *The West Briton* are rare. A complete bound set from the first issue on 20 July 1810 up to 1844 in the possession of the present writer comprises the personal file copies of John Heard, printer and publisher of the paper until his death in 1823, and thereafter of his widow, Elizabeth, who succeeded him in the same capacity. A few papers bear his annotations and signature. Apart from this set, the only three others known to exist are one in the British Museum—deposited there each week as legally required for copyright and other reasons—one at the Royal Institution of Cornwall at Truro and another owned by the Harmsworth group. Shortly before the Second World War, the latter became proprietors of *The West Briton*, which in 1951 absorbed its rival of almost one and a half centuries to become *The West Briton and Royal Cornwall Gazette*, the last named being older by a matter of seven years.

It should be stressed that in the nineteenth century *The West Briton* was a county-wide newspaper circulating everywhere in Cornwall and was not a district newspaper centred upon Truro, as is the case today.

Feock, 1970 *R. M. Barton*

INTRODUCTION

IN JULY 1810, THE APPEARANCE OF A SECOND COUNTY NEWSpaper in Cornwall, in opposition to *The Royal Cornwall Gazette*, then being published in Truro under Royal patronage and with strong financial backing from the Tories, was very much a sign of the times. The newcomer was *The West Briton*, a radical or 'Reform' newspaper promoted by a group of liberal-minded persons who, like others of the same pursuasion throughout the country, were dissatisfied with the established order of things and anxious to see a gradual and reasoned movement towards both social and parliamentary reform. With the French Revolution only two decades past, such ideas were causing general alarm among the upper classes who profited from the *status quo*, and even in the backwaters of Cornwall it was considered politic in the first issue of *The West Briton* to 'dispel the apprehensions of the timid, who have been led to expect a violence destructive of all order in society'. From that moment onwards, the editors of the two rival county newspapers waged political warfare in their columns for many years to come with unflagging enthusiasm.

A superficial reading of *The West Briton*, however, between its inception and 1835, reveals little of these undercurrents to the mainstream of national life but rather a quarter century filled with rousing event: the soldiering and sea-fights, the press-gangs and privateering of the Napoleonic Wars and the brief struggle with America; celebrations of great victory; the excitements of the copper mining hey-day in the county; cholera, hunger and riot in the 1830's; and the triumphant welcome of the Great Reform Bill, in 1832. Only on minute study of the 27,000 or more closely printed columns of newsprint is there revealed that 'order in society', that inequality of privilege and property, opportunity and wealth, which constituted the real fabric of Cornish life in what might loosely be termed the Regency period.

Not surprisingly, of the private lives of Cornwall's upper classes relatively little is learned. There is the rare glimpse of a grand mansion as a benevolent landlord entertains a few hundred deserving children on its wide lawns; a mention of this or that baronet and his lady quitting their country seat for the London season or a tour of the Continent; and there is published the occasional advertisement requiring a female domestic, a postillion, or threatening with punishment the poacher of game or salmon on a well stocked estate. One reads of a country house newly built in the fashionable Classical or Neo-Gothic style, or of a cottage orné as a country retreat. Fêtes champêtres are given, race-meetings attended and musical entertainments, given by some protegé of one of the upper society, graciously patronised. Truro, in lieu of the exuberant and fashionable metropolis, is dubbed Little London. The births and marriages, indispositions and final journeys of the well-to-do—often by sea or over rough turnpike from far afield to the family vault in Cornwall—are briefly recorded, but from beginning to end they remain, at least in their private lives, little more than names.

Of their public activities and commitments more is learned, for there is little of importance in the county, in the field of local or national government, in commerce or the law, over which they do not exert control. Corrupt or otherwise, they feature regularly in the lively reports of intrigue and bribery which attended the county and borough elections prior to 1832. As the owners of mineral and agricultural wealth, along with the merchants and professional men of the newly risen middle classes, thrifty, hard working and largely pro-Reform, they are involved in virtually every commercial activity in the county. It is the capital which they amass—the wages the poor are not paid—which goes into the development of mines, ports, railways, canals and an improved road network, into education and charitable institutions. In addition, as representatives of law and order, lord-lieutenants, grand jurors, magistrates, they make frequent appearance. In the latter capacity in particular, they meet the common people on their own level, clapping the drunk and disorderly into stocks, dealing first hand with riot and mutiny, selecting parish constables and overseers of the poor, supervising the prisons and lock-ups, the vagrants and paupers.

It is against this wide if sometimes shadowy backdrop of upper and middle class influence, prosperity and elegance that the real drama of early nineteenth century life in Cornwall—red blooded, crude and vigorous—is enacted in the pages of *The West Briton*. Week by week through twenty five years of newsprint, there is gradually revivified the daily pattern of life in the small and closely integrated community of Cornwall's working poor. There comes to detailed life, as if stepped out of the pages of a private journal, not only the familiar figures of working miner, farm labourer and fisherman, but a new and enlivening, more mobile population which has hitherto largely escaped the mesh of the historian: beggars and ballad singers; witches and wizards; conjurors, charmers, counterfeiters and convicts; slavers and their merchandise; highwaymen and footpads, to list but a small number. All emerge in the round, often in their exact reality, with minds we can enter and whose immediate fortunes we can share. They are uglier than imagined perhaps, these great-grandparents, grandparents even, of some of us; stunted and deformed by indifferent diet, marked or disfigured by disease, mutilated by war or by the ignorance and indifference which denied them safety in their ordinary pursuits, and all work-hardened and aged beyond their years. They are, too, probably grosser, crueller and more violent than expected, immoral and too often drunk, a people accustomed to the sight of public whippings and executions, to participating in the savageries of smuggling and wrecking, as well as such entertainments as bull-baiting and tail-piping. We encounter them in multifarious and often nefarious activities in a hundred and one places which fascinate because they are no more, savouring meanwhile sights, sounds and smells which our atrophied modern senses can barely encompass: the stink of fish and blown meat; of tanyard and shambles; of bodies unwashed, unburied; and the dank air of mine levels, or dark and sunless courts, piled with filth. We share, as well, the pandemonium of feasts, fairs and revels, of milling markets, running fights and wrestling matches. We enjoy the resource and sense of humour these people show at every turn, and particularly we relish their sense of occasion, with bells, bands, fireworks, flags and bonfires brought to the fore as frequently, perhaps, as we ourselves secretly should like. For whilst their lives were infinitely more harsh and hazardous than are ours, there remains the feeling, after having followed the fortunes of these ordinary Cornish folk during a lively quarter century, that they seemed to live life so much more *con brio*, and to enjoy it infinitely more, than most of us do today.

By 1835, although slower in this respect than 'up-country' England, the way of life in Cornwall was beginning to change—somewhat for the better. Advances in education, health and hygiene, a general improvement in morals, manners and sensibilities, in part due to the influence of Methodism, a greater respect for law and order, as well as an improved franchise, all contributed towards the making of a county more recognisable to modern eyes. More particularly, better communications put Cornwall in closer touch with the rest of England, already in advance in many of these respects. The local turnpikes were radically improved—under the supervision of Macadam's son, steamships plied regularly and swiftly to London and elsewhere, and the railway age, ushering in a new world, had made its beginnings in Cornwall. Yet these extracts from the early pages of *The West Briton* having been read, the newly forged link with the past cannot easily be broken and Cornwall seems never quite the same again. It is the principal and lasting pleasure of this book that it gives to the county a new dimension, filling it with lively ghosts—many of them skeletons in respectable family cupboards—whose names are difficult to forget and whose existence we recall at particular times and places as we move about Cornwall today.

A LETTER FROM PENZANCE

Our mackerel season is drawing to a close, having been a very successful one, perhaps the best known here for the last twenty years. The pilchard fishery commences this season on a very enlarged scale, considerable preparations have been made: in this place and St. Ives alone between forty and fifty seans have already been put on board. The adventurers have been principally induced to make these preparations in expectation of our increased demand in the West Indies. Wishing well to our country, we would avoid hazzarding an opinion that the preparations are more than commensurate to so contracted a market, which we fear will be overstocked. In such a case, it is above all things desirable, that the fish should be well cured, as a good article will always recommend itself, and do us credit.

20 July 1810

[During the Napoleonic Wars, European markets were largely closed to the pilchard industry, which sought outlets elsewhere. One such lay in the West Indies, where the cured fish was sold to plantation owners for their negro slaves. (See also p. 46)]

RENEWING TRURO'S WATER-BOUNDS

On Friday last the Mayor, Aldermen, and capital burgesses of this borough [Truro], attended by the custom-boat, and the band of the West Essex regiment of militia, proceeded from the quay, in the barge which on a similar occasion had been named the *Truro*, to renew the water-bounds of the borough. Having a fine breeze from the north, they soon reached the extremities of the port, and performed the accustomed ceremonies. From there they returned up the river, and anchored off Tregothnan Point, where with a large party of gentlemen, they partook of an excellent cold collation, provided by Mrs. Pearce of the Hotel. During the repast the band played several pieces of music, with the best effect; and at the close of the day, which was spent with great conviviality, the whole company reached this place highly delighted with the excursion.

27 July 1810

PRIZE SHIPS AT FOWEY

For sale by auction, at the Ship Inn, Fowey, on Wednesday, the 29th day of August, 1810, by eleven o'clock in the forenoon, the good chasse marees *San Joseph*, burthen about 35 tons, and *Saint Antonia L'Aventura*, burthen about 30 tons. Both strong well built vessels, calculated for the coasting trade, captured by the private ship of war *Violet*, Henry Dare, Commander, and condemned as prizes in the High Court of Admiralty.

Immediately after the sale of the vessels, will be sold, their entire cargoes; consisting of about 60 tons of Spanish iron ore of superior quality.

10 August 1810

[From 1807 any vessel sailing to a port under French control was seized as a prize by the British navy, unless it had already paid duty on its cargo in a British port. By this date Napoleon's France dominated the western European seaboard from Italy to Prussia, including Spain, whence these vessels sailed in 1810. In August of that year Wellington's armies were fighting the French in the midsummer heat of Spain.]

BOUND TO THE SEA-SERVICE

To Captains, masters of vessels &c, to be immediately bound to the sea service, two lads, one about 13, and the other 9 years old. Application (post-paid) to the Overseers, of St Thomas-street, Launceston. The boys being strong and healthy, are well worth the notice of persons of the above description. 17 August 1810

[Pauper children, those "on the parish", were normally apprenticed to some trade at the age of nine. The masters, to whom a premium was paid, often overworked and ill-treated these young people who in consequence frequently ran away (see p. 40 etc.)]

ESTABLISHING THE COUNTY ASYLUM

At a meeting of the High Sheriff, gentlemen, clergy, freeholders, and other inhabitants of the county of Cornwall, assembled at the Assizes at Bodmin, on the 22nd of August 1810, 1st—it was unanimously resolved to recommend to the magistrates of this county to direct notice to be given in conformity with the provisions of the 96 chap. of the 48th Geo. 3 in some public newspaper or newspapers circulating in the county, of their intention to take into consideration at their next General Quarter or General Annual Sessions, the expediency and propriety of providing a lunatic asylum, or house for the reception of lunatics, and other insane persons, within the said county.

2nd—That the magistrates of the county be requested forthwith, to take such measures as may appear to them to be proper for ascertaining the number of persons in their respective districts, for whose accommodation, comfort and cure it will be necessary in the first instance to provide.

24 August 1810

CORNWALL'S FIRST LIBRARY

Cornwall Library 30th August 1810. At a general meeting of subscribers held this day, Sir Christopher Hawkins, Bart. in the chair, it was resolved, that, as many books of value are now missing, no book be in future taken out of the library but by a subscriber in person, or by the librarian. Resolved, that the missing books be advertised twice in the Truro newspapers . . . Books missing. Lhuyd's Archaelogia Brittanica; Paley's Moral Philosophy, 2 vols; Junius's Letters, 2 vols; Andrew's History of England; Willyams's Treatise on Education; Collins's South Wales, 1st vol; Morit's Vindication of Homer; Encyclopaedia Brittanica, 6th vol; Liancourt's Travels, 1st vol; Life of Johnson, 3 vols; Steward's Anecdotes, 1st vol; Lord Lauderdale's Enquiry into the System of Government of India; Clarke's Sermons, 2d. vol . . . 31 August 1810

[The library, which was housed in the Public Rooms on Princes Street, Truro, was described elsewhere in *The West Briton* as "a valuable institution, patronised by the nobility and gentry of the county". Altogether 32 books, in like vein, were listed in the above advertisement, which was one of many asking for the return of missing volumes.]

TO CELEBRATE A WEDDING

Married on Monday last, at Kingston-Lacy, Edward Viscount Falmouth, to Miss Bankes, daughter of Henry Bankes, Esq. of Kingston-Hall, Dorsetshire. His Lordship with his usual benevolence has ordered a suit of clothes to be given to every poor person in the parish of St. Michael Penkevil. 31 August 1810

SUICIDE AT MEVAGISSEY

On Monday last Thomas Hunkin of Mevagissey hung himself in a small room in which he had been confined for some time, in consequence of his evidencing symptoms of derangement. He has left a wife and five children. 7 September 1810

A DISASTROUS PILCHARD SEASON

We are concerned to state that the pilchard season is passing away, without affording that quantity of nutriment for the winter, so requisite, and so universally made use of by the poor, that if the equinox should be settled in before many are taken the distress among the poor will be very serious. Since our last [issue], not more than 100 hogsheads have been taken at Mevagissey, and but 70 in Mount's-bay. 14 September 1810

ESCAPED FRENCH PRISONERS-OF-WAR

Caution to owners of boats, etc. The escapes of French prisoners-of-war in this country, and especially those on parole, having of late become exceedingly frequent, and such prisoners being in the practice of proceeding to the points of the sea coast nearest to the places from whence they abscond, and there seizing upon any boat or other vessel which they may not find properly guarded. A caution is hereby given to all owners of boats, etc. to be upon their guard against any such seizure; and they are recommended particularly to be careful not to leave any masts, sails, or oars in their boats, excepting when actually in use. 2 November 1810

ANTI-IMPETIGINES OR SOLOMON'S DROPS

Persons who have unfortunately made use of that dangerous mineral mercury would do well to weigh the consequences before it is too late, and resort to those medicines of established celebrity and character for a permanent and radical cure, and thereby establish their health upon the most firm and lasting foundation. The anti-impetigines, or Solomon's drops, prove of the highest utility in all cases of "depraved habit with infections of the skin"; hence its efficacy in cases of scurvy, scrofula or leprosy, as well as in the confirmed lues [*lues venerea* or syphilis]; and hence by its sanative power, it expels the virus out of the system, and restores it to convalescence. In scorbutic complaints, lues, etc. mercury, antimony and aquafortis have been recommended and tried but they reduce patients who have made use of them to the most deplorable state. Sold in 10s. 6d. and 33s. bottles . . . Every genuine bottle has a stamp which bears the proprietor's name and address, "Saml. Solomon, Liverpool", to imitate which is a felony. N.B. The postage of all letters to the doctor must be paid, and 10s.6d. as a fee enclosed for advice.

2 November 1810

TIDAL GRIST MILLS, ST. ISSEY

To be sold at the Fountain Inn, Wadebridge, . . . all those salt-water grist mills, called Trevorrick mills, situate in the parish of St. Issey, in the said county, late in the possession of Jethro Borrow, against whom a commission of bankrupt is awarded. The premises are well worth the public attention, being situate on a branch of the Padstow river, and in the heart of the best corn parish in the county, vessels of a moderate burthen can at high water lie alongside of the mill pier, and are exceedingly well calculated for mercantile business; the mill-house and machinery are quite new, and with the head-wear and pond-wall are in the most complete and thorough repair, upwards of one hundred bushels of corn per week may be ground at the mills. 2 November 1810

TO PACKETS'-MEN

It having been represented to me by Edward Angove, Esq., the Mayor, and the other respectable inhabitants of this port, that the packets'-men are desirous of returning to their duty, upon the assurance of their being received and protected on board their respective ships, I do therefore, hereby, give this public notice, that they shall be so received and protected, provided they return to their duty on or before Friday next, the 2nd of November, by twelve o'clock at noon, on that day, with the exception of the undermentioned persons, who cannot, on any account be admitted into the service of their Lordships His Majesty's Postmaster-General, namely,—Ezekiel Williams, Joseph Cane, George Wells, William Randtree, William Blackwell and John Parker. 2 November 1810

[On October 24th two packets about to leave Falmouth had been searched by Customs officers, and the crews' little "adventures"—a few articles to sell abroad upon which duty had not been paid—confiscated. In view of their low wages of 27s. per month, the removal of this privilege caused the men to refuse to take the packets to sea, with the result that their commanders thereupon handed them over to the press-gang and they were put on board the receiving ship in Falmouth harbour. Not unnaturally, other packets'-men working out of Falmouth were afraid to return to duty unprotected. As a result of investigation into these irregularities, and the riot which took place in the town, the packet station was removed to Plymouth until January 1811, to the temporary consternation of the people of Falmouth, who saw themselves facing ruin as a result.]

POSTILLION AND FOOTMAN WANTED

Servants wanted. A coachman, to drive as postillion, in the country; wages twenty guineas per annum; clothes, as in all gentlemen's families. Also a footman, wages twenty-four guineas per annum, and clothes as above. 9 November 1810

SPANISH SEAMEN IN PENZANCE

Several serious riots have occurred lately in Penzance by a number of Spanish seamen parading the streets with knives in their hands. Some of the inhabitants have been wounded by them. The Mayor has sworn in twenty additional constables to keep the peace, and it is hoped that the measures already adopted will prevent the recurrence of these scenes. 16 November 1810

SHIPWRECKS ON LOE BAR

In the gales of Thursday and Friday nights last two vessels were thrown ashore at the Bar near Helston the first, it has been learnt was a Spanish polacre [three masted Mediterranean merchant ship] with tent and fontinac on board bound for Plymouth; we are sorry to say every soul on board perished. Some of the wine was saved, and is now in the possession of Mr. Rogers, of Penrose, with whom it will remain a year and a day to give an opportunity for the claimants to appear. The other was a brig, with barilla on board, none of which could be saved. Two of the crew were drowned; several bodies have been since thrown ashore at Gunwallow and Porthleaven we have reason to believe that had the harbour at Porthleaven been completed these two vessels would have been saved the former vessel had been beating about in the bay for four and twenty hours before and could not clear the Lizard. 23 November 1810

[The cargoes comprised tent and fontinac (frontignac), both red wines, of which the former was used almost entirely for sacramental purposes, and barilla. Like kelp (see p. 138), this was a form of impure soda, used chiefly for glass and soap-making. It was imported mainly from Spain, Sicily and the Canaries, and obtained from the ashes of two plants, the salsola soda and the salicornia, grown along the sea coasts for this purpose.]

A STEAM ENGINE TO BE CARRIED

To Carriers. To be let by auction on Tuesday the 27th of this instant November, by ten o'clock in the forenoon, at West Wheal Unity, in the parish of Gwinear, a steam-engine (58-inch cylinder) to be carried to the Blue Hills [Mine] in St. Agnes, the boiler, cylinder and cistern to be put up in one lot, and all the other parts of the engine at per ton.

For any information respecting the above, apply to Mr. Jethro Hornblower, engineer, or to R. Penrose, auctioneer. 23 November 1810

A PUBLIC APOLOGY

Whereas I, Alexander Truscott, of the parish of St. Stephens in Brannell, in the county of Cornwall, yeoman, have, in conjunction with my son, William Truscott, unlawfully cut down certain timber trees on a farm called Down Derry in the said parish of St. Stephens, the property of the Right Hon. William Wyndham Lord Grenville and Anne Lady Grenville, for which they have justly commenced a prosecution against me, and which prosecution has been staid at my earnest solicitation, on my paying the costs incident thereto, and making this public acknowledgement as a warning to others not to be guilty of a similar offence; Now I do hereby most sincerely acknowledge my sorrow for having committed the said offence, and my thankfulness for the lenity which has been shewn to me. Witness my hand this thirteenth day of November, 1810. Alexander Truscott. 30 November 1810

A FALL DOWN A SHAFT

On Saturday last a man of the name of Sarah, in the neighbourhood of

Gwennap, left his home to put a traveller in the right road to Truro; on his return he unfortunately fell into the shaft of a mine and was killed; he has left a wife and eight children to lament his loss. 1 February 1811

DENTAL TREATMENT IN 1811

Mr. and Mrs. Boardman, dentists, at the house of Miss Parkyn, St. Nicholas Street, Truro, beg leave to inform the ladies and gentlemen of Truro and its neighbourhood that they render the teeth white and beautiful, though ever so tarnished, without impairing the enamel; such as are loose they fasten. They also fix real and artificial teeth, from one to a whole set, and human teeth in artificial gums. They engraft teeth also on old stumps, with gold pivots; the same in gold gums, and transplant them with the greatest safety. N.B. The most dangerous stumps drawn, without the use of a surgeon's implement. 8 February 1811

A WRECK CARGO FOR SALE

For sale by auction, at the Golden Lion Tavern, in Padstow, Cornwall, on Thursday the 28th day of this instant March, by 11 o'clock in the forenoon, about ninety tons (more or less) of stone barilla [lead ore], now lying in warehouses at Mawgan Porth, near Padstow, and there to be delivered; salved from the sloop *Janet*, Capt. Yule, wrecked near that place on her voyage from the Canaries to London. 8 March 1811

FOUND, A RED DOG

Found, a red dog, of the Mastiff kind, like one belonging to a tan-yard. It followed a carriage from near Ponsnooth. The owner, on paying the necessary charges, may have him again, by applying to Mr. Matthews, stationer, etc., Helston. 8 March 1811

TAN-YARD FOR SALE AT LAUNCESTON

To be sold by auction . . . all that desirable dwelling-house, tan-yard and appurtenances situate in St. Thomas, adjoining Launceston, now in the possession of Mr. Moses Symons, the proprietor. This house consists of a parlour, kitchen, pantry and dairy on the ground floor, and four very good lodging rooms over. The yard is 90 feet long by 48 broad, independent of the pound-house. Beam and drying ditto, stable and lofts, leather, bark and turf rooms; a back-kitchen and cellar, with two rooms over the same, those are contiguous to the dwelling-house; fourteen handlers, thirteen troughs, five latches (alias spenders), four lime pits, one watering ditto, and two capital drying ricks; likewise a walled garden, 45 feet by 39, adjoining the yard. The premises possess very superior advantages, having a never-failing stream of water at the top of the yard, which from its elevation may be carried to all the pits without the aid of pumps; situate in the centre of famous bark country; an extensive trade carrying on, and a sufficiency of room for improvements. 22 March 1811

THE ROYAL CORNWALL MILITIA

The Royal Cornwall Militia . . . have for some time past been doing prison duty at Dartmoor. We are happy to hear that the country at large is likely to derive considerable advantages from their services there. Forged Bank of England and provincial notes had been fabricated by the French prisoners, and previous to the arrival of the regiment had been circulated to a great amount. By the honesty of our countrymen in refusing considerable bribes to pass them out of the prison, and by their activity in seizing those offered to them, this ruinous and illegal traffic will be prevented, as the Bank of England has adopted measures to that effect. It appeared on examination before J. Elford, Esq., that more than fifty Frenchmen were daily employed in counterfeiting our paper money. 5 April 1811

[Dartmoor prison was built in 1809 to accommodate French prisoners of war].

MEN'S MERCER, TAILOR AND HABIT-MAKER

Robarts, men's mercer, tailor and habit-maker, near the coinage-hall, Truro, is just returned from London, with an elegant well-selected assortment of spring fashions, consisting of everything that is useful and ornamental in gentlemen's dresses and ladies' habits, of the first quality, and from some of the most fashionable houses in London. Grateful to the nobility and gentry, the inhabitants of Truro and the county in general, for past favours, and anxious to merit a continuance of the same, he will take the earliest opportunity of paying his personal respects to his friends and submitting his patterns, etc. for their inspection.

Ladies and gentlemen waited on at their houses on the shortest notice. Liveries of all kinds made to pattern. 10 May 1811

PARCHMENT MANUFACTORY AT PENRYN

The business which was carried on at Penryn in Cornwall as a parchment manufactory, under the firm of Penaluna and Co., was this day dissolved by mutual consent. As witness our hands this 7th day of May, 1811. William Penaluna, Joseph Smith. 10 May 1811

POLDAVY AND CANVAS WEAVERS

To be sold by auction, this present Friday, on the 17th day of May, by three o'clock in the afternoon, at the late workshop of Messrs. Tobias Martin and Sons, poldavy and canvas weavers, at St. John's, near Helston, 6 new looms, with sleas, harnesses, etc., complete; 4 new starching frames, 1 warping frame and spools, several spinning-wheels, quill-wheels, knives, and a variety of other articles. 17 May 1811

[Poldavy was a form of coarse sail-cloth in demand in the mining districts for ore-sacks (see pp. 25 and 39)].

THE WINDSOR FAIRY AT TRURO

The celebrated Windsor Fairy, better known by the title of Lady Morgan (a title which his present Majesty was pleased to confer upon her) is now travelling through this county, and we understand will be at Truro Fair, the Wednesday in Whitsun-week. This unparalleled woman is in the 54th year of her age, and only 18lb. weight. She was introduced to their Majesties at the Queen's Lodge, Windsor on the 4th of August 1781, by the recommendation of the late Dr. Hunter, when they were pleased to pronounce her the finest display of human nature in miniature they ever saw. We shall say no more of this wonder of nature, let those who honor her with a visit judge for themselves. 24 May 1811

NORWEGIAN AT RESTRONGUET PASSAGE

Ran away from his master, Captain Bendh Salveson, of the ship *Hope*, now lying at Restronguet Passage, near Truro, his apprentice, Johannes Tollisen, a Norwegian, about 14 years of age, 4 feet 9 inches in height, brown eyes, can speak but little English, and wore, when he left on Wednesday morning last, a blue jacket and trowsers.

Whoever will bring the above lad to Captain Salveson, at the Queen's Head Inn, Truro shall receive a guinea reward. And whoever harbours or employs the said boy after this notice will be prosecuted.

7 June 1811

[Norwegian ships brought timber for the Gwennap mines into Restronguet Pool, where they anchored. There the cargoes were discharged and the timber rafted up the creek at high water. The Norway Inn, at Perranarworthal, is a reminder of this former trade.]

WOOL SHORN WHILST WET

A caution to farmers in shearing their sheep. A farmer of considerable property in the neighbourhood of Camelford, sold his last year's shearing of wool (a few weeks since) to a respectable stapler, on opening of which it was found to have been shorn whilst wet, and the farmer in order to avoid a lawsuit [see p. 104], allowed the stapler the amount of eighty pounds of wool.

12 July 1811

LOSTWITHIEL QUARTER SESSIONS: BASTARDY CASES

The Quarter Sessions for this county commenced at Lostwithiel on Tuesday last. No business of general importance came before the Court. The following are the principal cases which occupied its attention . . . Peter Love, committed January 18, 1809, by Edward William Stackhouse, Esq., for want of sureties to indemnify the parish of Phillack in bastardy, and who has been confined on the same charge for two years and a half, was continued.

Mary Luke, committed December 16, 1809, by John Rogers, Esq. for refusing to declare the father of her bastard child, born in the parish of Breage, was continued; she is still persisting in her refusal.

Joseph Gill, committed February 6, 1811, by the Rev. H. Hawkins Tremayne, for want of sureties to indemnify the parish of St. Stephens in Brannell, in bastardy was continued.

John Baragwaneth, committed April 15, 1811, by B. Pender, Esq., for want of sureties to indemnify the parish of Wendron in bastardy, was discharged, there being no evidence that the woman had been delivered.

19 July 1811

[A woman was normally imprisoned for refusing to filiate her bastard child, a man similarly confined if he could offer no sureties to indemnify the parish obliged to support it. The prisons were crowded with penniless men unable to fulfil the necessary requirements, women usually being ready to name those responsible for their condition (see p. 137). Mary Luke was exceptional in that she spent four years in gaol for her silence, and her case aroused national interest and sympathy until it was rumoured that there were four earlier children by four different fathers and that, while she was in Bodmin prison, the fifth man of her choice was keeping her supplied with various material comforts she otherwise would never have enjoyed.]

ASSAULT IN ST. NEOT CHURCH

Cornwall Assizes—Richards v. Corse. This was an action for an assault committed in St. Neot Church. The parties being farmers of St. Neot, met in the Church on a Sunday afternoon, to settle parish accounts, when the plaintiff accused the defendant, who was the overseer, with cutting the leaves out of the parish book, and making improper entries. The defendant being provoked at this charge, struck the plaintiff, and gave him so severe a drubbing, that he was unable to attend to his concerns for several days. The assault was proved by several witnesses. The defendant's counsel made an admirable defence; he said it was impossible for any man possessing common feeling to pass over such a daring charge as this; it was in fact to accuse him of robbing the parish. The plaintiff was not satisfied with prosecuting in the ordinary way, but he has put the defendant in the Spiritual [Ecclesiastical] Court; one of the worst places a man could possibly be in. "I don't know, (said the learned counsel) where I would rather not be put than in the Spiritual Court. The defendant is already excommunicated, he cannot be admitted as a witness, nor do I believe the law will allow him ever to marry; so that if he had not the good fortune to have a wife already, he would be placed in a truly deplorable situation." A verdict must go for the plaintiff but he trusted the damages would be moderate, when the jury considered the great provocation given, and how materially the defendant had already suffered in the Spiritual Court. Verdict for plaintiff, 40s. 23 August 1811

TIN BOUNDS TO BE EXTINGUISHED

Notice is hereby given, that application will be made in the next session of Parliament for leave to bring in a bill for inclosing, dividing and allotting, and also for extinguishing all tin work bounds, within or upon certain commons or waste lands commonly called Coisgarne Downs, Chicoose Commons, Cold-Wind Common, Trevarth Common, Killiwherries Common, Feock Downs and Pennance Common, situate in the several parishes of Gwennap, Kea and Feock in the county of Cornwall.

30 August 1811

[Bounding, one of the most ancient privileges of the tinners in Cornwall and dating from at least the twelfth century, gave any man the right to search for tin on unenclosed—and sometimes enclosed—ground; to select the area he wished to work and mark out the bounds of this to the exclusion of all others. Thousands of tin bounds existed in the mining districts, many of them with extraordinary names (see pp. 129 and 150), each one being "renewed" annually by its owner or his descendants, although many of them were of no value once the alluvial tin had been worked out. The possibility of a rich lode being found beneath a bound was always there, however, and the proprietors of the tin-bounds described above held public meetings in strong opposition to the proposal to extinguish them, and with this possibility in mind were anxious to know what form compensation would take.]

BENEVOLENCE AT MARAZION

Mr. Blewett of Marazion, has most humanely supplied the poor of that place and its neighbourhood, with large quantities of pilchards at one shilling a hundred, and gave them as much salt as was sufficient to cure that quantity, for threepence; this at the ordinary rate, when duty is paid, would cost two shillings and sixpence. Many of the poor who were unable to purchase received fish and salt gratis from that gentleman.

6 September 1811

ROPE-WALK IN TRURO

To be sold by auction . . . that messuage, tenement and premises situate in Truro, consisting of a capital dwelling-house, store-houses and workshops, together with a long range of rope-walk and garden ground extending from Pydar Street to the leat leading from Truro to Carvedras.

27 September 1811

[Rope of all kinds was used in large quantities in the mining districts, as well as in the ports and harbours of Cornwall, so that "manufactories" were numerous at or near tide-water, where imported hemp was landed. In this same area, for instance, others were sited at Cometogood, Point, Penryn and Falmouth.]

THE THATCHED ROOFS OF TRURO

About twenty minutes past one o'clock on Wednesday morning last a fire was discovered in a part of the warehouses of Messrs. Plummer, woollen-manufacturers in Kenwyn Street. When first seen, the flames were bursting from the windows of a kiln and drying-house. The person who first discovered the fire resides at some distance from the place where it happened, and being awakened, as he supposes by the reflection of the light through his chamber window, he hurried to the spot, just in time to alarm the neighbourhood and rescue an old woman from the fury of the devouring element, which had already seized on the thatched roof of her dwelling . . .

We cannot omit noticing the very great danger of allowing houses in the streets of a populous town to remain covered with thatch; had the wind been high, or had the fire continued to rage undiscovered a quarter of an hour longer, the blaze produced by the burning thatch would have spread the devastation far and wide.

11 October 1811

A PUBLIC WHIPPING

At the Sessions, or Law Court, held at Launceston, on Wednesday last, Jonathan Barnes was found guilty of stealing oats, and sentenced to be publicly whipped on Saturday next.

18 October 1811

THE HATTER'S TRADE

Wanted, a woman who understands cutting rabbit skins. Apply to

Cotton Tuman (near Colonel Peter's) in St. Merrin, who will give sixpence per lb. more than is now given by any hatter in the county.

25 October 1811

MEDICINES OF 1811

Sleeman, druggist, Truro, has received the following valuable medicines from their respective proprietors, viz:—Cephalic snuff; Ching's worm lozenges; Charcoal tooth powder; Dalby's carminative [a drug for flatulence]; Daffy's elixir; Ford's balsam of horehound; German corn plaster; odontalgic, a specific for the tooth-ache; Pomade divine; Roche's embrocation for the hooping cough; Roseate powder for superfluous hairs; Taylor's remedy for deafness; Trotter's Asiatic tooth powder; Tolu lozenges.

25 October 1811

MULES FOR CARRYING COPPER ORE

To be sold by auction on Friday the 13th day of December next, by two o'clock in the afternoon, at the Oxford Inn, in the town of Redruth, twenty very capital young mules and horses. In good condition, with their saddles and sacks . . .

22 November 1811

[Mule trains, in which each animal was laden with sacks of ore resting on a wooden pack saddle, conveyed copper ore from the mines to the nearest point of shipment, until their replacement by mineral railways from about 1820.]

AN APPRENTICE ABSCONDED

Ran away from her master, Mark Richards, of St. Agnes, Innkeeper, Jane Snell, his apprentice, about 15 years of age, fair complexion, light hair, and about 4½ feet high; wore away a green stuff skirt, a blue coat, a buff-colour bed-gown, and a black silk bonnet. Whoever harbours or employs the apprentice after this public notice will be prosecuted.

22 November 1811

MISTAKING TREVOSE-HEAD FOR STRIPPER

In the gale on Monday evening last, H.M. Brig *Bloodhound*, Lieut. Bray, ran on shore in Harlyn Bay by mistaking Trevose-Head for Stripper, the western entrance to Padstow harbour, where she intended to go. This is the third vessel stranded near that place in the space of a month, by which eleven lives were lost; entirely for the want of the proposed light-house on Trevose-Head, which clearly proves the great necessity for the immediate erection thereof.

20 December 1811

[The loss of this vessel is commemorated in the name of Bloodhound Cove in Harlyn Bay.]

SALMON NETS AT FOWEY

The *Peggy* of Fowey, Cooper master, in working into that harbour, got foul of some salmon-nets, went on the rocks, and afterwards sunk in deep water; part of her stores are saved. 20 December 1811

OIL LIGHTS AT LIZARD POINT

Lights at the Lizard Point, Trinity-House, London, 9th January 1812. Notice is hereby given, that this corporation have, in compliance with the earnest and repeated request of the owners and master of ships trading in, and passing up and down, the British Channel, directed the two lights at the Lizard-Point, which have hitherto been shewn by coal fires, and found very defective, to be altered to oil lights, and the necessary lanthorns and apparatus for that purpose which are now erecting on the towers, will be completed by Thursday the 16th of January instant, from and after which time the said two lights at the Lizard will be exhibited upon the improved principle of Argand lamps and reflectors, producing lights of superior brilliancy, that will be visible to a great distance in every direction where requisite for the guidance of navigation. 17 January 1812

JOHN HICKS' HOUND

Hound lost. Stolen or strayed, from Launceston, on Saturday the 4th instant, a light-colour pied foxhound, 21 inches high, answers to the name of Delver, has a long tail not jointed, full-eared, with a little yellow over them, a brass collar on his neck, marked "John Hicks, Lawhitton", with the letter 'W' on the side, and about eleven months old. If strayed, a one pound note and one shilling will be given (in lieu of a guinea) to the bringer, by the said John Hicks; but if found in any person's possession after this notice, they will be prosecuted for its detention. 24 January 1812

SUMMER PASTURES ON BODMIN MOOR

Farms and summer pastures to be let . . . Lot 4. Hawke's Tor, Kerkees, Druglets and Scrible in the parish of Blisland, all inclosed and contiguous to each other, containing upwards of 800 acres of the best summer pastures for cattle and sheep in Cornwall, constantly supplied with large streams of fresh water, to which cattle always have access. A considerable sum has lately been laid out in clearing the leats [water conduits] draining and fencing these pastures, which will be completed in the ensuing summer. There is a dwelling house for a herd on these premises . . . Lot 5. Botreaux Tor, otherwise Butter Tor, in the parish of Simonsward, lately fallen into hand. Containing about 500 acres of inclosed pasture land, which has usually been let out for pasturing stock in summer, and through which a large stream of water constantly flows. 21 February 1812

TO THE INDIGENT BLIND

Mr. Dove, of St. Austell, surgeon and oculist, has reason to believe that there are many worthy and deserving persons in that part of Cornwall where he resides, who are labouring under all the evils attending a state of blindness, in consequence of their being unable, through poverty, to procure the assistance of a professional man; and, with a view to alleviating the miseries of this pitiable class of sufferers, Mr. D. wishes it to be publicly known, that he will attend to the cases of such persons, gratis, on application to him, at his surgery; but a certificate from some respectable person, that the applicant is a proper object and in indigent circumstances will be required. 20 March 1812

PENZANCE LIFEBOAT SEIZED FOR DEBT

We learn that the life-boat, at Penzance, which several years ago cost 150 guineas, though it has never been used, was on Monday last taken in distress for rent and sold for 20 guineas. The boat was purchased by subscription. Perhaps the gentlemen of Penzance and its neighbourhood feel themselves so burthened by providing the poor with provisions at this season, that they had nothing to spare for redeeming the life-boat ! ! 27 March 1812

[This lifeboat was bought in 1803, the first of its kind in Cornwall. That it had not been used is difficult to explain.]

MINERS' FOOD RIOTS

The present alarming scarcity of grain in this county, particularly of barley, which forms a chief part of the sustenance of the poor, [wheat was generally twice as dear as barley; the current prices per quarter were 117s. and 61s. respectively] has for some time induced an apprehension that the miners, pressed by the advanced price of grain and the difficulty of procuring it, would be led to resort to undue measures for lowering the price, and obtaining a supply. These apprehensions have been in part realised . . .

On Monday last the miners who reside between Redruth and Truro, assembled in great number and proceeded to the houses of several farmers, whom they induced to sign a written agreement to sell them wheat at 30 shillings, and barley at 15 shillings a Cornish bushel, of three Winchester bushels. Where this engagement was signed and corn delivered in compliance with it, the miners offered no violence, but contented themselves with soliciting a little bread, an article of food which some of them declared they had not tasted for several days . . .

On Tuesday the Sessions commenced at Truro, at which a number of magistrates and the High Sheriff attended. Information was received that the miners had assembled in considerable bodies near Redruth, and that serious apprehensions were entertained of their proceeding to violence. Shortly after Mr. Magor, one of the proprietors of Redruth Brewery informed the court, that the miners had taken posesssion of the brewery etc. for the purpose of obtaining the barley which might be there. Messrs. Magor and Co. have for some time sold barley to the poor in their neighbourhood at a price considerably less than that at which they bought it. Immediately a consultation was held on the Bench, and an order was signed by the Sheriff for calling out a part of the Monmouth and Brecon Militia, in garrison at Pendennis. 10 April 1812

[The miners suspected that farmers were hoarding grain in order to enhance the price, or that corn was being shipped "up-country" with the same end in view. The poor harvest which the county had experienced the previous season was typical of Britain as a whole, as were the hunger riots. In Cornwall, on their arrival at Falmouth or Truro, some cargoes of American flour were bought by the gentry and sold at reduced prices to the poor.]

THE SCARCITY OF FLOUR

At a meeting of the Associated Attornies of the County of Cornwall, assembled at the Easter sessions, held in Truro, on the 7th day of April 1812, it was proposed, and unanimously resolved, that during the present scarcity of corn, we will not permit pastry or puddings of any kind, of which flour shall form an ingredient, to be made use of in our respective families, and that we will in every other respect, as far as we possibly can, contribute to lessen the consumption of flour. 10 April 1812

MILITIAMEN IN TRAINING

At a general meeting of the deputy lieutenants of the said county [Cornwall] held, pursuant to the public advertisement, at Pearce's Hotel, in the borough of Truro, in the said county, the 8th day of April 1812, for taking into consideration his Royal Highness, the Prince Regent's pleasure, signified by one of his Majesty's principal Secretaries of State, that the Local Militia, of the said county, should be assembled for fourteen days for training and exercise, during the present year, exclusive of the days of arriving at, and departure from, and marching to, and from, the places of assembly. [The several regiments at this date were as follows:

The 1st or East Cornwall Regiment; the 2nd or Roseland Regiment; the 3rd or North Cornwall Regiment; the 4th or Mount's Bay Regiment; the 5th or Meneage Regiment; the 6th or Pendennis Artillery Regiment. Their places of assembly were Liskeard, Truro, Bodmin, Penzance, Helston and Falmouth respectively. Training was to take place during late May and early June.] Being the times and places adjudged least inconvenient to the public, regard having been had to the local circumstances of the county, and to the season most important to the farmers and fishermen within the same. And that, the whole of the local militia men, who have not been trained in any preceding year, be assembled for 7 extra days preceding the time . . . 24 April 1812

TOWN-DUNG AND SEA-SAND

To be sold by auction . . . all that part of the said barton of Penwarne, now in the occupation of Mr. Charles Thomas, jun. (whose term therein will expire at Michaelmas next) consisting of a good dwelling-house, all convenient outhouses, an excellent orchard of about one acre, in prime bearing, and 82 acres, or thereabouts, of exceedingly rich meadow, pasture and arable land. The above premises are most admirably situated for manure, being within half-a-mile of Mevagissey, where town-dung may be procured in any quantity, at the low price of one shilling per butt-load [a cart drawn by yoked oxen], and within a quarter of a mile of Porthmellin, whence sea-sand may be brought at a trifling expense.

1 May 1812

[Sea-sand was widely used in Cornwall to improve the soils, and for a farm to be near the coast was considered a great advantage. It enabled a farmer to obtain this heavy commodity more cheaply, as well as ore-weed (sea-weed), fishery salt, caff-fish (see p. 49) and lime from the numerous lime-kilns along the coast, all of which materials were used for the same purpose. Town-dung was obtained from cess-pits and street sweepings.]

PUBLIC EXECUTION AT BODMIN

The awful situation in which he [the prisoner Wyatt, convicted of the murder of Valentine, a Jew, at Fowey] was placed was so sensibly felt by the unhappy malefactor that it was with difficulty he could be supported on the platform, and when the clergyman had left him and the executioner was about to let the drop fall, the criminal fell off sidelong, the rope slipped on his neck, and the knot came nearly under his chin, so as to leave the windpipe, in a considerable degree, free from pressure; in this situation, the noise made by the miserable sufferer in endeavouring to breathe, was distinctly heard by the surrounding spectators,—nor was a period put to his existence for twenty minutes after he was suspended. The effect on the feelings of all present need not be described. This shocking scene was occasioned by the executioner's not letting the drop fall suddenly, by which means the rope, which was stronger than ordinary, as Wyatt was a large-sized man, and which had not been greased to make the knot slip readily, got in the position above described. After hanging the usual time, the body was delivered to the surgeons, who were waiting in the prison, by whom two incisions across the breast were made, and then delivered to Wyatt's friends by whom it was immediately interred. 8 May 1812

[In the early nineteenth century many crimes carried the penalty of capital punishment, although principally for offences against property rather than the person. Thus one was as readily hanged for stealing and killing a sheep, firing a hay rick or breaking-in and robbing a dwelling house, as for murder of the worst kind. Public executions—like public whippings—were intended to be a deterrent to others, but there is no doubt that the masses enjoyed such occasions. Executions were reported in grisly detail in the press, most of them far exceeding the above account in this respect, and doubtless made good reading for those unable to enjoy the morbid pleasures of such a spectacle at first hand.]

TWO MORE FOR THE GALLOWS

The old woman and her daughter, whom we mentioned last week as being accused of the murder of the latter's bastard child, at Lower St. Columb, were committed to Bodmin gaol on Friday last, the Coroner's inquest having returned a verdict of wilful murder against them. It appears from the circumstances that the child was a week old when it was strangled:—the stone under which it was found evidently being recently removed, the body was not putrid, and the mark of the cord round the neck quite fresh. . . . These wretches arrived at Bodmin during the time that the unfortunate Wyatt was being executed. 8 May 1812

[The harsh laws relating to bastardy were the cause of much human misery. Every effort was made to conceal an illegitimate birth and it is a matter of some surprise how many mothers survived the ordeal of secretly delivering themselves in the most unsalubrious surroundings during a brief break from their day's toils (see p. 129). Those infants not still-born were indifferently despatched and concealed, or left to die in some hidden spot.]

BROAD CLOTH MADE IN CAMELFORD

The annual meeting of the Cornwall Agricultural Society took place at Bodmin, on Tuesday last . . . The company were highly gratified by the exhibition of specimens of cloth manufactured by Messrs. R. E. and T. Pearse of Camelford, from the wool of merino sheep, grown in this county, which in texture, fineness, and finishing did great credit to the indefatigable exertions of Messrs. Pearse to establish and improve the manufacture of broad and narrow cloth in Cornwall. A proposal made, that every member shall appear at the next annual meeting, in a coat made of wool grown and manufactured in Cornwall, is likely to be adopted. Numerous orders were given for coats by persons present. 15 May 1812

[The "manufactory" had been established only a short period, what was claimed to be "the first piece of broadcloth ever manufactured in Cornwall" having been produced in November 1811. The first merino ram had been introduced into the county three years previously. (see also p. 43).]

CORNWALL INFIRMARY: A WEEKLY REPORT

May 21. Admitted this day one in-patient, and four out-patients, discharged one in-patient, greatly relieved—no bed vacant. Vaccinated 21 since our last report. The days for vaccinating the poor gratuitously, are Wednesdays and Saturdays at eleven o'clock. Professional gentlemen may receive a supply of recent vaccine lymph, by applying at the infirmary any forenoon, except Sunday. 22 May 1812

GATHERING SAMPHIRE

On Sunday last, John Brown, servant of Mr. S. Wade, of Tintagell, went to King Arthur's Island, in order to see some sheep which his master had there. It is supposed he went to gather samphire, and that he fell from the cliff into the sea, as he has not since been heard of. 5 June 1812

[Samphire (once *herbe de St. Pierre*, hence its present name) is a cliff plant with salty, fleshy leaves, and formerly was widely gathered in Cornwall for pickling.]

THE PRESS GANG IN FALMOUTH

Whilst Col. Burgess, the officers, etc. of the Pendennis Local Artillery Militia were at dinner, after the inspection of the corps on Tuesday last; some verses composed by the Laureat of Cornwall, on the occasion, were handed to the colonel, who was about to read them to his company, when he was interrupted by a bustle in consequence of one of the regiment having been impressed, and that too though he was in regimentals, by the gang at Falmouth. He is now on board the *Experiment* receiving ship at that port. This we scruple not to call an almost unprecedented outrage;—these poor fellows must repair to the place of training where they are summoned, or they are to be treated as deserters, and when they arrive there, they are liable to be torn from their families by the impress service.

5 June 1812

[The navy at this date was badly undermanned, due to harsh conditions of service, and the press gangs were very active as a result. The policy of British cruisers in halting American merchantmen on the high seas and impressing men who may or may not have been deserters from the Royal Navy, was one of the causes leading to the Anglo-American War of 1812 (see pp. 37 and 39).]

WRESTLING AT HELSTON

Helston Annual Games. To be wrestled for, at Mr. Ash's Farm, Helston, on Thursday and Friday the 25th and 26th of June instant, the following prizes:—First best man, a capital silver watch, with chain and seal, value £4.4s.; second best man, a prime pair of buff breeches; third best man a gold laced hat value £1. 11s. 6d., and fourth best man a gold laced hat value £1. 6s. The players to be subject to such conditions as will be read on the ground. The wrestling to begin at nine o'clock in the morning of each day. Booths with every accommodation on the ground.

19 June 1812

[Formerly wrestling was the most popular of all Cornish sports and the prizes to be won were usually of a kind to which only the gentry could aspire—fine gloves, an elegant watch, or the gold and silver laced hats or hat-bands which were then fashionable among the upper orders of society.]

FISH SALT FOR SCILLY

The situation of the poorer inhabitants of the Scilly Islands, during the last winter, was truly distressing. These persons chiefly depend for their support in winter, on the fish caught and cured by them in the summer months but such has been the pressure of the times even upon these poor islanders, that they were unable to purchase the salt necessary for curing the fish caught last summer; there being no market to which they could have recourse, the sufferings of the poor became very alarming, as very little fish is caught during the winter. The situation of the Islands being reported to the Bishop of Exeter, his Lordship most humanely laid their case before the Lords of the Treasury, who have most properly allowed a quantity of salt to be shipped at Penzance, for the Scilly Islands, which is to be sold to the poor, free of duty in quantities not exceeding half a bushel to each person. The sloop *Neptune* of Scilly, arrived at the Island of St. Mary's on the 15th instant, with 855 bushels of salt on board, in consequence of orders received from Government for that purpose.

26 June 1812

RIGHTS OF TURBARY

St. Just in Penwith. Sundry estates [in the tenement of Gorland] to be leased, in lots, for terms of 99 years, determinable by the deaths of three lives of the purchaser's nomination. The town-place, cliff, and moors, containing about 33 acres, are in common. The premises are capable of great improvement, lying close to Whitsand-Bay, whence sand and ore-weed [seaweed] may be procured. Each lot will be entitled to cut and carry home from Bartinney Forest, in the same parish, upwards of 3100 turves annually. 31 July 1812

MAIL-COACH AT POULSON BRIDGE

On Friday last, as the mail-coach was passing over Poulson Bridge, which separates Cornwall from Devonshire, one of the wheels came in contact with an angle in the wall, and the coach overset. There were four outside passengers on the coach; three of whom were precipitated over the bridge; the fourth hung by his hands on the top of the wall, until he was delivered by the guard. A Mr. Williams of London, one of the passengers, had his right leg badly fractured, and one of his ribs broken; another a Portuguese, received several wounds and contusions in different parts of his body; the third escaped with a slight wound on his knee. The coachman was seriously hurt and the guard slightly. 14 August 1812

RE-ESTABLISHMENT OF THE CORUNNA PACKET

On Friday last, the Post-Office announced the re-establishment of packets to Corunna, so that we may expect increased facilities in the transmission of intelligence from the head-quarters of our army in Spain. 4 September 1812

[In 1689, at the beginning of the long period of wars with France, Falmouth first became a packet station with the establishment of a mail service to Corunna in north Spain. Formerly the mails had gone overland through France. The Continental war caused the service to Corunna to be discontinued until 1812, when Wellington's final victory in the Peninsular War was imminent.]

ESCAPE FROM BODMIN GAOL

Escape of two prisoners from Bodmin Gaol, August 27, 1812. George Kendall, a blacksmith, five feet ten inches high, aged 33 years, swarthy complexion, brown hair, grey eyes, a large scar on the left cheek, stout made, and one foot larger than the other. John Bayley, a travelling tinker, five feet five inches high, aged 33 years, grey hollow eyes, swarthy complexion, light sandy hair, lost two joints of his forefinger on the right hand.

Whosoever will apprehend and lodge them in one of his Majesty's gaols, and give notice of the same to the gaoler of Bodmin Gaol, shall receive ten guineas reward, or five guineas for either of them.

11 September 1812

CRANTOCK, A THATCHED VILLAGE

On Saturday morning last, about ten o'clock, a dreadful fire broke out in Crantock church-town, on the premises of Mr. William Johns, a respectable farmer of that place. This afflicting event was occasioned by a spark which flew from a smith's forge, which adjoined Mr. John's mowhay, and fell on a mow of corn, which immediately caught fire, and in ten minutes, 400 bushels of wheat, and 500 bushels of barley in the straw; fifty tons of hay, the barns, stables, out-houses, winnowing and threshing machines, and the smith's dwelling-house and shop, exhibited one tremendous blaze, the heat of which prevented the affrighted spectators from approaching the burning mass. All that could be done was to prevent the progress of the destructive element which threatened to involve the whole village in one general ruin, as the houses are almost all thatched. Winnowing sheets were spread on the roofs, and these being kept constantly wet, gave time to extinguish the burning straw, which the wind scattered in all directions; but for this device, it would have been impossible to save the village, as the thatch, from the long continuance of dry weather, was combustible in the highest degree. 18 September 1812

EXPORT OF CORN PREVENTED

At Padstow, a vessel laden with wheat, for Plymouth, was discovered leaky; upon examining her, a large hole (made with an augur) was discovered in her side, supposed to have been purposely done by some of the poorer sort of people, who have for a long time been so much distressed by the high price of corn. 2 October 1812

PRE-ELECTION CALM

"The close boroughs, of course, are unagitated. Liskeard, St. Germans, Michell, St. Mawes, &c. &c. enjoy profound repose. When the day of election comes, the freemen will be informed whom it is that their patrons 'favourably recommend' for the honor of their votes. There can be no doubt that the recommendations will be successful, and the electors will have the honor to eat venison and drink wine with the new members, if they should be present, if not, with their Lord's steward and friends."

2 October 1812

[Prior to the Reform Bill of 1832 corruption and scandal attended parliamentary elections in Cornwall, as elsewhere. There were in the county 21 boroughs each returning two members and two members were also elected to represent Cornwall itself. Most of the boroughs were insignificant settlements, mere hamlets sometimes, such as Tintagel. Often the electors were very few in number and their votes, in consequence, easily "bought" and controlled by wealthy patrons who nominated candidates to serve their particular interests. Those nominated usually had little connection with or concern for the people they represented, and the boroughs were neglected. At this time the franchise differed from borough to borough, sometimes being vested in the ratepayers, or the owners of certain properties, in the members of the corporation, and so on, or as in the case of Tregony, in the "pot-wallopers", a loose term including all those who were able to provide their own food and boil it in their own pot. Less easily controlled were the two county seats, where the franchise was held by all men owning freehold property valued at 40 shillings a year. Nevertheless, the whole system was open to every form of bribery, menace and underhand manoeuvre, and as *The West Briton* was a "Reform" newspaper, the election campaigns were always reported with relish.]

THE 'POT-WALLOPERS' OF TREGONY

Tregony has most unexpectedly shewed symptoms of deserting the old interest, and voting against the proprietor of the borough. The right of election here is in all the householders, commonly called 'pot-boilers', or 'pot-wallopers', and after having kept their plans secret for some time, lest they should be turned out before the dissolution of Parliament; they suddenly turned round, and invited *somebody* to stand for the borough. They have found two persons, and if they can 'raise the wind', they will be returned, if not, the landed property will prevail. 9 October 1812

TIN-STREAM IN SPATE

On Monday last, a girl who was at work on a tin-stream at St. Agnes, went to pick up a hat which a boy had let fall into the water. The stream being greatly swoln by the rains, the girl was carried off, and was picked up half a mile from the place, much cut and bruised.

13 November 1812

A MONITORIAL SCHOOL IN TRURO

The girls' school at Truro, on the system of Dr. Bell, we understand, was opened on Monday last, with about twenty scholars, who it is intended shall be brought forward to take the place of monitresses over Christmas, when it is proposed to encrease the number of the scholars to fifty or sixty. The committee having resolved to request the ladies of Truro to undertake the superintendence of this excellent institution; we have much satisfaction in informing our readers, that several ladies have already undertaken this highly meritorious office. 13 November 1812

[Dr. Bell, an Anglican clergyman, had recently devised the method of making use of one or more older pupils, properly instructed, to teach many others younger. Their knowledge was acquired only by boring repetition of facts but it was better than nothing, and the system served to emphasise the need for properly trained teachers.]

THREAT TO A CUSTOMS-MAN

Custom-House, London, December 1812. Whereas it has been represented to the Commissioners of His Majesty's Customs, that a threatening letter was on the 28th ult, received by Joseph Platt, an officer of the Customs, at the port of Falmouth, of which the following is a copy:—"Pray to God to forgive you, Joseph Platt, your doom is fixed as Perceval [the recently assassinated Prime Minister], received his death by a ball, so you shall fall. Your late proceedings with the packets, has driven me to despair, & ere I leave this earth, my determination is fixed to put an end to your wicked and cruel existance, unless you discontinue your committing such robberies as you and your crew has perpetrated for some time past. I give you, J. Platt, to consider of this as above until 30th March 1813, my Dr. friend although my cruel enemie, and my ruien, for the sake of your soul, pray to Jesus to forgive you, I say again your fate is fixed. A friend to the community, Falmouth 28th Novr. 1812."

The said commissioners of His Majesty's Customs, in order to bring to justice the person who wrote or sent the said letter, are hereby pleased to offer a reward of fifty pounds to any person or persons who shall discover and apprehend or cause to be discovered and apprehended the person or persons who wrote the said letter . . . 25 December 1812

A CASE OF DISTRESS AT CHACEWATER

There is now living near the village of Chacewater, a poor but once industrious man, named Hannibal Thomas, who has for two years past, laboured under that most dreadful of maladies, mental derangement. This unfortunate man, with his wife and five small children, has been chiefly supported by the parish for some time. On Thursday se'nnight, by the death of one of the children, the deplorable state of this miserable family was discovered. In the single room which they inhabit, the father was found confined to the bed, raving in all the wildness of frenzy; the mother also was confined by illness, and near her lay the corps of her infant; and the other children crying for food, which their wretched parent was unable to supply, their pittance not enabling them to secure a sufficiency of barley-bread or potatoes. At this a season of almost general festivity, their case is recommended to the attention of those whose hearts feel for human misery. 25 December 1812

RELIEF FOR THE RUSSIANS

At a meeting of the inhabitants of the said borough [Truro], convened by public advertisement, by the Mayor, at the townhall, on the 15th day of January 1813, for the purpose of considering of a subscription for the relief of the people of Russia, suffering the severest privations and distress, in consequence of the French invasion [Napoleon's Moscow campaign of 1812], Wm. Paull, Esq., Mayor, in the Chair; resolved unanimously, that a subscription now be opened and that the bankers in Truro be requested to receive the sums subscribed . . . 22 January 1813

FALMOUTH PACKET'S EPIC FIGHT

On several occasions, during the present war, the Falmouth packets have been distinguished, by beating off vessels of superior force to themselves, and on some occasions, capturing the assailants. We have this day to record an action, which, in point of gallantry, has not been exceeded we believe, in any instance during the war, though the issue was not as fortunate as that of some others.

The *Townshend* packet, Captain Cock, which sailed from Falmouth for Jamaica in October last, on the 23rd November, whilst in sight of Barbadoes, fell in with two American privateers, by which she was soon brought to close action. Captain Cock and his gallant crew, with four passengers, sustained the unequal conflict with the greatest gallantry for two hours and a half, during which time the crews of the privateers made several attempts to board, but were beaten off with considerable loss. At length the packet having five feet of water in her hold; the main-mast ready to fall over the side; the bowsprit and fore-top-mast gone; the master killed and ten of the crew and three of the passengers wounded, there being besides no prospect of the vessel continuing to swim, Capt. Cock reluctantly struck his colours.

The privateers finding that it would be impossible to keep the packet afloat, plundered her of everything valuable, and then gave her up to the captain and his crew, in order that they might proceed to Barbadoes, into which island they succeeded in carrying her, and where the remains of the master, Mr. Sedgmond, were interred with military honours.

5 February 1813

HARVESTING SEA-WEED IN MOUNT'S BAY

A number of boats were employed last week and the beginning of this, in Mount's Bay collecting sea-weed from the rocks, which are left dry at low water, particularly during spring tides. This weed makes excellent manure for potatoes, and the farmers round Penzance give six shillings for a small boat load of it: these boats are generally managed by a man and a boy, who contrive to gather two loads a day. 5 February 1813

NAVAL TIMBER FOR SALE

Capital naval and other timber. On Monday the 15th day of March next, by five o'clock in the afternoon, a public auction will be holden at the house of Thomas Cory, innkeeper, in the borough of Lostwithiel, in the county of Cornwall, for selling 575 capital oak, ash and beech trees of very large size; now standing in Pelyn Wood, in the parish of Lanlivery. . . . The timber is of very large dimensions, and will answer to the purpose of shipbuilding. 19 February 1813

COUNTERFEIT OF SCORRIER TOKENS

Scorrier House, Feb. 11, 1813. Whereas a considerable quantity of copper penny pieces, having on the one side the device of a steam-engine-house, and the figures "1811", with the words "Cornish Penny", in the margin, and, on the other side, the device of a fish between blocks of tin and cakes of copper, and the words "For the accommodation of the county", in the margin, have been issued by me, and I stand engaged to the public to accept all the penny-pieces at any time issued by me, and pay for them at the rate of one penny each. And whereas Augustus Morcom, of Kenwyn-street, Truro, spirit-merchant, and William Trahar, of Lemon-street, Truro, flour-dealer, have since industriously circulated considerable quantities of other copper penny-pieces, which were never issued by me, or with my knowledge, though they bear the same stamp or device, and have the same figures and words as those above described. I hereby give notice that I intend to call in all the penny-pieces above described which have been issued by me . . . John Williams.

19 February 1813

[The high price of copper caused the Government to issue insufficient small change, in consequence of which it was made lawful for others to circulate copper tokens in lieu. These were each to be one ounce in weight, and their issuers were bound to redeem them on demand in Bank of England money. Many were issued in Cornwall not only because of the county's great production of the mineral during this period but also because of the resulting industrial and trading activity which created a need for them. Generally they were acceptable by all traders and shopkeepers, although underweight and counterfeit tokens had always to be guarded against.]

ORE FROM CRINNIS MINE

To be let, by tender, for one year certain, from the first of April next, with three months notice from either party, for the discontinuance of the same, all the copper ore raised from Crinnis Mine, near St. Austle, to Charlestown, distance about one mile, on level road. All tenders, to be sealed, sent to Mr. Joshua Rowe, at the above mine . . . The number of mules necessary to carry the said ores is supposed to be from 25 to 30.

12 March 1813

ONE DAY'S ARRIVALS AND DEPARTURES, FALMOUTH

Falmouth, Wednesday,—arrived the *Nocton* packet, Leonard, with mails from Bermuda, 22 days passage, all the frigates had sailed from thence on cruises; the *Paz* schooner had arrived out; the *Chichester* and *Freeling* packets, have both sailed with flags of truce for New York. Several captures and recaptures have been carried into Bermuda. The *Nocton* packet was captured on her voyage from the Brazils, by the American frigate *Essex*, and recaptured by H.M. Ship *Belvidera*; all the specie, about £16,000 value, was taken out of the *Nocton* by the *Essex*. Arrived off this port H.M. Ship *Dauntless*, of 18 guns, Capt. Parkin, with a mail from Gibraltar, 21 days passage. It is said she brings an account of H.M. Ship *Java*, of 50 guns, the Hon. Capt. Lambert, having been sunk, after a desperate action, by the *Constitution*, American frigate; the British are said to have had 60 killed, and 105 wounded; the Americans only 8 killed, and 15 wounded; no date nor place mentioned where the action took place, so that hopes are entertained that it will not prove true. The *Java* passed this port, in November last, with a fleet under convoy for the East Indies. H.M. Ship *Bonne Citoyenne*, is said to have passed this port this afternoon, with specie on board from the Brazils. 19 March 1813

[The legal trade of packets was in bullion and passengers (see p. 217). British ships at this time were being intercepted by those of America on account of the state of war then existing between the two countries. This had been declared by America in 1812, basically because of the British Navy's interference with her, as a neutral, shipping produce to France, as well as its impressing of crews of American merchantmen (see p. 32). The dispute was finally resolved in 1814.]

ROYAL MAIL COACH

Goud, Windsor, Stevens, Lang and Co. respectfully inform the nobility, gentry and commercial gentlemen, and the public in general, that on the 5th of April next the Royal Mail Coach from Falmouth to Plymouth will, in future, start from the following places, viz. Commin's Hotel, Falmouth; Stevens's, Red Lion, Truro; Queen's Head, St. Austell; Town Arms,

Lostwithiel; Fountain Inn, Liskeard; Lang's, Ferry-house, Torpoint. Passengers and parcels booked at the above houses. Runs to Goud's Hotel, Plymouth-Dock, and Windsor's, King's Arms, Plymouth; where it meets the London Mail, to Exeter, Bath, etc., also a coach every morning at eight o'clock for London. 26 March 1813

LIFE PRESERVERS FOR SEAMEN

An experiment of great importance to seamen in general, was made at Falmouth on Monday last. A mattress so contrived as to answer the double purpose of a seaman's bed and a life preserver, was exhibited before a great number of spectators, who were fully satisfied that the inventor has attained the desirable object which he proposed. The buoyance of this life preserver and its capability of supporting a human body for any length of time were made evident. A hole in the centre, into which a cushion falls, admits the head, and the cushion is so contrived as to answer the purpose of a cap which preserves the head from injury. It is recommended to the Packet service and is likely to come into general use. 2 April 1813

A SEQUEL TO THE FIRE AT CRANTOCK

Crantock, March 29, 1813. Deeply impressed with a sense of gratitude to my friends for their kindness in proposing, conducting and so liberally bestowing their contributions towards alleviating my late misfortune, I take this opportunity of acknowledging the obligation, and of returning them my sincere and hearty thanks for their favours bestowed, and beg leave to subscribe myself, with the utmost gratitude, their most obliged and humble servant. William Johns. 9 April 1813

[The report of the fire at Johns' farm at Crantock occurs on 18 September 1812. None of the property was insured and Johns, with a family of eight infant children, stood to lose about £2000.]

PARISH APPRENTICE RUNS AWAY

Ran away from his master (Mr. Samuel Peter, of the parish of Lewannick, in the county of Cornwall) on the morning of the 13th of March last, William Jenkins, his parish apprentice, aged about 18 years, has flaxen hair, grey eyes, small legs, is in-kneed, and speaks remarkably quick; wore away and carried with him a blue jacket, a check cloth ditto, one pair of corduroy, and one pair of Russia drab trousers, and is supposed to be in the neighbourhood of Helston.

If the said apprentice will return to his master, he will be kindly received and forgiven for the past, but if callous to this caution, and found in any person's employ after this notice, both he and them will be dealt with as by law presented, and any person who may bring him back, shall receive one pound reward, by applying as above. 9 April 1813

THE MAYOR OF ST. MAWES

Sir, I hope you will allow me, through the medium of your paper, to call the attention of the public to the very great hardship and oppression which the tradesmen of Falmouth endure, in consequence of a new mode of procedure adapted by the officers of the Customs at that port . . . [They] lay hold on various articles of British manufacture, not otherwise liable to be detained *because they are suspicious that there is cause to suspect that they are destined for the packet trade* . . . Mr. Williamson had a parcel of goods of British manufacture on board his own boat; the worshipful Mr. Jago, Mayor of the respectable borough of St. Mawes, and an officer of his Majesty's Customs, took it into his head, that it would be for the benefit of the revenue or of some body connected with it, to seize the boat and what it contained; so he followed Mr. Williamson, who had landed at Trefusis Point, and put the broad arrow upon the boat and its contents. Seeing that Mr. Williamson, who had left the boat, and was proceeding from the beach, had a box under his arm, one of his worship's men followed him, and seizing upon him with the grasp of a highwayman, he cried in the tone of one of that fraternity; "d - - n you deliver what you have." This exclamation was followed by a struggle, in which Mr. Williamson was compelled by force to resign to the mayor of St. Mawes, a very valuable box of British jewelry. But the most extraordinary part of the business is, that this box never reached the Custom-house; mind, Sir, I can't say how this has happened; his worship may have lost or mislaid it; I dare say it will be found yet . . . Yours etc. Job. Thornberry. 23 April 1813

[The mayor and his co-officers, having been indicted for assault, settled the matter out of court by the payment of compensation.

BANKRUPT'S EFFECTS AT CHARLESTOWN

To be sold by auction, (by order of the assignees of the estate of Joseph Dingle, a bankrupt) on Monday, the 10th of May next, by four o'clock in the afternoon, at the Charlestown Hotel, all those stop and tuck pilchard seans, boats and materials, with their stocks of salt, viz. the Porthmeor Sean, the Charlestown Sean, the 3 Sisters Sean, one-16th in the Friend's Endeavour Sean, and one-32nd in the Parr sean, and also all the cellar utensils viz. washing troughs, bucklers, press-poles, oil stands, lade-buckets, fish-stands, scoops, barrows etc., etc. 23 April 1813

TURF-STEALING AT ALTERNUN

Elizabeth Williams, of Alternun, was charged with having stolen 100 tabs and 100 turfs, the property of William Hooper. The parties are poor cottagers, who live near a common, where they cut turf for fuel. They had each a rick of turf on the common, and near each other; and some suspicion being entertained by the daughter of the prosecutor, that the prisoner visited her father's rick instead of her own, she watched her on the 25th of February last, when she saw her go to Hooper's rick and fill her sack, on which she went up to her and charged her with the theft. This the prisoner denied, and said she had taken the turf from her own rick. The prisoner produced no witnesses, but declared the turf was her own. She was acquitted. 30 April 1813

HOUSES OF ILL-FAME AT FALMOUTH

Catherine Mitchell being found guilty of keeping a house of ill-fame in Falmouth, was sentenced to be imprisoned for two months and to pay a fine of ten pounds; and to be farther imprisoned until it was paid. Elizabeth Tresidder, for committing a similar offence in the parish of Budock, was sentenced to be imprisoned a fortnight, and fined one shilling. Ann Lampshire, who surrendered in discharge of her bail, was found guilty of keeping a disorderly house in the parish of Budock, and was ordered to be imprisoned one month, and fined a shilling. Matilda Lisle, charged with frequenting houses of ill-fame, was reprimanded by the chairman and discharged. 30 April 1813

COACH AND HARNESS MAKERS IN TRURO

Messrs. Jenking, Force, Treganowan and Co. (from London), Coach and Harness Makers, beg leave respectfully to inform the nobility and gentry of Cornwall, innkeepers, and public in general, that they have recently opened a manufactory in the above-mentioned lines, at the back of Lemon Street, near Russell's Waggon-yard, Truro; where they hope, as well by the superior execution of their work, as attending to their customers and dispatch of orders, to merit and acquire the patronage of the county at large, and of Truro and its neighbourhood in particular.

Landaus, landaulets, chariots, post-chaises, cars, mourning-coaches, hearses, stage-coaches, gigs etc. made, repaired, and painted, in the best modern London fashions. N.B. Old carriages taken in exchange.

28 May 1813

GATHERING SAMPHIRE ON THE CLIFFS

On Tuesday last, a poor man named Mark Thomas, and his wife, left four infant children at St. Agnes, where they resided, to gather samphire [see p.31] on the cliffs near Perran. Whilst engaged in their hazardous employment, the man stood on a projecting part of the cliff; with one hand he held a part of the rock above him, and with the other he pulled the samphire, which he handed to his wife, who stood a few yards below him. Unfortunately the part on which he stood gave way, and he fell upon the woman, both of whom were precipitated down a tremendous precipice, about 100 feet from the spot where they stood, and fell within about three yards of each other . . . These poor creatures it seems, were compelled by extreme poverty to resort to this dangerous occupation in order to procure the means of support for their children; and it is remarkable, that they did so in order to avoid the necessity of applying to the parish for relief.

11 June 1813

SEANS FOR SALE AT ST. MAWES

St. Mawes Pilchard Fishery &c. To be sold by public auction on Thursday the 8th day of July next, by three o'clock in the afternoon, at the Hamburg Arms, in the borough of St. Mawes, the following shares in seans &c. One-16th of the Cumberland stop and tuck sean, sean-boat, follower and lurker, with all materials thereunto belonging. Three-16ths and a half of the Gallipot stop and tuck sean, sean-boat and follower, with all materials thereunto belonging. About 600 bushels Liverpool salt, 340 barrels for pickling pilchards, 40 oil or cider casks, 2000 barrel staves, 2500 pilchard cask staves, 4000 puncheon heading, 6000 cooper's rods cleft, several bundles of rush, some hhd. hoops &c. 2 July 1813

MERINO RAMS IN CORNWALL

To be sold, on reasonable terms, 45 pure blood merino rams, mostly imported from the Escurial flocks, in 1811 [see also p. 31], and the others from the flock of Lord Somerville. Apply to the Shepherd at Boconnoc, near Lostwithiel, previous to the 20th instant. 9 July 1813

STEALING MILK FROM A COW

Cornwall Quarter Sessions. Ann Holman was found guilty of stealing milk from a cow belonging to James Grey, and sentenced to two months imprisonment. The ease with which this species of felony may be committed, and its frequency, induced the Bench to inflict a punishment, that might otherwise be considered as rather severe. 16 July 1813

A SOCIETY FOR THE PROSECUTION OF THIEVES

A society for the prosecution of thieves and other depradators has been formed in Truro, under patronage of Mr. Paul, the mayor. The society offer a reward of five guineas for the apprehension of such persons as shall be convicted of burglary, high-way robbery, stealing horses or cattle;

stealing corn or lead, or of receiving any goods knowing them to be stolen. They offer a reward of two pounds for apprehension of persons who shall be convicted of stealing hogs; husbandry implements, or shop-lifting; one pound on the apprehension of persons who shall be convicted of robbing orchards or gardens, or barking or cutting trees; and for the apprehension and conviction of persons charged with breaking hedges; stealing gates, &c., garden vegetables, hay or straw, or robbing fish ponds, they offer a reward of ten shillings. 16 July 1813

TURTLES FOR SALE AT FALMOUTH

To be sold, a few very fine turtle, now lying on board the ship *Apollo*, Captain Atkin, just arrived from New Providence. Price 3s. 6d. to 2s. 6d. per pound. For further information, apply to the captain on board in Carrack-Road or to Richard Carne and Son, merchants, Falmouth.

16 July 1813

A MIXED CARGO AT THE MOUNT

St. Michael's Mount. For sale, on Tuesday the 27th of July instant, at two o'clock in the afternoon, about 15 cwt. prime Somersetshire cheese; 2,000 scouring bricks; 400 feet elm; 2,000 feet inch and half-inch elm plank; 3 keel pieces, from 28 to 32 feet long, by 14 inches square; creases [ridge tiles], tiles, bricks &c. The above goods are now landing from the sloop *Bird*, of Bridgwater, and will be sold in small lots, for the accommodation of purchasers. Likewise for sale, a few bolts of Russia canvas.

23 July 1813

LORD WELLINGTON'S VICTORY

The town of Falmouth was brilliantly illuminated on Monday last, in honor of the late splendid victory of Vittoria [in the Peninsular War]. As the inhabitants were desirous of manifesting their exultation on this glorious event, in a suitable manner, they were forced to allow some time for preparation, in order to prevent accidents in a town where the streets are rather confined, and to afford different individuals an opportunity of displaying their tastes in transparencies [topical subjects painted on glass, and illuminated] etc.

At the house of Mrs. Fletcher there was no transparency, but in one of her shop windows was erected a tent, at the entrance of which was a centinel, and inside appeared a number of French flags, eagles, &c. round a table covered with ornamental velvet, and on which lay a book. A well executed figure of Lord Wellington in the uniform of a British field-marshal, over which was thrown a Spanish robe, appeared as stopping to give some orders before he entered the tent, whilst Fame approached to

crown him with laurel. At some distance appeared a monument on which was written, "To commemorate the achievements of Field-marshal the Marquis of Wellington." 30 July 1813
[see also pp. 14 and 33].

STOLEN OR STRAYED FROM REDRUTH FAIR

Stolen or strayed from Redruth fair, on Tuesday the 3rd instant, an old red cow, with a tip on the right ear, and a wen on the right fore leg above the knee, and a white udder. Whoever will bring information, so that she may be had again, shall receive one guinea reward, by applying to Peter Phillips, of the parish of Stithians; or at the Queen's Head, Truro; or to Walter Bray, Redruth. 13 August 1813

CORNWALL ASSIZES

John Budge was convicted of taking the mark of white thread out of a quantity of cordage belonging to his Majesty, and sentenced to be transported for fourteen years. Elizabeth Osborne was convicted of having set fire to a mow of corn belonging to Mr. John Lobb, and sentenced to be hanged. William Wallis was found guilty of stealing and killing a sheep belonging to Mr. Thomas Pethick and received sentence of death. James Northey was found guilty of house breaking and robbing, in the dwelling of John Woolcock, and was sentenced to be hanged. 20 August 1813

[A white strand was incorporated in the King's cordage to distinguish it from all other, and this mark Budge's workmen were found removing from fifty foot lengths of rope in his ropewalk at Torpoint. Second-hand King's cordage was sold only in six foot lengths.]

BURIED WHERE FOUR ROADS MEET

On Sunday last, the body of a young woman was buried at a place where four roads meet, in the parish of Morvah, near Land's End. This unfortunate creature having become pregnant in consequence of an illicit intercourse, resolved to put a period to her existence. She purchased a quantity of arsenic under pretence of a purpose to poison rats . . .

20 August 1813

[At this date suicides were buried at night without the usual religious ceremonies. Over fourteen years had to elapse before the law permitted burial within a churchyard, but still without a funeral service.]

THE CORNWALL MUSICAL FESTIVAL

The Cornwall Musical Festival will commence at Truro on Tuesday next. From the numerous applications for lodgings it has been ascertained that it will be attended by almost all the gentry in the county. The chief magnet in the company is Madame Catalini, who has completely charmed the good people at Exeter, and we doubt not will have equal success here.

27 August 1813

[The festival was one of a number of cultural activities which characterised Truro in the early nineteenth century. It was held in the Assembly Rooms, the façade of which still stands in High Cross, beside the cathedral. On this occasion, because of the general shortage of change (see p. 38), no tickets could be bought at the door.]

VICTORY CELEBRATIONS AT MADRON

On Monday evening, the villages of Newlyn and Madron were illuminated [in honor of Lord Wellington's victory]. Three tar-barrels were set on fire on the top of Madron tower, which had a very singular appearance, and was discernable for several miles round. 27 August 1813

PILCHARDS FOR THE WEST INDIES

The shutting up of those foreign markets to which the adventurers in our pilchard fishery were wont to look for remuneration, has given an inferior degree of interest, to this once valuable source of employment for the lower classes on our coast. A comparatively small quantity has of late been cured and pickled for the West India islands, where they are purchased by planters for the use of their negroes; and the poor in many parts of this county make cured pilchards a considerable article of their food. These, with those sold fresh, during what is called the pilchard season, are almost all that the war has left the ordinary markets for this excellent fish, which annually visit the shores of Cornwall, in vast shoals, and for the appearance of which we used to look with much anxiety. However, it is gratifying to reflect that human ingenuity is rich in expedients, and though it is impossible to put off the pilchards that are taken in the ordinary way, it has been found practicable to make them conduce to human support in another; when mixed with a proper quantity of earth, they form a rich manure, and for some years several seans have been purchased and sent out by farmers, in order to obtain them for this purpose. 2 September 1813

SERIOUS ALARM AT NEWLYN

On Wednesday evening last, some persons at Newlyn discovered a light at a distance in Mount's Bay. As it approached it became more conspicuous, and at length was discovered to be a vessel on fire. As the burning vessel drove directly towards the town, the inhabitants became alarmed, fearing she might be one of the armed ships stationed off the Land's End,

&c., and dreading the explosion of the magazine. As the vessel approached, flaming to the mast head, the sight was awfully grand; at length she took the ground, and continued to burn until the fire reached the water's edge. She proves to be the *Happy Return* of Gweek, bound for Cork.

24 September 1813

GRAMPOUND YARN MANUFACTORY

A person who well understands the management of carding and scribbling engines, billies, jennies, &c., is wanted at the above manufactory, as a foreman; and if a religious character the more acceptable. Apply to Thomas Seccombe, Grampound. 19 November 1813

WATERING SHIPS OF WAR AT CAWSAND

A proposition having been made to Government for watering the ships of war lying at Cawsand Bay, by means of leather hose carried from a reservoir on the adjacent heights, an experiment was made on Thursday last to ascertain the practicability; when by means of an engine worked by four men, a cask which was placed in a boat a mile from the shore was filled with water. The reservoir being on a height above the level of shipping will render an engine unnecessary. 17 December 1813

CORNISH GRANITE FOR A LONDON BRIDGE

Notice is hereby given, that in consequence of the column-stones, acquired for building the Strand-bridge, running something larger than the rest, and the captains' complaining they are more difficult stowage, the freight on such stones [from Penryn] will in future be advanced two shillings per ton, and one shilling per ton on the same, as primage to the captains.

17 December 1813

THE SEVERE WINTER OF 1814

Within the last few days the weather has been more severe than any that has been experienced in Cornwall since the winter of 1794. On Monday night and Tuesday morning the fall of snow was so great as to render travelling, in any direction, exceedingly dangerous. The mail coach which left Truro for Exeter had proceeded about six miles on the road to Bodmin, when at a place called Michell-common, the coachman was wholly incapable of distinguishing the road, and notwithstanding his utmost caution, the coach was overturned . . . After some time the coach was got up and with the addition of a pair of horses was enabled to get as far as the first stage; but it was found impracticable to proceed; the snow, in many places, was as high as the horses' shoulders and it was impossible to ascertain the road across Goss Moor, in which there are several stream-works, and the excavations made in searching for tin being near the road in many places, a deviation on either side might have proved fatal.

14 January 1814

LOSS OF THE 'QUEEN' TRANSPORT

The ship *Queen*, Captain Carr, belonging to London, a transport bound from Lisbon and Cadiz to Portsmouth, with invalids &c. from Lord Wellington's army [see also pp. 14, 33, and 44], put into Falmouth on Monday se'nnight, and brought up in Carrick Roads where she remained . . . until the Thursday following. On that day a gale commenced . . . she parted her cable and went on shore at Trefusis Point, where she became a complete wreck in 20 minutes after she struck. At this awful moment there were upwards of 330 persons on board . . . The horror and confusion that ensued is indescribable; those who got on deck were either swept off by the waves . . . or maimed by the fragments of the rigging and spars that flew about in all directions. Numbers could not make their way up, and as the vessel's bottom was speedily beaten to pieces, they were drowned or crushed to death by the floating planks and timbers.

Some of the unfortunate sufferers who had got on shore as soon as the vessel struck, ran to the little town of Flushing, the inhabitants of which were immediately alarmed . . . The return of day presented a shocking spectacle . . . dead bodies of men, women and children, many of them mangled, several of them naked and others scarcely half dressed, strewed the shore. It has been ascertained that two hundred and thirteen perished. Such of the bodies as were found have been interred in a becoming manner.

21 January 1814

THE LAX CLERGY

Sir, A good deal has been said relative to the evils arising from the non-residence of the clergy . . . The parishes of St. Buryan, Sennen and St. Leven, known as the Deanery, are held by a Rev. Gentleman who resides near London, and who, I believe, never saw these parishes, though he receives between seven and eight hundred pounds per annum for attending to the spiritual concerns of the inhabitants . . . I can assure you that two out of the three parishes are left totally unprovided for, and that in neither of them has divine service been performed since October last. As no banns can be published, even the poor labourers . . . are compelled to purchase a licence, or dispense with the service altogether . . . Parents are obliged to take their infants to the neighbouring parishes, in order to get them baptized . . . The people being without public worship are left to find some mode of employing their time on each succeeding sabbath. A few Sundays since, the inhabitants of Sennen resolved to chase a fox—armed with guns, pitchforks, sticks &c., and after a famous chase, succeeded in taking the depradator, whose head was exhibited on a pike, amidst shouts of triumph. 28 January 1814

RUSSELL'S FLY WAGGONS

Robert Russell, proprietor of the daily fly waggons, which set out from London, the Bell, No. 12, Friday-street to Falmouth, Market-place, feels much pleasure in being able, owing to the blessings derived from the late harvest, to reduce the advances he lately made on carriage.

The proprietor gives public notice, that he will not hold himself answerable or accountable for any article unless the same shall be entered by the book-keeper, or landlord . . . No more than five pounds will be paid for the damage or loss of any article whatever of less weight than a quarter of a hundred (28lb.) . . . No laces, silks, ribbons, muslins, gauze, cambricks, lawns, gloves, books, maps, pictures, prints, umbrellas, chairs, or other furniture, will be paid for in any degree if damaged in the carriage, unless packed in proper boxes or cases . . . Nor will any animal be paid for though lost, hurt, or killed on the journey, by accident. The proprietor requests that any person or persons sending aqua-fortis, spirit of vitriol, or any other ardent spirits, will write on the direction the contents . . . Carriages drawn at the end of waggons will be charged according to their weight . . .

4 February 1814

[Fly or stage waggons, slow and uncomfortable, were a means of transport used only by the lower classes, and served also as carriers of light goods. In addition specie, brought by the packets into Falmouth (see p. 217) was sent to London, a journey of several weeks, in guarded stage waggons. Fares and charges varied according to the price of corn fed to the waggoners' horses, and thus according to the success or otherwise of the harvest.]

FARM TO LET NEAR GORRAN HAVEN

To let, by tender . . . all that capital Barton of Treveage, in the parish of Gorran, now in the occupation of Mr. James Guy. Consisting of one hundred acres of very good orchard, arable, meadow and pasture land, with a very good dwelling-house, and all convenient out-houses.

This estate lies in a ring-fence, is not racked out, and very advantageous for manure, being a quarter of a mile from Gorran-Haven, where lime, sand, ore-weed [sea-weed], caff-fish, and old salt, may be had in the greatest abundance, and conveyed with two oxen and two horses to any part of the estate. 18 March 1814

[The waste products of the fishing industry, old salt used for curing pilchards, and caff-fish, or those unfit for sale, were valuable to farmers as manure, in addition to sand, seaweed, town-dung and lime (see p. 196). The fish were buried for several months before spreading or ploughing in.]

AN IRISHMAN AND A CATHOLIC

Our duty to the public will not allow us to pass over in silence a circumstance which must excite disgust and indignation in every mind not wholly devoid of humanity. After the condemnation of the wretched man [William Burns, who murdered a signal-man of the Land's End signal station, see p. 51] on Tuesday last, some of the witnesses who came from Penzance to attend the trial, prepared to return in triumph. The horses and the driver of the chaise in which they were to proceed, were dressed in ribbons, as symbols of the exultation which they felt on the occasion. Of the guilt of the prisoner no doubt could be entertained, even before his confession; but the display of inhuman joy at his fate, however deserved, would disgrace savages; it was diabolical, even though he was an *Irishman* and a *Catholic*. 1 April 1814

TURF CUTTING ON BOFARNAL DOWNS

St. Winnow, in the County of Cornwall, As great depredations have been committed on Bofarnal Downs a caution to those who are employed in the cutting of turf, or the employer or carrier of the same, who are not duly authorised, Take Notice, that if they are found committing the like trespass again, after this public caution given, a prosecution will be commenced against them by the freeholders of the same. 15 April 1814

PUBLIC REJOICINGS IN CORNWALL

The entrance of the Allied Army into Paris, and the subsequent dethronement of Bonaparte was received in every part of Cornwall, with almost extravagant demonstrations of joy.

Penzance and Newlyn were very brilliantly illuminated on Tuesday se'nnight; the populace erected bonfires in several of the streets, and their more opulent neighbours regaled them with several barrels of beer. The white cockade was universally worn. On Thursday, Marazion and St. Michael's Mount were illuminated; the castle which crowns the summit of the latter, was magnificently lighted and produced a very striking effect: the bells in the tower of the castle, which had not been rung for many years, were set in motion on this occasion. The fishermen . . . of Mousehole manifested their joy . . . when Bonaparte was burnt in effigy. The inhabitants of Liskeard . . . went in a body to meet the mail coach, which forty young men drew into the town. Tomorrow, the proprietors of Crinnis Mine entertain the captains, miners and work people in their employ . . . The captains dine together, and are allowed 12 dozen of wine. The work people will be treated with a very fine ox, which is to be roasted whole, one thousand loaves, and ten hogsheads of beer. In the evening there is to be a grand display of fireworks for the amusement of the jovial company. 22 April 1814

[Napoleon was sent to Elba, escaped, and fought the Allies again at Waterloo. He was then banished to St. Helena.]

THE DRY DOCK AT PENZANCE

The ship *Mary*, Broem master, from Oporto to Liverpool, was driven on shore on the Scilly Islands, in the gale of January last. She was afterwards got off and the cargo landed. The vessel arrived in Penzance on Friday se'nnight, in order to undergo a thorough repair in Mr. Matthews' dry dock, at that place, which is considered by all the nautical men who have seen it, to be the first dry dock in the West of England. The dock has been cut out of solid rock, and cost Mr. Matthews a considerable sum of money; but it is to be expected that he will be amply repaid; as such vessels as may enter the bay in a damaged state, must find it most advantageous to be repaired without the delay of working by tides, as is done when they are laid on a beach. 6 May 1814

[Hitherto vessels were fixed on blocks on the open beach and repaired there but were frequently shifted from their supports during gales. Their repair within the dry dock was cheaper, as well as being accomplished in a quarter of the time.]

PHILLACK WOOL FAIR

An annual shew fair for wool, as well as cattle of all sorts, will be held at Phillack Church-town, on the 30th of June. A considerable quantity of wool, grown on the Phillack and Gwithian Sands, which has long been esteemed some of the finest in the West of England, will be exhibited at the ensuing fair, which will render it well worth the attention of wool traders in general. 13 May 1814

[The north coast towans or sand-hills supported a singular breed of sheep, compact and small, which produced unusually fine wool and flavoursome meat. The latter was attributed to the numerous snails on the towan grass, the sheep apparently relishing the one as much as the other.]

THE THREAT OF INVASION GONE

The Lords of the Admiralty have given notice, that all the signals along the coast of Great Britain and Ireland are ordered to be discontinued, excepting the stations from North Yarmouth to the Land's End, both inclusive; and also from Ballynacotta to Disney Island, both inclusive, which are to remain for the present. 20 May 1814

AN IMMENSE FLOORING SLATE

Last week a flooring slate was sold by Messrs. Tyeth, Shilson and Co., the proprietors of Tresmarrow quarry, to Mr. William Thomas, and placed opposite to his dwelling, against the Town-hall, in Launceston, where its size attracted universal attention. It is two inches thick and contains 84 superficial feet. At the time it was removed there was in the quarry, a slate 30 feet long and 9 wide, containing 270 superficial feet, which it is presumed, is the largest slate ever seen in the kingdom. The rags and scantle in this quarry are also remarkably large. 27 May 1814

CORDIAL BALM OF GILEAD

The greatest discovery in the memory of man is universally allowed to be the celebrated Cordial Balm of Gilead which is a certain and effectual remedy for nervous disorders, juvenile indiscretions, lowness of spirits, female complaints, headache, debility, loss of appetite, relaxations, indigestion, coughs and colds, bilious cases, consumptions, gout in the stomach, impurities of the blood, gleets, seminal weakness &c. &c. Prepared only by S. Solomon M.D. (Author of the 'Guide to Health' and other valuable works) Gilead-House, near Liverpool, Dr. Solomon expects, when consulted by letter, the usual compliment of a one pound note to be enclosed, addressed "Money Letter", Dr. Solomon, Gilead-House, near Liverpool. Paid double postage. 3 June 1814

A PUBLISHED APOLOGY

I, John Hooper, of the parish of Gwennap, in the county of Cornwall, yeoman, do hereby acknowledge that I have, to the injury of the character of Samuel Phillips, of the parish of Redruth, miller, said that he had a quantity of china-clay found in his mill, which I cannot prove, and do verily believe to be false, and have obtained forgiveness, on my publishing this in the *West Briton*, and *Cornwall Gazette*, newspapers, twice. As witness my hand, John Hooper. Gwennap May 30th, 1814.

10 June 1814

[Owing to the general shortage of flour, adulteration with foreign matter, in order to increase its bulk, was not uncommon. The first case of this kind in Cornwall had been discovered a few weeks earlier at the Treyew grist mills, Truro, where china-clay was being incorporated with the flour produced. Its consumption had caused illness not only in Cornwall but also among the French prisoners-of-war in Dartmoor (see p. 20) and Wellington's Peninsular army].

CELEBRATIONS ON THE MINES

[At Dolcoath], tables and benches were prepared for 1500 under the windows of the counting-house, where some of the principal adventurers and their friends met to celebrate together with their men, the return of peace. Flags of all nations were displayed throughout the mine, which with innumerable triumphal arches, added much to the gaity of the scene, and the whole was rendered complete by a cloudless sky. On a signal given by a cannon, the captains marched in their companies of men, women and children, preceded by a band of music to their appointed tables: half a loaf, two pounds of beef, and three pints of porter were allotted to each individual.

At the United Mines, Michael Williams Esq., presided; here 1200 persons sat down to dinner at tables which formed a square, the extent of which measured 138 feet on the outside, and 102 on the inside; the whole of this space was enclosed by boughs of trees, which produced a pleasing effect. There were but two entrances to this square, over which were placed boughs of trees to represent triumphal arches; there were also flags displayed at proper intervals, with mottoes painted thereon, descriptive of the happy event. In the centre of the square, a booth was judiciously erected, measuring 34 feet by 17, and which contained the provisions, &c., 29 cwt. of excellent beef, was dressed, 1,200 lbs. of bread and 600 gallons of strong beer, was provided. The gentlemen with their agents assisted the labourers at their table, nor did they sit down to their own repast until their dinner was concluded. 1 July 1814

TO THE CHARITABLE AND HUMANE

The charitable feelings of the public are called upon on behalf of Grace, the truly distressed widow of Joseph Burnett, who was unfortunately shot in the public street of Lostwithiel, on Sunday the 21st of this present August, and is thereby left a widow with nine children, six of whom are wholly unable to get their bread, viz. Mary, aged 11 years, Jane 9, Grace 7, Helena 5, Joseph 3 and Hannah, only 10 weeks old.

2 September 1814

AT THE PORT OF GWEEK

By order of the Hon. Commissioners of His Majesty's Customs on Tuesday the 20th day of September, 1814, at ten o'clock in the forenoon, will be exposed to public sale, at the Custom-house, in this port, the following goods, viz. 12 pair of silk gloves, 47 leather ditto, 452 cotton hose, 249 worsted ditto, 153 scissors, 8 doz gilt watch chains, 5 doz silk handkerchiefs, 30 doz clasp knives different sorts, 7 doz and 11 razors, 1 doz spectacles, 12 lace veils, 15 telescopes, 500 quills, 2 double bridles, 11 worsted night caps, 2 grose of thimbles, 4 grose of chain buttons, 1 pound of snuff . . . 16 September 1814

FRAUD AND COUNTERFEITING

A tall stout woman of a tolerably decent appearance who has something of the Irish accent, in company with a stout set made man about five feet nine or ten inches high with a dark beard and sallow complexion, has lately been travelling through the county and, especially at fairs, circulating base silver, mostly shillings. In doing this their chief instrument is a little girl, who is supposed to be about ten or eleven years of age.

A gang of women, with false papers as soldiers' wives, have been obtaining money from the Overseers of the Poor in the West of England. It appears this species of deception has been much practised through the county . . .

Two men, convicted of an attempt to impose on the Mayor of this town by false passes, &c. were publicly whipped on Saturday last.

9 December 1814

[With the return of peace in 1814, thousands of troops returned home penniless. Having no prospects, many drifted into a life of vagrancy and crime, sometimes with their womenfolk. Petty offences of all kinds were very numerous, and in Cornwall the authorities were too badly organised and indolent effectively to deal with the situation].

BULL BAITING IN PENZANCE

The unfortunate animal was led through the streets [of Penzance] adorned with ribbons, surrounded by a savage crew, eager to glut their eyes in beholding its tortures . . . On the next morning at ten o'clock, the miserable bull was led to the field of torture, where, with the docility of a lamb, it allowed itself to be fastened to a stake, and the dogs being loosed, it was worried for four or five hours, until it sunk exhausted to the earth; it was a considerable time before it could be got on its legs again . . . Notwithstanding the mangled state of the animal, its brutal tormentors proposed to put it to grass for a week, in order that they might have another day's sport. But happily, as grass is scarce, they could get no-one to take it in. The chief reason assigned for the wish to beat the bull a second time was, that the dogs had not fairly pinned it . . . to seize on its tongue; and that unless the tongue is nearly torn off, the sport is imperfect.

Such . . . was the scene exhibited in the 19th century in the most civilised country of the globe. 16 December 1814

NEGLECTED BOROUGHS

The constitution of some of our boroughs, especially where the scot and lot are votes, and the landed property almost entirely in the hands of one or two persons, is certainly hostile to every effort towards improvement. Of our 21 boroughs, post-chaises are kept only in 7; some have no post-office, others no market. A stranger entering Cornwall at Poulston-bridge, is struck with the distant view of Launceston and the grandeur of its castle. On approaching the town, however, his fears are awakened and he thinks himself lucky in having ascended the hill and passed the south-gate. The access to the castle he finds hazardous from neglect; the mound is studded with pig-sties and the lofty keep undermined by gardens . . . Passing on to Bodmin, should he reach the town at night, he probably encounters a lamp-post (lamp-irons and posts *only* have been fixed at Bodmin for some years). Avoiding this, he stumbles on a clean assemblage of pigs, or is precipitated over a butcher's block into the neighbouring gutter; for though Bodmin is resorted to, at times, by all the rank and beauty of the county . . . it has not yet been found practicable out of decency to strangers, and for preventing the slaughtered carcases in summer from frying, to erect there a market-house . . . At Penryn and Falmouth he will find cause for wishing himself out of their narrow and incommodious streets. And should he return by the south, and escape all other difficulties, let him beware of foundering, as some who have gone before him have done, between the Looes (particularly on the few yards of road leading from West Looe to the bridge), the Scylla and Charybdis of Cornwall.

23 December 1814

ENGLAND'S FINEST HARBOUR

The West Indian fleet, &c. amounting in the whole to nearly 300 sail, left Falmouth on Sunday last, after having rode out all the late heavy gales, *with scarcely any damage; a thing unprecedented in any other port in Great Britain*. The whole fleet got out without the smallest incident.

30 December 1814

[Falmouth was very sensitive to Plymouth's claim to being a better harbour of refuge, particularly since the temporary removal of the packet station from one to the other in 1810 (see p. 17).]

THEFT OF CANDLES

Cornwall Quarter Sessions. John Morcom was found guilty of stealing three pounds of candles from a chandling-house on the United Mines, and sentenced to be imprisoned for one month, and to be publicly whipped at the mine.

20 January 1815

SMUGGLING EXTRAORDINARY

A French vessel not liking the company that wished to join her off

Fowey, ran directly into that harbour . . . During the forenoon she was taken possession of by the Fowey Custom-House officers and with her cargo amounting to 118 casks soon brought within a convenient distance of the Custom-House. Here followed a most disgraceful scene; almost all concerned, including numerous officers, extra-men, curiosity-men, and pilfering-men, began to taste the welcome stuff. Such a division of the prey was productive of everything but harmony among the hunters, from words they came to blows . . . We cannot learn that the Magistrates interfered. The Recorder we know lives a long way off! The Mayor is also non-resident *without* a deputy! The Deputy Recorder was perhaps too busily engaged in calculating his poundage as Collector! The senior Alderman (poor creature) is bed-ridden; The Senior Free-Burgess is Lord knows where, having paid his debt to nature near half a century since!

3 February 1815

'TAIL-PIPING' A DOG

On Saturday last, near Penzance, some men and boys, accompanied by two young women, amused themselves with tail-piping a dog, which they had procured for that purpose. Having fastened a bullock's horn to its tail, they turned the affrighted animal loose and followed it with brutal exultation. The dog, pursued by its savage tormentors, ran down a road called Trereife-lane, when meeting a cart . . . the horses took fright; the driver who was sitting on the shafts of the cart was thrown off, and the wheels passing over his head, he was killed on the spot . . . and the young women on coming up, found that the lad just killed was their brother. We shall not attempt to describe their feelings.

The practice of tail-piping, or, as it is there called, pralling dogs, we believe, ranks as an amusement, next to bull-baiting, in the estimation of the lower orders in the neighbourhood of Penzance.

10 February 1815

SHEEP STEALING IN MADRON

Cornwall Assizes. William Carbis, sen, William Carbis jun. and Francis Bassett, a father, son and son-in-law, were indicted for stealing two ewe sheep . . . From some suspicious circumstances, a search-warrant was procured . . . In a little room called a spense [in Bassett's house] they found a sheep's head, and in the bed-room above stairs, they discovered a fore and hind quarter, with some other parts of a sheep; in a box they got about five pounds of mutton tallow . . . From Bassett's they went to the house of the elder Carbis . . . an old woman, who was apparently ill, refused to get out of bed and the constables were obliged to lift her up, where they found a quantity of mutton between the sacking and bed-tie, and in a vessel by the bed side they got some mutton tallow. They next proceeded to the house of the younger Carbis . . . Carbis was from home and his wife refused to get up. In the bedroom, they found a basket covered with a cloth, in which was a large quantity of mutton . . .

The prisoners are sea-faring men, it appearing they went to sea immediately after the discovery above stated. The Jury found them guilty, and the Judge proceeded to pass sentence of death upon them.

7 April 1815

WARNING FIRES FOR SMUGGLERS

Cornwall Assizes. Richard Cock was tried by a special jury, under the Act for preventing fires from being made during the night on any part of the coast, as signal to smuggling vessels. Nicholas Marshall stated that he is sitter of the preventative boat at Cawsand, which belongs to the port of Plymouth. On the evening of the 7th of December last, the witness with some of his people, was on shore between Rame Head and Penlee Point. About half-past eight o'clock they saw two fires and proceeded towards them; when they came within a few yards of the first fire, the person who was attending it ran away and escaped. On going towards the second fire, which was within 20 or 30 yards of the first, they saw the defendant. Richard Cock, with an instrument called a fire-fork, holding up the reed of which the fire was made, in order that it might blaze . . .

7 April 1815

[Cock had little prospect of being acquitted. According to law, the burden of proof that the fire had been lighted for another purpose fell upon him, and at such a time and in so remote a place, it was obvious what he was doing.]

UPLAND SUMMER PASTURES

Summering of cattle at Hawke's-Tor and Butter's Tor in Blisland and Symonward; containing altogether 1500 acres of inclosed land, well fenced and drained, and plentifully supplied with water, being the best summer pastures in Cornwall, at six shillings per head; horses and colts double the price of cattle.

The cattle will be received and returned to the owners at the times and places following: At Michell, Roach, and Luxullion Church-town, on Monday, May 15; and returned September 18: At Wadebridge, Resprin-Bridge, and Poundscawse, on Wednesday, May 17; and returned September 20: Proper herdsmen have been appointed. 14 April 1815

THE DEATH OF GIANT CHILLCOTT

Died last week, aged 60, at Trenaw, in the parish of Tintagel, in consequence of an apoplectic fit, a person commonly known by the appelation of, Giant Chillcott. His height was six foot four inches, without shoes: he measured round the breast, six feet nine inches: round the full part of the thigh, three feet four inches: and weighed about 460 lbs. He was almost constantly smoking: the stem of the pipe he used was about two inches long, and he consumed three pounds of tobacco weekly. One of his stockings held six gallons of wheat. The curiosity of strangers who came to visit him, gave him evident pleasure, and his usual address on such occasions was, "come under my arm, little fellow." 14 April 1815

WRECKING AT GODREAVY

On Friday last, the brig *Neptune*, of Fish Gard, Griffiths, master, was driven on shore, near Godreavy, in St. Ives Bay . . . Should the weather continue favourable and it be found possible to prevent the swarms of plunderers from a neighbouring depot from carrying her away piecemeal, hopes are entertained that the vessel may be got off by the next spring tides. It is scarcely credible, though unfortunately too true, that some of the ruffians who assembled under pretence of protecting the property, actually robbed the Captain of his watch and plundered all the unfortunate seamen of the clothes they endeavoured to save at the risk of their lives. One of the crew who got on shore almost naked, saw a number of miscreants employed in carrying off some rope, and remonstrated with them on the atrocity of their conduct, when he was told that unless he immediately departed and refrained from molesting them in securing their lawful spoil, they would strangle him on the spot. 21 April 1815

HELFORD OYSTER BEDS

To be let . . . all that oysterage and shrimpage of and in the harbour of Helford in the County of Cornwall; and the creeks and shallows of water thereunto belonging, within the Royalty of the Manor of Penryn Forryn, now and for many years last past in the occupation of Joseph Toy. The oyster beds are in a very flourishing state, and the quality of the Helford Oysters too well known to require any recommendation. 5 May 1815

BODMIN CHURCH IN DISREPAIR

The application to Parliament, for a bill to inclose the commons round Bodmin, in order to defray the expense of repairing the church, having proved unsuccessful, the farther prosecution in that very necessary undertaking has been suspended. Great part of the roof of the building is off, and part of the wall is down; so that this venerable fabric is likely to become a heap of ruins; neither the corporation, their noble patron, nor the parishioners will be at the expense of providing a place of worship for the town. At the last visitation the new churchwardens refused to be sworn, lest they should become liable to be prosecuted for not repairing the church. 12 May 1815.

[Bodmin church was no exception, many others in the county being in a serious state of neglect by the beginning of the nineteenth century (see also p. 69).]

CORN MILLS FOR SALE

To be sold . . . Treovis Mills, in the parish of Stoke-Climsland, in the county of Cornwall. Consisting of a roomy and convenient mill-house, with corn and flour binns, 3 pair of stones; a full-sized bolting-mill; mill for stripping clover; smut and other machines; kiln and all conveniences for making groats; a large and comfortable dwelling-house; pigs-houses; courtilage; and two orchards, fully planted with choice fruit trees, in good bearing.

The mills are well accustomed . . . being situate in a very extensive corn parish, and distant only five miles from Cotele-quay, from whence the produce may be conveyed at very small expence to Plymouth and Dock. 12 May 1815

ROBBERY IN CROWAN

Whereas, William Williams, alias William Cornish, did on Monday last, the 15th instant, rob and carry away, from the house of Captn. Jennings, of Tregear, in the parish of Crowan, various articles of wearing apparel, viz. a bottle-green coat, with yellow buttons, a yellow kerseymere waistcoat, a pair of light kerseymere trowsers, a nankeen short coat, a pair of green corduroy trowsers and many other articles. A reward of three pounds is hereby offered to any person or persons who will apprehend . . . the said William Cornish . . . He is about five feet six inches high, of full complexion, blue eyes, dark hair, has the wound of a bayonet on the left side of his neck, and wore away when he left, a light jacket and grey trowsers, and is supposed to have taken the road to Padstow or Bodmin. 19 May 1815

A STEAM VESSEL IN HAYLE, 1815

A great number of persons assembled at the port of Hayle, on Sunday and Monday last, to view a vessel worked by steam, which arrived there on her way from Scotland, where she was built, to London. The vessel is constructed on a large scale, and is worked by means of a small steam engine, which is placed nearly in the centre. By this the machinery is set in motion which impels her through the water; the vessel in question came from Milford to Hayle in between 12 and 13 hours, with a head wind; a distance of upwards of 120 miles. 9 June 1815

A RINGING MATCH, ST. AUSTELL

On Tuesday, the 27th day of June next, will be rung for, at St. Austell, on a fine new peal of eight bells, the following prizes viz. for the first best peal, the sum of 8 guineas, for the second ditto 4 pounds, for the third ditto, 2 pounds, and for the fourth ditto (if there be more than five sets to ring), a silver bell.

And as a further encouragement to ringers who live more than 20 miles from St. Austell, and shall not have tried the bells previous to the day of ringing for the prizes, they will be permitted to ring one peal on the morning of the said day. N.B. Each set of ringers must bring an umpire with them. No ringers will be allowed to ring on the day before the ringing, after seven o'clock in the evening. 16 June 1815

BUONAPARTE IN PLYMOUTH SOUND

A letter from our Plymouth-Dock correspondent informs us, that at ten o'clock on Wednesday morning the *Bellerophon* appeared in the offing, and at four the same evening she anchored in the Sound; she was accompanied by the *Slaney* and the *Myrmidon*, which have the baggage of the ex-Emperor and his suite on board. As soon as the *Bellerophon* cast anchor, every boat in the port of Plymouth was put into requisition; but by order of the Government, guard boats stationed round her, prevented any near approach of the curious observers . . . About six o'clock, Buonaparte appeared on deck, and instantly every officer there, British as well as French, uncovered. 28 July 1815

[Napoleon was on his way to exile on St. Helena, having been defeated at Waterloo in June.]

FRENCH SALT FOR THE PILCHARD FISHERY

Le Barbier Pradun [of Croisie, Brittany], most respectfully informs his Cornish friends, concerned in the fishery, that as the causes which lately interrupted their commercial relations with France are happily removed, with the flattering hope of those relations being immediately re-established under more auspicious circumstances, he avails himself of the earliest opportunity to return this thankful acknowledgments for past favors, and begs leave to solicit a continuation thereof.

His friends may rely on the utmost dispatch, on his part, in the execution of their orders, and obtaining salt of the best quality at the lowest rate. The present price of last year's best salt is 58 francs per muid, free on board; but as the weather has hitherto been unfavourable for making new salt, should it still continue unsettled, an advance will most probably take place. N.B. No vessel whatever, laden with salt, can clear out of a French port, unless she admeasures full 70 tons. 11 August 1815

AT ARWENACK ROPE-WALK, FALMOUTH

For sale by public auction, on the spot, on Tuesday the 3rd October next, by ten o'clock in the forenoon, about two tons damaged hemp; now lying at Arwenack rope-walk, Falmouth which may be viewed the day before the sale, by applying to Mr. Peter Roberts, the foreman of the said rope-walk. 29 September 1815

SUPERSTITIONS OF THE FISHERMEN

The season for the pilchard fishery is now closed; and, we are sorry to say, it has been far from a successful one. It is curious to remark, the various reasons assigned by the disappointed fishermen, for this lamented desertion of their shores by their annual finny visitants. Some place it to the account of a brutal outrage offered to them a few years ago, by some fishermen, who finding that the smaller fish swarmed by their boats in such multitudes, as to obstruct them in the use of the hook and line, determined to fright them away by the following barbarous expedient. They caught and scarified, a number of the intruders, and in this state, cast them alive into the sea. It is positively asserted, that these poor tortured animals found means to convey to their companions the sad tale of their wrongs . . . Others, however, assert that the above is not the sole cause of the disappointment experienced by the sean-owners. About the middle of the last century, the most opulent of them obtained an Act of Parliament to prevent the drift fishermen from casting their nets within three miles of the shore, in order that they might not disturb the shoals of pilchards which the sean boats were intended to inclose, on their coming into shallow water . . . A superior power was determined to avenge the cause of the drifters; as an aquatic monster, such as human eye had never before viewed, appeared upon the coast, and, wonderful to relate! whilst it passed the drifters, without molesting the fish by which they were surrounded, it bent the whole weight of its fury upon the shoals the ill-fated seaners were about to inclose; swallowed them by the myriads, spread destruction and consternation on every side . . . The failure of the late season is attributed to the reappearance of this monster, or, at least, one of its kindred. 20 October 1815

THE WRECKERS OF BREAGUE AND GERMOE

The Russian galliot, *Flora*, Thot, master, from Bordeaux to Riga, went on shore at Praar Sand in Mount's Bay. It being high water when she struck, she was left dry at the ebb tide; when the barbarians of Breague and Germoe came down in such numbers, that before assistance could proceed from Marazion, they had nearly torn the vessel to pieces and carried great part of her and the cargo, with the seamen's clothes, &c., into the country. A detachment of the local militia which arrived shortly after the plundering had commenced, could scarcely restrain the wretches from completing the work they had so actively begun. 27 October 1815

CHILD SCALDED TO DEATH

A child two years old, belonging to a person who lives at Higher-town, near Truro, was last week scalded to death by drinking boiling water out of a tea-kettle which was just taken from the fire. The infant lived two days in great agony. This, with many circumstances of a like nature, should operate as a caution to those who have the care of children to place boiling water and dangerous liquids out of their reach. A practice too common among the poor, of giving young children drink from a tea-pot, should be carefully avoided. 27 October 1815

'IMPROVED BOOKS' FOR CHILDREN

A list of improved books, &c. for children . . . orders for which are thankfully received by J. Heard, bookseller, Truro. (1) The Yellow Shoe-strings; or the good effects of obedience to parents, price 1s. (2) The Modern Goody two-shoes exemplifying the good consequence of early attention to learning and virtue, price 1s. (3) Learning better than house and land, 2s. 6d. half bound. (4) The adventures of the celebrated little Thomas Dellow, who was stolen from his parents on the 18th of November, 1811, and restored to them on the 3rd of January 1812, price 1s. (5) The first, or mother's catechism, containing common things necessary to be known at an early age, price 9d. (6) Mary and her Cat, a tale for good children, chiefly in words of two syllables, price 1s. (7) Juvenile Plutarch, containing accounts of the lives of celebrated children, and of the infancy of persons who have been illustrious for their virtues or talents, with plates, two vols., price 5s. (8) The mice and their pic-nic; an allegorical tale, representing the manner and customs of the present age; in contentment—a fashionable visitor—high breeding—the effects of fashion—the epicure—an invitation—a consultation and journey—a season in London—etiquette, &c., price 1s. (9) The good boy's soliloquy; containing his parents' instructions relative to his disposition and manners, price 1s. (10) Signor Topsy Turvy's wonderful magic lanthorn; or the world turned upside down, price 3s. 6d. half bound. (11) Industry and Idleness, a pleasing and instructive tale for good little girls, in words not exceeding two syllables, price 1s. 3 November 1815

[Altogether nearly 60 books were listed, on similar themes].

ESCAPED FROM JUSTICE

Elizabeth Phillips, late of the parish of Wendron, in Cornwall, single woman, who was charged by the verdict of a coroner's inquest with the murder of her infant child, escaped from the parish officers at Wendron church-town, on the evening of the 27th of September last. Notice is hereby given that whoever will apprehend and bring the said Elizabeth Phillips before Mr. Pearce Rogers, the coroner . . . shall receive five pounds reward. Description: Elizabeth Phillips, is about 23 years of age but looks rather older, about five feet eight inches high, well made, features long, and nose large, grey eyes, light color hair and marked with the small pox. At the time of her escape she had only been delivered six days, and had on a black silk bonnet, and a brown pelisse. 24 November 1815

EVERY MAN HIS OWN DOCTOR

By the efficacy of Dr. Boerhaave's infallible Red Pill (4s. 6d. *only* per box) persons of either sex (assisted by the invaluable copious directions therewith given) are enabled to eradicate effectually a certain insidious disease, and to facilitate the recovery of health, with ease and certainty, in a few days. 1 December 1815

GINGERBREAD BAKERS FROM REDRUTH

On Sunday morning last, about three o'clock, as several gingerbread-bakers, of Redruth, were crossing the sands from Lelant to Hayle [before the building of the causeway in 1825], on their way home from St. Ives fair, which had been held the previous day, one of the carts, drawn by a single horse, and having six persons on it, stuck fast nearly in the centre of Lelant River. Those in the vehicle immediately jumped out. Five of them safely reached the shore; but one woman, far advanced in pregnancy, was unable to extricate herself from the tide, which was then rapidly flowing, and the morning being very dark. A man who had crossed before, with his cart, heard her cries and went back to her assistance. He succeeded in getting the body out of the water, and had it conveyed to the house of Mr. Trenery, innkeeper, where it was put in a warm bed. Mr. Gurney, a surgeon in the neighbourhood, was immediately called; but his active exertions to restore suspended animation were unfortunately ineffectual.

8 December 1815

BRUSH AND BELLOWS MANUFACTORY

R. Evans begs to acquaint the public, that he has connected the bellows with the brush manufactory [King Street, Truro], and having engaged one of the best workmen in the former business from the metropolis, he hopes by good articles and moderate terms to merit the public favour. N.B. Forge and small bellows repaired in the neatest manner.

5 January 1816

ONE GUINEA REWARD

Whereas the body of Benjamin Christopher, who was drowned on the 16th day of December last, near Plymouth breakwater, has not yet been discovered, it is hoped that whoever may find the body, will give immediate information to his mother, Mrs. Elizabeth Hooper, of Looe Island, who will give the above reward, and take charge of the body.

He was about 30 years old, 5 feet 10 inches high, well made, fair complexion, very light hair; had on a blue cloth jacket and trowsers, blue frock, light worsted stockings, and yellow silk handkerchief.

5 January 1816

[Benjamin Christopher, who lived with his mother on Looe Island, had left there for Plymouth in an open boat, with lobsters.]

ASSAULT ON THE ST. IVES CUSTOMS MEN

Custom-house, London, 4th December 1815. Whereas it has been represented to the Commissioners of His Majesty's Customs, that in the night of the 23rd day of November last, Richard Hosking, sitter of the preventive boat in the service of the Customs, stationed at the port of St. Ives, in the county of Cornwall, seized on shore within the said port, between two hundred and three hundred casks of smuggled spirits; after which, the said Richard Hosking and his assistants were violently assaulted, and obstructed by a great number of smugglers unknown, who rescued and carried away the said goods.

The Commissioners of His Majesty's Customs, in order to bring the offenders to justice, are hereby pleased to offer a reward of £200 to any person or persons who shall discover and apprehend, or cause to be discovered and apprehended, any one or more of the said offenders, to be paid by the Collector of Customs at the port of St. Ives, upon conviction.

5 January 1816

HUNTING ON CHACEWATER MINE

On Monday last, the celebrated pack of hounds belonging to John Vivian, Esq. of Truro, were running a hare on the downs in the neighbourhood of Chacewater. On crossing Chacewater mine, the hare jumped into a shaft, 40 fathoms deep, and was followed by nine of the pack.

A street scene in Launceston

Penzance and its harbour

Every exertion was made to rescue the animals from their dreadful situation; but on getting to them, seven of the nine that plunged into the shaft were found dead at the bottom; the other two were greatly injured. 12 January 1816

ESCAPE FROM THE FRENCH WRECKERS

The brig, *Mary*, Bruce, late master of and from Belfast, for Lisbon, with a general cargo, came into Penzance on Friday last. She had been on shore on the French coast near Saintes, and has a French captain and crew, with two French custom-house officers on board. They were proceeding to Brest with her, and were driven off the coast by the late gales . . . The French people came down by hundreds, like our Breage and Germoe men, with saws, axes, &c, to cut her up. The persons who had charge of her were obliged to fire on them; when two were killed and several wounded. The vessel is detained. 9 February 1816

LANREATH GARLAND FAIR

To farmers, butchers, graziers, &c., Lanreath Garland Fair, annually held the third Tuesday after Shrove-Monday, will now fall on the 19th day of March, and as it has for several years past been considered one of the first show fairs of cattle in the county, it is duly understood, that this year will far exceed any of the former, as the farmers in the vicinity have kept their cattle to promote this highly esteemed fair. 1 March 1816

[It is interesting to note that the prize-winning ox or cow sometimes had a small prize, such as a snuff-box, concealed in the garland placed round its neck.]

A TATTOOED APPRENTICE

Ran away from his master, Mr. James Bennett, tailor, Truro, George Treweek, his apprentice, on Monday the 26th of February last. He is about five feet high, fair complexion, light hair, and has a purple mark, worked in with a needle, on the left hand; wore away a green coat and black pantaloons. This is, therefore, to caution all persons from harbouring or employing the said George Treweek after this notice, as whosoever is found so doing, will be prosecuted according to law. 8 March 1816

CAPTAIN MANBY'S APPARATUS AT PENZANCE

Two small mortars, with lines, &c. on Captain Manby's plan, for conveying a rope to a stranded vessel, have been received at Penzance from London. 15 March 1816

[At the beginning of June, St. Ives and Hayle also received Manby's apparatus.]

UTTERING BASE COIN AT KINGSAND

On Tuesday last two men and a woman were taken up at Kingsand, for making and uttering base coin. These persons had for some time been travelling in this county as rat-catchers; under which appearance they contrived to vend their counterfeits without detection, but suspicion being at length excited, their lodging was searched, and two of them detected in the act of preparing counterfeit shillings for circulation. They were immediately committed to Bodmin prison. 19 April 1816

COPPICE WOOD FOR SALE

About twelve acres of coppice wood, standing and growing in Cosawes-wood in the parish of Gluvias, in the county of Cornwall, being in fine condition and upwards of twenty-one years' growth.

The above proportion of wood intended for sale, will be found within the following limits (that is to say), to the westward of the road leading from Truro to Penryn, within a quarter of a mile of Sticken-bridge; and from thence to the road leading towards the powder-mills; and bounded on the north by the road leading to the powder-mills direct, and on the southward by a certain foot-path leading to the said powder-mills; subject to the reservation of 153 standards. 26 April 1816

[Coppice woods, always of oak, were constantly being felled for their bark, which was bought by tanners, and their timber which was charred for use in blowing-houses. The brushwood was sold for domestic fuel. In view of the widespread felling of timber in earlier years, especially of oak for shipwrights, it was usual at this date to reserve a number of standards or saplings with an eye to the future. So little oak bark was to be had for tanning that a substitute was being eagerly sought at this time.]

CORNWALL EASTER SESSIONS

William Harvey and Henry Pengelley were indicted for stealing a number of flower-roots, belonging to Mr. John Chapple [who] keeps a nursery in the vicinity of Truro; the prisoner Harvey was his apprentice, and the prisoner Pengelley lived at Penwithers, in the neighbourhood of the same place. Harvey absconded from his master's service about nine weeks since, and from his own confession before the magistrate who committed him, it appeared that he and Pengelley laid a plan for robbing the nursery of the prosecutor . . . They took up and carried off a number of plants; but the only one to which the prosecutor would swear was an American flowering shrub called a rhododendron . . . W. Harvey was sentenced to six months hard labour, and at the expiration of that time to be publicly whipped through the town of Truro; and Henry Pengelley to six months imprisonment. 26 April 1816

PUBLIC WORSHIP IN BODMIN ASSIZE HALL

The church at Bodmin, has long been in a ruinous state, and public worship has been performed in the Assize-hall; nor is there any probability that the case will be speedily altered. The corporation are, by prescription, liable to keep the church in repair; but their funds, we understand, are inadequate to the expence which these repairs would now require. We are informed that, a short time since, a meeting of the inhabitants of the borough and parish was called by the Mayor; when the town clerk informed them, that the Corporation was no longer able to repair the church, as their funds were wholly exhausted. They had borrowed £1500, which was expended, and their credit was so low, that they could borrow no more; the inhabitants must, therefore, take the repairs into their own hands. One of the persons present said, that before the inhabitants took the repairs upon them, the Corporation should show their books, that it might be clearly ascertained they were insolvent. On this the Mayor addressed the person who made the observation in the following terms; "You d———d scoundrel, you shall never see the books." After calling the Vicar of Bodmin a liar, and threatening to knock the head off the shoulders of another Rev. gentleman, who was present, his Worship left the meeting, which broke up in confusion. 3 May 1816

LANIVET ANNUAL REVEL

On Sunday last, the commencement of the annual revel at Lanivet, drew to the parish church-town a number of the inhabitants of Bodmin. As soon as the service of the church was concluded the younger part of the congregation adjourned to the adjoining public-house, to qualify themselves for commencing their amusements with proper spirit. Here, it seems, the lads of Roach and Luxillion shewed some jealousy of the youths of Bodmin, whom they regarded as intruders. From jeers the parties proceeded to blows, but after a short skirmish, the Bodmin men were overpowered by numbers, and forced to make a precipitate retreat.

The sports on Monday passed without any serious disturbance; but on Tuesday, the attraction of wrestling brought out a number of young persons from Bodmin; one of whom entered the ring and threw two Roach men. This success was immediately followed by an attack on the Bodmin men, and a general battle commenced. After having for some time contended in the pugilistic style, the combatants armed themselves with bludgeons from a large wood-rick in the church-town; thus equipped, the fight was renewed with fury; heads were laid open; teeth knocked out, and the field of battle was quickly strewn with the maimed. After the contest had continued for about two hours, and when twilight had commenced, victory still hung doubtful; but about this time, the Roach and Luxillion men were reinforced by a considerable detachment from the neighbouring mines. This fresh body of forces soon decided the fate of the day, and the Bodmin men were forced to fly in disorder.

3 May 1816

VOTES IN NEWPORT

To be sold . . . all that very desirable and convenient dwelling-house and walled garden, situate at Newport, near Launceston, in the county of Cornwall . . . The whole forming a charming residence for a genteel family, and the purchaser, residing thereon, will be entitled to vote for members to serve in Parliament for the ancient borough of Newport, or should he choose to divide the premises, it would constitute two votes, being held under two distinct leases.

31 May 1816

THE WELL-KNOWN WATER-DOCTOR

The public are respectfully informed, that Dr. Taylor, the well-known water-doctor, from Manchester, who has performed so many cures in this neighbourhood, from the multiplicity of business in the vicinity of Bodmin and Truro, has not been able to attend to the patients as well as he could have wished, which has obliged them to remain all night, to their great inconvenience and additional expence; the doctor has now the pleasure to announce that, for the accommodation of his numerous patients, he will attend at the following places every market-day, where man, woman or child, bringing or sending their morning urine, may be told whether they are curable or not, free of any expence, as he charges nothing for his advice whatever.

Dr. Taylor may be consulted at the New Inn, Falmouth, every Tuesday, at the White Hart, Truro, every Wednesday; at the Star Inn, Penzance, every Thursday; at the London Inn, Redruth, every Friday; and at the Fountain Inn, Liskeard, every Saturday . . .

31 May 1816

TRENGROUSE'S ROCKET APPARATUS

Mr. Trengrouse's contrivance for throwing a line is admirably simple in construction, and not the less easy and successful in execution. The experiment was three times repeated, across the mouth of Porthleven harbour, in the presence of the Mayor of Helston, and several other gentlemen, to all of whom it afforded the utmost satisfaction.

Nothing of the sort could well be conceived to exceed, in point of facility and expedition, the manner in which a man was safely conveyed, four successive times, across the harbour, a distance of about 160 yards; twice in a flexible chair; which by means of two rollers, ran, in a state of suspension, along a tightened hawser; and twice upon the surface of the water, enwrapped in a float of cork, which encompassed the body, like a pair of stays, without in any measure, impeding the free motion of the limbs. 14 June 1816

MIDSUMMER EVE AT PENZANCE

Midsummer Eve was kept at Penzance with all the accustomed éclat of bonfires, fire-works &c. The streets appeared in a blaze, and were crowded with lads and lasses from the neighbourhood, in their holiday clothes. Midsummer day being very fine, numbers flocked to the quay-fair, where they were indulged with one or two pennyworth of sea, by the fishermen, who attended in their boats decorated with such flags as they could procure. During their aquatic excursion, the company in each boat were treated with national airs, &c, by a fiddler or fifer, employed for the occasion. Dr. Paris gave to a number of the gentlemen and ladies of the town and neighbourhood tea and a ball, at the new bathing-rooms; during which some excellent fire-works were let off on the beach. 28 June 1816

TO MANUFACTURERS AND FARMERS

Wanted, for about fifteen or twenty healthy boys and girls, from 8 to 12 years of age, masters who will undertake to teach them to get their livelihood. For particulars, application may be made, if by letter post-paid, to Mr. Thomas Simmons, or Mr. Richard Sampson, overseers of the parish of Gwennap. 12 July 1816

BARGES ON TRURO RIVER

To shippers of tin, Truro, July 9, 1816. We, whose names are hereunder subscribed, being the masters and men belonging to the *Charlotte* and *Truro* barges, employed in carrying tin, goods and merchandize, in and from Truro, to Falmouth, Penryn and St. Mawes, have unanimously agreed to carry down tin in either of the said barges, at the following reduced prices, in respect of what is now paid to other barges in Truro river, viz.

To any place or station below Turner-wear, and within the rock of Falmouth, at or for twenty shillings per load, that is, from one ton to twenty. And from Truro quay to any place or station at or above Turner-wear, towards Truro, for fifteen shillings per load, of the weight above mentioned. John Buzza, master of the *Charlotte*, Nicholas Scobell, master of the *Truro*, Thomas Martin, Thomas Thomas, Joseph Buzza, Richard Buzza. 12 July 1816

SHARES IN MOUNT'S BAY SEANS

To be sold by auction, on Saturday the 27th day of July instant by four o'clock in the afternoon, at the Union Hotel, in Penzance, the several shares in the following seans, viz. nine 32nds in the Delight and Diligent Seans, at Newlyn; one 8th in the Resolute, Defence and Ardent Seans, at ditto; one 8th in the Vigilant Sean, at ditto; one 16th in the Endeavour Sean at ditto; one 16th in the Mary and Ann Sean, at ditto; eight 32nds in the Lord Nelson Sean, at St. Michael's Mount; eight 32nds in the Marazion Sean, at ditto; three 64ths in the Blewett fish cellar at ditto.

19 July 1816

CADGWITH SMUGGLERS PRESS-GANGED

The *Hind* revenue cutter sent into Falmouth on Tuesday last a boat belonging to Cadgwith, having on board 50 ankers of spirits. Four men, who were on board the smuggler, have been taken to Plymouth for the purpose of being put on board the fleet about to sail under Lord Exmouth, against the Algerines. 26 July 1816

[This fleet, of 25 ships, sailed from Plymouth with the purpose of bombarding Algiers in an endeavour to put an end to the depredations of Barbary pirates and the seizure of men from British ships for slavery. Fortunately for the four smugglers, the expedition was a total success, and it is probable that eventually they returned to England.]

FRENCH SMUGGLERS IN LOOE

On Thursday last a small French vessel was observed to be nearly on shore, not far from Looe harbour; happily by the exertions of persons belonging to the port, she was got in safely . . . The vessel is chiefly laden with fruit, and having entered it at the Custom-house at Looe, a great part of the cargo was speedily disposed of. The custom-house officers took particular notice of twelve elegantly formed toys, in the shape of horses, the bodies of which were about four inches in diameter; and on handling them, they were led to suppose that they were more valuable than they appeared to be. Accordingly, one of them was embowelled, which led to a similar examination of the rest. The result was, the finding of 51 pair of silk stockings and 9 silk shawls which had been carefully secreted in the bodies of these elegant play-things. The King's broad arrow has been placed on the vessel and cargo, in consequence of this unlucky discovery.

23 August 1816

WATERWHEELS AT PERRANPORTH

To be sold by auction, at St. George Mine, in the parish of Perranzabuloe, in the county of Cornwall, on Thursday the 3rd day of October next, and every following Tuesday and Thursday, until the whole is sold, the following materials, viz. one water-wheel 40 feet diameter, and 3 feet wide over the breast; one 34 feet ditto and 3 feet ditto; one 23 feet ditto and 3 feet ditto; one 34 feet ditto and 2 feet ditto . . .

20 September 1816

CROSSING TO ST. MICHAEL'S MOUNT

On Monday last, during the time of flood tide, as a carriage, drawn by two oxen and three horses, was attempting to pass on the causeway that unites St. Michael's Mount to Marazion, and which is completely covered by the tide some time before high water, they were swept off into deep water, and all would have been lost but for the timely assistance of boats from the Mount which succeeded in saving all but one horse, which was drowned.

4 October 1816

A CARGO FOR ST. HELENA

The brig *Adolphus*, which put into Falmouth, on Tuesday last, is bound for St. Helena and the Cape of Good Hope. She has on board 50 tons of iron railing, for the enclosing a park, &c. for Bonaparte.

4 October 1816

PONSANOOTH WOOLLEN MANUFACTORY

To be sold by auction, on Wednesday the 20th November inst. by three o'clock in the afternoon, at the Red Lion Inn, in the borough of Penryn, all that valuable leasehold property, determinable on the deaths of two good lives, now in the occupation of Mrs. Susanna Williams, situate at Ponsanooth, where an extensive woollen manufactory has been carried on for at least 200 years, with tucking-mills, racks &c, acknowledged to be one of the first water-courses in the county . . .

15 November 1816

THE WORST STORM FOR DECADES

On Sunday last, soon after dark, a violent gale of wind came on from the south-east, which about midnight increased to one of the most tremendous storms which the oldest inhabitants recollect to have witnessed, being scarcely equalled by that which carried away the Eddystone lighthouse many years ago . . .

Kingsand and Cawsand have suffered considerably; the damages done at these places is estimated at upwards of five thousand pounds. One house, with a man who dwelt in it, was completely swept away. Some of the fish-cellars, with nets, &c, were swept into the ocean. Nearly all the quays for loading lime-stone, &c, round the port, are either damaged or wholly swept away; of one lately built by Mr. Fuge, which cost upwards of £600, not a stone is left on another. . . .

Looe: In consequence of the violent gale on Sunday night, the tide on

Monday morning rose to a height scarcely ever before remembered here; the lower parts of the town were inundated; the quays damaged; the cannon, 18-pounders, washed off the platforms; cellar doors burst in, and property to a considerable amount damaged or destroyed. In the lower streets, the inhabitants were confined to the upper stories, being unable to escape. A vessel of 60 tons burthen was thrown upon the quay by one wave, and shortly afterwards carried off by another. When the tide ebbed, the streets were found covered with ore-weed, &c. The damages at this place are estimated at £1000.

At Polperro the ruin is dreadful; out of 45 fishing boats belonging to the place, 30 have been dashed to atoms; most of those remaining are incapable of being repaired. Upwards of 60 families are deprived of bread. The pier is nearly destroyed and several dwellings and cellars have been washed away. Two seans are totally lost, and the greater part of the fish-salt in the town is washed away. Three new boats; all the timber, tools, &c. which were in a shipwright's yard, have been carried away, and the adjoining dwelling-house much injured. The loss to the proprietor, Mr. John Rundle, is nearly £800. The entire damage alone at Polperro is upwards of £6000.

Penzance, Marazion, &c: In the course of the night the storm increased to a hurricane. At day-break a most awful scene presented itself. The sea was mountains high, and impelled by the wind ran up much farther than was ever remembered. The May-pole at Marazion which had, for many years braved the fury of the storm, was washed away, with the cliff on which it stood . . . At Penzance, the waves broke higher than the mast-heads of the vessels, carrying everything before them . . . A storm somewhat similar to that on Sunday night, was experienced on Dec. 7, 1771. At that time a moor-stone pig's trough, at Mousehole was, with the piggery to which it belonged, carried away by the sea, nor could it ever be found. During the gale of Sunday night it was cast on shore.

24 January 1817

THE BREAGE AND GERMOE WRECKERS AGAIN

On Saturday last, during a thick fog, and the wind at south, an account was received at Penzance and Marazion that a large brig was anchored in a most perilous situation, within half a mile of the shore, near Porthleven . . . The shore was covered by hundreds of barbarians belonging to Breage and Germoe, eagerly watching for an opportunity to plunder.

31 January 1817

PAUPERS' HOUSES BURNED AT ST. BURYAN

About 12 o'clock on the night of Saturday last, a range of houses occupied by the poor of the parish of St. Buryan, about 6 miles from Penzance, was discovered to be on fire, and as no engine could be procured, the flames spread with such rapidity as to bid defiance to every effort to arrest their progress, until the whole was reduced to a heap of ruins. There were 27 paupers in the houses at the time of the accident; 21 of these saved themselves by jumping out of the windows, but two men and four women were unable to escape, and unhappily perished, one of these was a poor girl, 19 years of age, who being subject to fits and occasional derangement, was lately removed to the poor-house, because the overseers thought two shillings a week too much for her maintenance; her father is an industrious fisherman, with a large family; her mother is blind. The unfortunate girl became violent on being separated from her friends, and was secured by a chain. She was seen struggling in the flames but could not free herself from the fetters, and no assistance could be afforded her.

28 February 1817

CAMBORNE MINERS PLUNDER A WRECK

On Thursday morning last, about 4 o'clock, during the fall of snow, and in a strong gale from the north, the Brig *Mary*, of Ilfracombe, Capt. James Bowden, laden with culm, was driven on shore at Fassel Geaver cove in the parish of Camborne, a little to the eastwards of St. Ives . . . On the second evening a party of Camborne miners came down, determined for a wreck, they cut the ship's cable, carried off two of her small anchors, stole all the beef and biscuit on board, and even had the hardihood, before it became dark, to steal some of the seamen's cloathes at Gwithian church-town, which having been washed by the people of the village for the poor fellows, had been hung up to dry. In pillaging the ship they set the watch at defiance, by threatening to cut them down with dags or hatchets . . .

28 March 1817

BACK-BREAKING LOADS OF ORE

From a period long antecedent to the memory of any person living, it has been a practice in the mines of Cornwall to use what is called a standard barrow in carrying copper ore. This barrow contains three hundred weight; and allowing for the weight of the barrow and of the water held by the pulverised ore recently washed, the whole weight can be little less than four hundred weight. This is an enormous burthen, which is borne by all descriptions of persons who are employed in dressing and weighing . . . Labour so disproportionate to the degree of strength possessed by ordinary individuals, has given rise to a most pernicious custom, generally adopted by persons, women as well as men, who are employed in mixing, dividing and weighing ore; that of drinking large quantities of spirituous liquors, from a false idea, that they are thereby invigorated to perform the labour required of them . . .

About thirty years since, the carriers of tin ore used a sack which contained three hundred weight; that is, the regular load of a horse or mule. The manner in which these beasts were loaded was as follows. Two men lifted the sack above described on the shoulder of the carrier, and he carried it to the animal and threw it across its back. In this manner were 20, 30 or 40 mules or horses loaded several times a day. So many carriers were, at length, found to have been injured by the practice that the seam or load was divided, and put into two sacks. This was found an effectual remedy. What has been done in the case of the load of tin ore will, I hope, be shortly accomplished in that of weighing copper ore . . .

25 April 1817

[Extract from a letter written in consequence of the death of a young man at Crenver mine who burst a blood vessel while weighing copper ore.]

TO PORCELAIN MANUFACTURERS

To be let . . . the very extensive and newly-discovered china clay pits called Halvigan and Carne, in the parish of St. Mewan, in Cornwall. These pits are situate several miles nearer Charlestown from whence all the china clay raised in Cornwall is shipped, than any other clay pits now discovered, being within three miles, and the clay is of a very superior quality.

9 May 1817

TURNPIKE TOLLS

Notice is hereby given that in pursuance of an Act passed in the present session of Parliament, on the 2nd day of July next, the tolls now payable at the toll-gates on these roads, will cease, and be no longer payable. And that, on and after that day, there will be demanded and taken the tolls following, viz.

For every horse, or other beast of draught, drawing any coach, chariot, landau, berlin, chaise, chaise-marine, calash, chair, caravan, hearse, litter, or other such carriage, the sum of sixpence.

For every horse or other beast of draught drawing any waggon, wain, butt, cart, or other such carriage, the sum of sixpence. For every horse, mule, ass or other beast of burden, laden or not laden, and not drawing, the sum of two-pence.

For every drove of oxen, cows or neat cattle, the sum of one shilling and three-pence per score, and so in proportion for any less number.

For every drove of calves, swine, sheep, lambs, or goats, the sum of eightpence per score, and so in proportion for any less number. And on Sundays one-half over and above such respective tolls.

27 June 1817

CASE OF EXTRAORDINARY DISTRESS

At a public meeting of the inhabitants of the town and neighbourhood of Penzance, held at the Guildhall there, on Wednesday, the 18th of June, 1817, pursuant to a notice from the High-Sheriff, for the purpose of enquiring into the circumstances of the unfortunate sufferers by the late storm. Resolved.—That it appears to this meeting, that early in the morning of the 13th instant, the boats employed in the mackerel fishery in Mount's Bay, were suddenly overtaken by a tremendous tempest, in which two large boats, each containing seven men, with their crews, were totally lost. That these fourteen men had all their little property in fishing materials, to the value of above £300, embarked with them. That they have left eleven widows, thirty children, (mostly infants) and nine relatives, who were dependant on their labour for support, and that several of the widows are also near the time of their confinement, unprovided with even common necessaries. That these fifty unfortunate persons are left altogether destitute, except of their legal aid on a parish already overburthened, or the aid of benevolence.

Resolved.—That this is a case of extraordinary distress; and that a public subscription for its relief be now opened. 27 June 1817

PETER SKEWES: A MINER-FARMER

Peter Skewes [a miner at Wheal Unity] resides at Blackwater, in the parish of St. Agnes; he holds a small tenement consisting of about an acre and three quarters of land, the soil of which is naturally steril. This is divided into two nearly equal plots. One of these he plants with potatoes; the other he tills to wheat; and so on alternately; every year one of his little fields producing potatoes and the other wheat. By proper attention in the cultivation he has on average, 80 Cornish bushels of potatoes, and nine of wheat, each season. He keeps two donkies which graze on the neighbouring common during the summer, and are partly fed with the straw of his wheat in the winter; with these he carries coals, &c. for his neighbours, and collects manure for his ground. The refuse potatoes, &c. enable him to feed a pig which, with fish, purchased in the season, affords all that is required for food, in addition to the produce of his fields, and little garden. In this way has Peter Skewes passed the last seven years, and supported a wife and family; now consisting of six children, not only without parish aid; but with a degree of comfort and independence of which there are not many examples in his situation in life. 4 July 1817

WINDOW TAX

For the information of farmers. By virtue of the Act 57. Geo. III, cap. 23, a farmer, being the tenant of the farm, is exempt for one glazed window either in the dairy or cheese-room, or in a room used for both purposes, provided the house be solely used as a farm-house. It should be observed, that he is allowed only one glazed window, not one in the dairy and another in the cheese-room. 11 July 1817

A SINGULAR COW

Mr. Little of Hessenford, in this county, has a cow, one of the forelegs of which was accidentally broken some time since. Unwilling to kill the animal, which was far from being fat, the leg was amputated below the knee joint, and when sufficiently healed, a wooden leg was braced on it. With this the animal walks about, lies down, and rises with as much facility as a wounded seaman similarly circumstanced could be supposed to do. 18 July 1817

THE BELLS OF GWENNAP

On Tuesday last, there was a ringing match at Gwennap; the Camborne ringers got the first prize, which was six silver-laced hats; the Redruth ringers got the second, a gold-laced hat; and the Gluvias ringers the third, six pairs of gloves. 1 August 1817

COMETOGOOD FARM AND ROPE-WALK

To be let, with possession from Michaelmas next, for such term as may be agreed on, all that farm called Cometogood, situate in the parish of Kea, and adjoining Feock Downs; consisting of a good dwelling-house, barn, stable, and other suitable outhouses, with about thirty acres of land, orchards, gardens, crofts, &c. Together with that old-established rope-walk thereon; consisting of a rope-house, hemp-loft, and other houses, with a large copper furnace, capstan, heads, jacks, and other necessary working materials for carrying on the rope-making business. The rope-walk, being situate near the mines, and wharfs on Falmouth harbour, is a desirable object for a company, or any person connected with the mines, who may wish to enter into the rope-making line. 5 September 1817

RODE OFF A BLACK MARE

Whereas John Cock, my servant, did on the 2nd day of September inst., without my consent, collect some money and rode off a black mare, about 14 hands high, 7 years of age; her both knees has been cut very much, and the near knee very large; has a white star on her forehead, and the mark of a cut over her right eye. The said John Cock, is about 27 years of age, 5 feet high, pale complexion, dark hair, and wore off a baragan coat, and fustian trowsers, and appeared in the habit of a miller, and has several marks with Indian ink on his arm.

Whoever will apprehend the said John Cock, and lodge him in any of His Majesty's gaols, on conviction thereof, shall receive five pounds reward; and whoever will give information of the said mare, so that she may be had again, shall receive ten shillings reward, and all reasonable expenses paid, by applying to me, Thos. Brewer, of Golden-Mills, in the parish of Probus. N.B. The said John Cock was seen passing through Lostwithiel by eleven o'clock the same night. 5 September 1817

THE FIRST METHODIST SOCIETY

Died at Redruth, on Tuesday last, at an advanced age, Mrs. Phillipa Andrew, widow of Mr. Joseph Andrew, a respectable grocer of that town. Mr. and Mrs. Andrews formed part of the first Methodist Society established by the Rev. John Wesley in this county; from which time, to the day of their decease, they continued firmly attached to the principles they embraced. 12 September 1817

SUDDEN DEATH

On Saturday last, Thomas Richards, a miner of Illogan, dropped down dead, immediately after having been shaved in the mine to which he belonged, without having complained of any previous indisposition.

10 October 1817

[Miners paid "barber's pence", normally 3d. each per month, for being shaved on the mine where they worked.]

A MAN TRAP AN SPIKES

Take notes that thear is a man trap an spikes are soat in those turnaps. If aney parson is cacht steling or puling up turnaps from this ground shall ailmeggently be takin up and sent to geaill and tak the punishment of the law. 10 October 1817

[The above notice was reported to have been fixed on the gate of a field of turnips near Penzance.]

SMUGGLERS NEAR MULLION

On Thursday last, the *Hind* and *Dolphin* revenue cutters, with the preventive-boat, stationed at King's-cove, Mount's-Bay, got up between 90 and 100 kegs of foreign spirits, which had been sunk by smugglers near Mullion. 2 January 1818

THE ANCIENT BOROUGH OF TINTAGEL

We understand, that there is likely to be a contested election, in the ancient borough of Tintagel. The electors, nine in number, are split into two parties, who are strongly opposed to each other; both claiming the title of worthy and independent. The proceedings on the approaching election must be highly interesting. These candidates, no doubt, will publish addresses, as we learn that the mayor and one or two more of the electors are actually able to read; a proof of the extension of information in this enlightened age. 20 February 1818

GUILTY OF FELONY

Whereas, John Harry, of Truro, stationer, stands charged upon oath, with being guilty of felony; whoever will apprehend him, and bring him to justice, shall, on conviction, receive ten guineas reward.

The said John Harry, brought up to the business of a stationer, with his uncle, at Truro, was born either in the parish of Madron or Gulval, near Penzance; is about 38 or 40 years of age; 5 feet 2 or 3 inches high; of an ordinary size; brown cropped hair; large dark eyes, long face, red nose, and moderately florid complexion; has a squeaking effeminate voice; an insinuating, or rather a canting hypocritical manner of expression; addressing himself with great assiduity to the confidence of the person with whom he converses; and by a kind of whining familiarity, peculiarly his own, deceives, and imposes upon every one, with whom he gains the least footing of friendship.

He is supposed to have gone from Truro to St. Austell, in a gig, disguised as a female, on Thursday night, the 12th of February instant.

20 February 1818

A FALL FROM THE KIBBAL

On Thursday last, a miner named Collins, belonging to Gwennap, was killed in Poldory mine. He had just exploded a hole which contained six pounds of powder, and went down to see that the blast had properly taken effect. Finding the smoke which had not cleared out of the shaft too powerful, he desired to be drawn up. Just as he came to the surface, but before he could be laid hold on, he fell from the bucket or kibbal in which he stood, and being precipitated to the bottom, was killed on the spot. The unfortunate man has left a wife and six children.

27 February 1818

WRECKED VESSELS AT ST. MINVER

Since the wreck of three vessels at St. Minver, near Padstow . . . the shore near the place where these disasters occurred, has been visited by numbers of the peasantry, who have picked up quantities of bacon, &c. these vessels being laden with provisions from Ireland. On Friday last, two men who had ventured too far into the sea, in endeavouring to secure a bale of bacon, were overwhelmed by the waves, and unfortunately drowned. They were both married and have left, the one four, the other three children. 6 March 1818

[A schooner, a sloop and a brig were wrecked near Hell Bay in the Camel estuary on February 24th. Butter, bacon, lard, pork and beef were washed ashore from two of the vessels. A few days after the above incident, another man was drowned while endeavouring to secure some of the food. He left a wife and five children.]

WARLEGGAN CHURCH TOWER SPLIT ASUNDER

On Saturday last, during a tremendous thunderstorm, the tower of Warleggan church was struck by lightning, and split nearly from top to bottom. One part fell on the church and destroyed the roof and all the pews, except one. The damage is estimated at £600. 13 March 1818

GAS LIGHTING AT LISKEARD

On Tuesday evening, the inhabitants of Liskeard were much pleased, at seeing the shop of Mr. George Geach, watch-maker, of that place, lighted with gas. The gas is produced by a simple and cheap apparatus, placed in the chimney of Mrs. Geach's kitchen. The brilliancy of the light and the saving produced by the mode of producing it, promise to render the adoption of the apparatus general. 13 March 1818

ON THE CLIFFS AT ST. TEATH

Two lads, both about fourteen years of age, named Hodge and Hora, went on the cliffs, at St. Teath, on Good Friday, to pick muscles, and have not since been heard of, though the most diligent search has been made after them by their parents and friends. There is not the least doubt of their being drowned. 27 March 1818

GREAT CRINNIS MINE

Cornwall Assizes, Hanley versus Wood. Richard Hooper [witness] is acquainted with Great Crinnis, Little Crinnis, and Campdown mines. Remembers when Hanley had these mines [1806-8]; witness was employed as one of the captains. Hanley drove an adit from the level of the sea, until he cut a lode in Great Crinnis. The adit was driven westward. They discovered a little copper, but not sufficient to make any return; it was not sold. There was no shaft sunk, but four pins were driven into the ground, to mark the place where Hanley intended to sink a shaft. There were no buildings erected on Great Crinnis. Witness superintended the working at Little Crinnis under Hanley. They found an old shaft which had been sunk near the edge of the cliff and they erected a windlass over it; they also erected ladders in the shaft, and a small hut near it, for the workmen to change their clothes in, when they came from underground. The shaft went to the level of the sea, and they sunk it deeper, so as to bring it to a level with the low-water mark. They had a valve in the adit, to let out the sea-water that might get into the mine, and to keep out the water on the rising of the tide. They pursued the lode westward, and sunk a wins or underground shaft, from the former level. They discovered some copper ore in sinking the wins, and raised fifteen or sixteen tons of it, which they dressed for smelting. The lode was promising, and they sunk a new shaft over the wins, on which they erected a whim to draw up the stuff: there was a small house for holding the workmen's tools, called a material-house; it was part of the hut or shed in which the workmen changed their clothes. Witness was also captain of Campdown mine, where they found a shaft on the edge of the cliff; they sunk a wins and discovered some ore; they also erected a horse engine to draw off the water. Another shaft was sunk, from the surface, a little farther west, and a small changing-house built, [cut out of the hillside, and with a turf front and roof.] A small smith's shop was built near the changing-house; and, after a time, a little count-house was taken from the changing-house. Witness had seen the mines in the last fortnight. The counting-house had been converted into a dwelling house . . . He had lately seen Great Crinnis mine; there are many buildings on it now which were not there at the time of Hanley's death. There are fire-engines and every thing necessary to carry on a great mine.

3 April 1818

[One of the richest lodes of ore ever found in Britain was discovered at Great Crinnis, but not by Hanley (see p. 39), who had relinquished the mine on account of its inauspicious beginnings.]

TO CARRIERS

We, whose names are hereto subscribed [the principals of the main mining, smelting and mine merchanting companies], considering the very heavy expenses attending the repairs of the highways in the mining districts, and the great damage done to them by the carriage of unlimited weights, on narrow wheels, are of the opinion that the general use of wide wheels, if made flat and cylindrical, would greatly tend to remedy the evil, without subjecting the carrier to any material inconvenience, and with that view, we consider it a duty we owe to the public, as well as to ourselves, to give notice, that from and after the first of October next, we will not employ any carrier with carts and waggons who shall not keep and use for the carriage of coals, copper ore, tin and tin stuff, timber, iron, candles and other articles, wheels having the tire of the fellies, at least six inches in breadth.

Market stalls in Boscawen Street, Truro

Hay making near Bodmin

And we, the proprietors and freeholders of the sand banks, in Gwithian and Phillack [five signatures were subscribed], sensible of the advantages the public will derive from the general use of wide wheels, do also give notice, that from and after the first of October next, we will not permit any person to take and carry sand from our freeholds aforesaid, who shall not keep and use for that purpose wide wheels of the description above-mentioned, save and except one-horse carts, or two-horse carts drawn by horses under thirteen hands high. 17 April 1818

SEAMEN'S HOSPITAL AT FALMOUTH

We are informed that the Merchant Seamen's Committee at Falmouth, have it in contemplation to purchase a part of the materials of the temporary barracks [a war-time establishment, including a hospital], at Pendennis garrison, for the purpose of erecting a Merchant Seamen's Hospital for that port. 24 April 1818

[This hospital was successfully established, for the relief of disabled seamen and their widows. Crews of vessels registered in Falmouth each paid 6d. per month towards this end, and by 1825 there were 70 regular pensioners attached to the establishment.]

THE BUTTER MARKET AT PENZANCE

A custom long prevailed in Penzance, as it has in most towns of the county, of selling 18 ounces to the pound of fresh butter. Some time since, the keepers of the dairies near that place, resolved that they would give no more than 16 ounces to the pound, in future [because Irish and Welsh butters were being sold at the latter rate]. As large quantities of this article are purchased in Penzance, for the purpose of re-selling in other parts of the county, the alteration created no small degree of confusion; but it was at length acquiesced in. On Thursday last, Mr. Penneck, the mayor, and a number of constables, suddenly entered the market and, having shut and secured the doors, proceeded to weigh the butter offered for sale. It soon appeared that some of the dairy-keepers had as strong objections to 16 as they had had to 18 ounces to the pound. Above one hundred pounds of butter was seized for being short of weight; some of which was deficient an ounce on the pound. One basket full was wholly abandoned; no owner being found for it. The mayor has declared his determination to inflict the penalties incurred by the offenders.

24 April 1818

A RAFT OF CONTRABAND SPIRITS

On Saturday last, the preventive boats of Polperro and Wrinkle, took up a raft of contraband spirits, near Looe Island, containing 106 ankers, which they lodged in the excise warehouse at Looe. 15 May 1818

EARLY EMIGRANTS TO AMERICA

On Wednesday morning, sailed from the port of Charlestown, the *Charlestown*, Williams, master, with about 50 persons on board, as passengers for America; amongst whom are some whole families, including infants at the breast. In the number of those who have thus bid adieu to the land of their nativity, in pursuit of better fortune on a distant shore, is a woman 70 years of age, whose husband emigrated seven months since. 22 May 1818

THE STOPPAGE-BOOK ON PAY-DAY

[There is] a practice which has long prevailed amongst many of the mines in this county . . . that of compelling the labourers to purchase their necessaries at particular shops. For this purpose, if their necessaries are urgent, as they too generally are, they are favoured with a written order, upon which they are furnished with what they need, as far as the amount stated in that order extends. An account is kept of these orders, and on each pay-day, the amount is deducted from those who received them. But it sometimes happens, that another mode is adopted of effecting the same object. In place of issuing orders, the favoured shopkeeper or shopkeepers, who are invariably connected with some of the agents, and not infrequently their partners, obtain correct and regular information at the counting-house of the mine, as to what amount this credit may extend. At the pay-day they send to the counting-house what is called a stoppage-book, in which is entered the amount each labourer is indebted to them. This money is stopped, by the captains, frequently to the amount of £200 in a single pay-day. Thus the business goes on; the unfortunate laborers are forced to go into debt, in order to exist; and they are forced to pay what they are charged; complaint is unavailing; no credit can be obtained by them elsewhere, as the favorites are sure to be paid first. In consequence . . . persons have been known to take up from a shopkeeper so situated, goods which they did not want, and sell them again at an enormous loss, in order to obtain articles of necessity, which they could not obtain where they were allowed credit. You will easily perceive how good a thing it is to be a favorite or partner of the purser of a great mine. 19 June 1818

ACCOUNT DAY

By immemorial custom, an account-day [on a mine] is a species of feast. Such of the adventurers as choose to attend, of whom the merchants and their friends form a decided majority, sit down to an excellent dinner, in which the good old English cheer, of roast beef and plum-pudding makes a conspicuous part. This is followed by flowing bowls of excellent punch, for the manufacture of which mine captains are celebrated. After a full and substantial meal has been properly diluted, by drinking the usual sentiments in this exhilarating beverage, the manager, who is usually in the chair, produces the Cost Book . . . 17 July 1818

FÊTE CHAMPÊTRE AT MOUNT EDGCUMBE

On the 14th instant, the Earl of Mount Edgcumbe and Lady Emma Edgcumbe, gave a breakfast to a select party in the flower gardens at his Lordship's beautiful seat near Plymouth. Lord and Lady Exmouth, and most of the gentry of the neighbourhood were present. The guests began to arrive before two o'clock. After breakfast they promenaded the gardens, the walks of which are shaded by cedars, magnolias, cork-trees, &c. At four o'clock they partook of a cold collation, intermixed with hot soups, in the orangery, a noble building of the Doric order, one hundred feet in length. After this repast, the company adjourned to a spacious platform, fitted as a temporary ball-room, at each end of which was a circular tent, where refreshments were provided. Here dancing commenced. At nine o'clock, the gardens were illuminated with a profusion of variegated lamps. The whole company partook of tea, and at twelve o'clock, of supper. At one o'clock the visitors retired, highly gratified with the beauties of the place, and the politeness and hospitality of their noble host and his amiable and lovely daughter. 24 July 1818

DISTRESS ON SCILLY

At a meeting of the magistrates of the county of Cornwall, acting for the western division of the hundred of Penwith, held for the purpose of taking into consideration the distressed state of the inhabitants of the Scilly Isles, which has now first come to their knowledge from statements in the public papers, Sir Rose Price, Bart. in the chair, the following resolutions were passed:—

1st. That from the information personally given to them by Lieut.-Governor Vigoreux, who had previously made known the situation of the inhabitants to the Government, and had, in consequence of that representation, obtained a donation of £500 for their relief, it is the opinion of the meeting that the distresses, which were chiefly confined to the off Islands, have been great, but at present are not numerous, nor more severe than in many parts of Cornwall.

2nd. That these distresses, which originated in a failure in the potatoe crop, and which have been partially increased by the suppression of smuggling, have not been diminished by any appeal to the proper authorities for enforcing the Poor Laws.

3rd. That the present efficacious mode of preventing smuggling, though it may be a cause of temporary distress, will ultimately tend to the real prosperity and happiness of the inhabitants.

4th. That in consequence of this change of system, it is the more necessary that the inhabitants should be encouraged and assisted in gaining an honest livelihood by burning kelp, improving their lands, and extending their fisheries, from which their late habits rendered them averse.

5th. That any further pecuniary aid at this season of the year would tend to check industry.

24 July 1818

[The report caused a public outcry and as a result a deputation was sent to investigate the state of affairs in Scilly at first hand. It was thereafter decided to equip the islanders with all the means to commence a proper mackerel and pilchard fishery, the necessary money (over £7,500) being subscribed on the mainland, and the equipment bought. By 1823 the new industry had been abandoned for no apparently good reason.]

THE PILCHARD CATCH

After being thus enclosed [by the stop-sean], the fish are taken from the sean by the tuck-net, and hoisted into boats, which convey them to the cellars to be cured. Tucking is effected by placing the follower [boat] within the ropes, and stationing other boats on the outside, to receive the fish which are taken from the stop-sean by the tuck-net, and to carry them to the shore. This operation is always performed at low water; and when it takes place on a fine calm moon-light evening, the scene is interesting beyond expression. The number of boats sailing or rowing in all directions around the sean; the quantity of persons employed in baling up the fish with baskets; the refulgent appearance of the scaly tribe, struggling, springing, and gleaming to the moon in every direction; the busy and contented hum of the fishermen, together with the plashing of the frequent-plying oar, altogether form a picture to which language is incapable of doing justice.

31 July 1818

THE PILOTS OF PENZANCE

The sloop *Jones*, of Dartmouth, bound to Bridgewater, during the gale on Monday last, made for Penzance pier, which not being able to weather, she came to anchor outside it, and made a signal for a pilot. A boat put off to her assistance, but, according to custom, the persons on board determined to extort as much as possible for their aid, and refused to come on board the sloop unless the master promised to comply with their exorbitant demands. During the delay occasioned by this proceeding, the sloop parted her cable, and immediately drove on shore. She sustained considerable damage; but fortunately was got off next tide. Is there no mode of punishing such conduct, on the part of pilots?

25 September 1818

ASPHYXIATED IN WHEAL FANNY

Two men who were at work, underground, in a remote part of Wheal Fanny mine, on Monday last, were found by their comrades, lying beside each other and totally insensible. They were got out as speedily as possible, and every means used for their recovery. After some time, one was restored: but in the other, the vital spark was totally extinct; the disaster was occasioned by foul air.

25 September 1818

TANDEAN HAMMER-MILL

To be sold by auction, for ready money . . . all the materials, walls, and roof of Tandean hammer-mill, situate in the parish of Perranarworthal on Carnon Stream, and near Carnon turnpike; consisting of one water-wheel, 13 feet diameter, 3 feet breast, (oak); one ditto, 13 feet ditto, 22 inches ditto, (oak); four large bellows (suitable for blowing houses); sundry lots of wrought iron, useful for smiths; two smiths' anvils, a bench vice, and working tools; roofs of forge, about 15 square of slating; brick walls and stacks, about 30,000 bricks; sundry large pieces of oak; one piece of ash, and sundry lots of timber and boards; some tons of cast iron, &c, &c.

16 October 1818

AT BODMIN MARKET

A man named Walter, of the parish of Lanivet, led forward his wife, by a halter, which was fastened round her waist and publicly offered her for sale. A person called Sobey, who has lately been discharged from the 28th regiment, bid sixpence for her, and was immediately declared the purchaser. He led off his bargain in triumph, amidst the shouts of the crowd; and to the great apparent satisfaction of her late owner.

13 November 1818

A DISTRESS FOR RENT

On Wednesday last, prematurely, at Launceston, occasioned by a fright, in consequence of the landlord of the house she occupies, levying a distress for rent, which was not due to him, Mrs. French, of two sons.

4 December 1818

FALMOUTH PACKETS

Order of sailing: For Lisbon, every Friday evening from the 5th of

April to the 10th of October, and on Saturday morning from the 10th of October to the 5th of April.

For Barbadoes and Jamaica, and America, on the Sunday after the first Wednesday in every month.

Leeward Islands, on the Sunday after the third Wednesday in every month.

Brazils, on the Saturday after the first Tuesday in every month.

Mediterranean, on Saturday once in three weeks.

The return of the packets is calculated thus; to Jamaica and back, 17 weeks—America and back, 15 weeks—Leeward Islands and back, 13 weeks—Mediterranean and back, 12 weeks—Brazils and back, 18 weeks.

1 January, 1819

TO GENTLEMEN OF FORTUNE

Any two gentlemen, who would wish to secure seats at the next Parliament, may be accommodated at the borough of Launceston. There are but 15 votes, majority 3. All letters directed for A.B. to be left at the Exeter post-office, will be duly attended to. 29 January 1819

DIED ON THE ROAD

On Thursday last, a miner named John Jewel who resided at Wendron, had his arm broken and received some other injuries by an accident in a mine at Camborne. Having had his arm set, he thought he was able to walk home [a distance of five miles]; but after attempting to do so, he found he could not proceed, and died on the road. What renders the case more distressing is the fact that he has left five small children, all ill of the measles, to lament his death. 29 January 1819

BALL MAIDENS VICTORIOUS

The country people in the neighbourhood of Padstow have been rather busily employed, for some time, in securing the part of the cargo of the vessel lately wrecked on their coast. On Wednesday evening last, a box of figs, part of this cargo, was discovered on St. Minver Commons, which gave rise to a serious affray between a party of damsels who were on the look-out for secreted plunder, and some ball maidens who were returning from a mine. The contest lasted for two hours, in the course of which some of the combatants were reduced to a state approaching nudity. In the end the ball maidens were victorious, and carried off the prize.

5 February 1819

STEM-BOOKS MISSING

The account-house [on United Mines] is a large building, containing several apartments, with a kitchen, for the purpose of dressing dinners for the adventurers, agents, and captains on account-days, &c. In a particular room, one of the captains is stationed on duty, every night, and the key of the office, where the books of account, &c. are kept, is placed, for security, in this room. On the night in question [when the stem-books were stolen] the key was brought into the captain's room, as usual, and the captain on duty never suspected what had occurred, until the door of the office was found open in the morning. During the night, he was absent from the room about two hours, examining some work going on at a distant part of the mine; this opportunity must have been taken by the person who stole the books, and who, it is evident, must have been on watch to enter the captain's room . . . The loss of the books put a stop to all further investigations . . . 5 February 1819

[Enquiries were about to be made into suspected frauds in the charging of "stems", that is extra periods of work done by the miners and paid at a fixed rate. As hundreds of men were working at United mines, the practice of considerable fraud was easy. A twenty-five guineas reward was offered for the recovery of the books, carried off towards Redruth it was thought, by a boy seen leaving the mines with a heavy green bag.]

FLOGGED THROUGH THE FORE STREET

The town of Bodmin having been lately much infested by vagrants, the Mayor issued a notice on Saturday last, that any wanderers who should after that day be found within the precincts of the borough should be dealt with according to law. This intimation not being attended to, some of the offenders were seized on Monday, and being convicted of begging in the borough, were sentenced to be flogged through the fore-street, which is of considerable length. The sentence was forthwith carried into execution, though rather leniently, and the delinquents dismissed with an intimation that if they again offended, they would be treated more severely. How are these unhappy creatures to avoid beggary, or where are they to obtain employment? Are they to be whipped from parish to parish until they perish under the lash, or expire from want, in a ditch?

5 March 1819

A GHOST AT PADSTOW

Messrs. Ryan and Sheppard, of Padstow, having bought from the poor of the neighbourhood all the bones they could collect, for the purpose of shipping them for Bristol, a report was circulated that a quantity of human bones was mixed with those collected for sale. This report was confirmed by the alleged appearance of a ghost near the store in which the bones were collected; and which the good folk of the town supposed was that of some individual that wished to prevent its mortal relics from being removed from their native soil, and profaned by being put to common use. The alarm was spread, and to prevent the serious interference of the mobility, a sloop was hastily engaged and the bones shipped off without delay, to the no small mortification of those who had determined on opposing such a measure, until they were satisfied that there were none of the mortal remains of their ancestors amongst them. 12 March 1819

GUILTY OF FORGERY

A short time since a fellow came to the office of Messrs. Rashleigh and Coode, St. Austell, and demanded £3.12s. for the interment of dead bodies found on the shore at Zennor, near Land's-End. He produced eleven certificates, signed, as he asserted, by a magistrate in that neighbourhood. Suspicion being excited, it was discovered that the whole were forgeries; and subsequently the fellow admitted that his name was Floyd, and that he lived at Modbury, in Devonshire. He was committed to take his trial at the Assizes. 19 March 1819

[On arrest, the prisoner was found to possess a bundle of blank orders to be filled up, for the interment of bodies washed on shore. He was found guilty of forgery, and sentenced to death.]

TO BOTANY BAY

Cornwall Assizes. Pascoe Walters, aged 19 years, was indicted for stealing sundry articles of wearing apparel from the house of Thomas Varcoe, of Roach. From the evidence it appeared that the prisoner took the articles from the prosecutor's house for the purpose of being transported, in order to join his father and mother, who are both at Botany Bay. He avowed this purpose when he was apprehended, and put himself in the way of the prosecutor, in order to be committed. His Lordship said it was evident the prisoner had not taken the property with a felonious intent, and therefore he must be acquitted. 2 April 1819

[In fact, first offenders, and any young criminals under the age of sixteen, served their transportation sentences on prison hulks (usually old ships of war, such as the *Bellerophon*, converted at Plymouth in 1826) in naval dockyards, where they were put to work. Conditions were similar to those on board slave ships, so that the hardened offenders transported overseas to Botany Bay and Van Diemen's Land, were much more fortunate, being released on arrival. In 1826 a change was made in Government policy, 150 superintendents being sent out to commence a system of supervised hard labour among the convicts.]

FISHING INSIDE THE LIMITS

A prosecution having been commenced against us, the undersigned,

Edward Scantlebery, of Polruan, and Nicholas Thomas, of Mevagissey, fishermen, for having in the month of September last taken pilchards with drift nets within the distance of one league and a half from the shore of this county, contrary to an Act of Parliament, passed in the reign of King Charles the II, for the protection of the pilchard fishery; and Mr. Thomas Stark, acting on behalf of himself and others concerned in the pilchard fishery, having consented to withdraw the prosecution on our payment of the court fees and making this public acknowledgment of our guilt; we hereby express our thanks to Mr. Stark, and the persons on whose behalf the said prosecution was instituted, for the lenity shewn in withdrawing such prosecution, and we do hereby promise not to offend in like manner again. As witness our hands, this 22nd April, 1819: The mark of Edw. X Scantlebery. Nicholas Thomas.. 30 April 1819

HELP FOR THE SCILLONIANS

The Industrious Society proposes employing all those widows, infirm, and aged women, and distressed orphans, whom the fisheries could not relieve. It is now commencing operations. The female committee are teaching straw-plait, widows and children are knitting stockings, and a woman from Essex is gone to Scilly to with a new spinning wheel, to instruct them in spinning, with both hands, shoe thread and line twine. All these goods will be sent to a warehouse in Penzance, and disposed of under the management of a committee. 7 May 1819

[Sufficient money having been obtained by subscription to establish a fishing industry on the islands, the above society was formed early in April to assist those who would not benefit from the pilchard and mackerel fisheries. Its patron was the Prince Regent, Duke of Cornwall, its officers leading personages in the county at that time.]

SPRINGTIME, 1819

No spring, in the memory of the oldest inhabitants, was ever more promising, early, or more beautiful than the present. The apple trees are showing their blossoms; the vines putting forth the clusters; and the young corn crops have the most gratifying appearance throughout the country. 14 May 1819

NET-BRAIDERS OF NEWLYN

Fourteen girls from Newlyn and Mousehole are placed on the Islands [of Scilly] . . . to instruct the islanders in braiding nets. 14 May 1819

GOOD SPEED TIN MINE

To be sold by private contract 32-60ths, doles or shares in Good Speed tin mine, commonly called Black Pepper, situate near Beam mine, in the parish of Roach. The ores make grain tin of the best quality, and the set is large. There are two stamping-mills, and a water engine on the mine, and a great quantity of tin has been returned. 21 May 1819

ENTERTAINMENT IN TRURO

By permission of the Worshipful the Mayor, for two nights only, on Monday and Tuesday next, at the Assembly-rooms, Truro, the two wonderful Russian fire-proof phenomena, Monsieur and Mademoiselle Chabert, brother and sister, who have had the honour of exhibiting before the University and city of Oxford, with universal approbation, of whom the London papers have made so much mention, and who lately caused so much astonishment in London and Paris, also at Petersburgh, by going into an oven, in presence of the Royal Faculty of Physicians, with a leg of mutton, and remaining with it until the meat was well baked. This experiment he will have the honour of performing again [in London], whenever a liberal subscription [£500] shall be made for that purpose . . .

28 May 1819

[The performances at Truro were to be of a somewhat more ordinary nature, such as holding in the mouth boiling oil, melted sealing wax, burning charcoal, and molten lead, as well as "eating a lighted torch, with a fork, as if it were sallad"].

ENTERTAINMENT IN PENZANCE

Mons. Chabert, the celebrated fire-eater, exhibited his wonderful capability of resisting the effects of heat, at the theatre, Penzance, on the night of Monday last. After going through the various feats of standing in melting lead, eating burning torches, etc., &c. he concluded by getting into a frame-work on which was hung a number of rockets, and to which he was to set fire, whilst he remained exposed to the flame, until his clothes were literally burnt from his body. On exhibiting this experiment. the house became filled with smoke, and the sulphureous smell became intolerable, that the auditors were quickly forced to seek a purer atmosphere. But as the means of egress did not allow of their doing this as speedily as was necessary, several persons fainted, and a scene of general confusion ensued. The screams for assistance became loud and piercing; a cry of fire was raised, and the crowd which quickly assembled, lost no time in breaking through the roof, in order to extricate those imprisoned within, who by tumbling over each other, had nearly blocked up the ordinary passages. Happily this expedient, by allowing the smoke to evaporate, and giving an opportunity to remove to the open air, those who had become insensible, prevented a fatal termination of the disaster, which, in all probability, would have otherwise occurred.

18 June 1819

ROYAL STOCKINGS FROM SCILLY

When the School of Industry for the Scilly Isles was formed, his Royal Highness condescended to become its patron. Impressed with gratitude for this honor, the committee gave directions that two pair of lamb's-wool stockings should be knit by some poor families on the Islands, as a present to their illustrious patron. A few days since the stockings reached Penzance, and were generally admired by most of the respectable inhabitants of that town; many persons considered them almost as fine as if they had been wove, and, certainly, much more durable. G.P.R. as initials, were neatly wrought in crimson silk, and surrounded with a fanciful wreath on each stocking. This humble present was accompanied with a most respectful letter from the female committee at St. Mary's, addressed to his Royal Highness, soliciting his acceptance of the first fruits of that institution he had deigned to patronize. 2 July 1819

[Worsted and lamb's-wool stockings, men's frocks, nightcaps, gloves, braces, straw hats, and shoe-thread were the usual articles sent by the School of Industry to the distribution depot set up in Penzance.]

VAGRANTS IN TRURO

On Wednesday, the magistrates being informed that an unusual number of vagrants had arrived here, they ordered the constables to visit the different lodging houses where travellers of this description put up. In consequence of this visitation, which was very unwelcome to the objects of it, thirty-seven vagabonds were accommodated with a lodging in our prison, for the night; and yesterday the whole posse underwent an examination before the magistrates. The result was that twenty-six were allowed to *go about their business*, two were ordered to be publicly whipped, which sentence was carried into effect in Boscawen-street, and the remainder were sent to the county bridewell. 16 July 1819

PAVING STONES OUT OF MOUNT'S BAY

Two labouring men who were employed to procure stone for paving the streets of Penzance from a reef of rock in Mount's-Bay, that stretches about half a mile into the sea, between Penzance and Chyandour, had a very narrow escape of being drowned on Monday last. As the top of the reef is above water, except at spring tides, the men supposed themselves perfectly safe, but the wind blowing hard from the S.W. on Sunday and Monday, caused a high tide, which soon left them but a very small space to stand on. In this extremity they drove a crow-bar into an opening of the rock, and fastened themselves to it, whilst they endeavoured to attract the attention of those on shore by waving their hats. Fortunately they were observed by a woman who immediately gave notice of their danger. Mr. Bolitho of Chyandour fearing that a boat from that place could not reach them in time, having to row against the wind, sent off a man and horse to Penzance, from which a boat put off to their assistance, and reached the poor men just in time to rescue them from their perilous situation. 23 July 1819

THEFT OF TIN AT ST. GERMANS

Cornwall Assizes. William Screetch and John Harris were indicted for stealing three blocks of tin, weighing 900 lbs, belonging to the Drinkwall [Drakewalls] Company, at St. Germans in May last. It appeared that the prisoners contrived to carry off the tin, which they cut into small pieces, and melted in an iron frying-pan. They sold the tin for pewter, to a brazier named Luke, at Saltash, for six-pence a pound . . . 20 August 1819

BODMIN RACES

It being represented to the stewards that on account of the many shooting parties being formed for the first of September; the races at Bodmin are not likely to be as fully attended as heretofore, they have in consequence been induced to alter the date from the 1st and 2nd to Tuesday and Wednesday the 7th and 8th of September.

20 August 1819

THE POOR HOUSE AT PADSTOW

Cornwall Assizes. Phillippa May, a pauper belonging to Padstow, was put to the bar, charged with the murder of Mary Jeffry. It appeared that the prisoner had been insane for two years before, and was confined with a chain at the poor-house at Padstow. The prisoner was chained to a beam, and the deceased, who was 73 years of age, slept in the same room with her. On the night of the 19th of May last, the prisoner contrived to get loose from the chain and strangled the poor old woman by grasping her throat. The groans of the sufferer awaked the keeper of the poor-house, who came to her assistance, but she was dead before the surgeon arrived. Not guilty, being insane at the time the act was committed.

20 August 1819

FROM ST. STEPHENS TO ILLINOIS

Dear Cousin, If any of our friends are coming to America, let them provide for themselves, boxes to put their provision and clothes in, and find themselves on their passage; for it is the cheapest and best way.

They should provide a good stock of strong shoes, above every thing else. When we left Alexandria, Gilbert White, mason of Saint Stephens, worked at the fort near that place; his wages were 2¼ dollars per day, with liquor twice a day. A blacksmith is a very good calling here; iron is 8d. per lb, and he gets 2½ dollars for a set of shoes. A shoe-maker is also a good calling, as sole leather is only 18d. per lb, and other leather in proportion, and a pair of shoes comes to 3½ dollars. Carpenters' wages are 2 dollars per day. Tailors, they say, are best off of any tradesmen in America . . . It is a most beautiful country that I ever saw; the prairies level and grass plenty, surrounded by beautiful woods, very handy for building houses and fences. The houses are all of timber, and so are almost all fences. I would not pursuade any persons to come here, let them observe their own mind. I have heard there are one or two gone back to England, giving an evil report of a very good land; I suppose they could get three times as much in America as they can in England. H.C. was telling about coming, when we came; if he intends to come where we are, it would be best for him to go to Mr. Charles Slade, merchant, of Alexandria, as we live very near his son . . . Mr. Richard Truscott, of Roach, and Mr. William Truscott, of St. Stephens, live in our neighbourhood; we are all very well at present. I wish all my friends in England were here with us, as I am sure they would do better here than at home. Mills are very scarce with us as yet; it is about thirty-four miles from us to a grist-mill, which makes the flour dear and scarce. We hope there will be a wind-mill erected near us. We often wish Mr. Y—— [probably Yelland], the miller, was here with us, as he has a large family, and that is a great advantage in this country . . . If any of our friends inquire how we do, tell them we are well satisfied with our new country, for it is a very good one. Myself and Mr. William Truscott, and Mr. Richard Truscott, have bought two quarter sections of land, which are 320 acres . . . You may tell Mr. Richard Arthur that his son Samuel is very well in health and getting money very fast . . . Edward Coad. 3 September 1819

[From a long and glowing account of the conditions of life in Illinois, in a letter from Coad to his cousin Edward Coad, cordwainer, in St. Stephen-in-Brannel. The surnames mentioned are those still common in this Cornish parish, and probably the emigrants went out as a group.]

FIRES GUIDE THE FISHERMEN

Several shoals of pilchards appeared in Mount's Bay on Wednesday evening, and about 16 seans were shot all of which have inclosed fish. One sean sent in about 70 hogsheads, on Thursday morning. As fires were seen during the night on the high lands near Mullion and Gunwalloe, as signals for the boats from Newlyn and Mousehole to proceed to enclose the fish which were near the shore at the former places, it is hoped a considerable quantity has been taken. 3 September 1819

AGAINST PROFANE SWEARING

The Act against profane swearing, which has become nearly a dead letter, was read at St. Mary's Church, Truro, on Sunday last, after divine service. The law requires that this Act be read in all churches, four times a year. 8 October 1819

NICHOLAS BRAY TREVUZO

Whereas Nicholas Bray Trevuzo, of the parish of Kea, in the County of Cornwall, has absconded, and left his wife and family chargeable to the said parish. He is about 5 feet 11½ inches high, has black eyes, brown hair, of fresh complexion, and has a large wart on one of his thumbs, has a demure countenance, and did, and is now supposed to, belong to the Methodist connexion.

Whoever will apprehend the said Nicholas Bray Trevuzo, and bring him to the overseers of the parish of Kea, shall receive a reward of twenty shillings, and all reasonable expenses. 8 October 1819

THE MERRY BELL-RINGERS

On Tuesday last, William Coath of Liskeard, was brought before the justices assembled at Callington, on a charge of having stolen the key of the church at Pillaton. This key was missed after the ringers had been treating the neighbourhood with a merry peal, in consequence of a wedding; but as none of them were less than half-seas-over, they could not tell who locked the door or how the key was lost. The loss of the key of the church being the theme of conversation in the neighbourhood, it was discovered that Coath had pledged it at Landrake, for a shilling's worth of beer. The offender was taken up; but as he insisted he had found the key on the high road, and as none of the party could tell whether the key was lost or stolen, the magistrates dismissed the charge. The churchwardens had above five pounds to pay for witnesses, &c. after having been compelled to break open the church doors, in order to read the burial service at a funeral which took place before the key was found.

12 November 1819

TO THE EDITOR OF THE WEST BRITON

Sir, A few days since I received a letter from Upper Canada, North America, written by a person unknown to me, stating the death of Thomas

Turner, which took place in that province, on the 28th of July last. The writer states that the deceased was a native of this county, where he left a wife and family, and requests me to make inquiry for them. As I am wholly unacquainted with the persons described, I request you will insert this notice in your next paper, where it may meet the eye of the widow or the relatives of the deceased, who are requested to apply to me, at the Methodist chapel, in this place. J. Hodson, Redruth.

19 November 1819

BURNING LIME AT PHILLEIGH

On Friday evening last, two men who were left to attend to a lime kiln belonging to J. P. Peters, Esq. at Philleigh, were overpowered, as it is supposed, by the gas which arose from the kiln, as they were pressing down the burning lime with an iron bar, in order to put more on the top. They fell on the burning mass, and the bodies were found the next morning reduced to ashes; nothing remaining but part of the scull of each. Both were married and have left children. 26 November 1819

FIRE AT GLYNN

About three o'clock on Friday morning, the inhabitants of Bodmin were roused from their sleep by the ringing of the fire-bell, and the sound of bugles of the staff of the Cornwall Militia. This alarm was occasioned by a fire which had broken out at Glynn, the elegant mansion of that public spirited and highly esteemed magistrate E. J. Glynn, Esq. A similar alarm was spread at Lostwithiel, and assistance obtained from both places. Many of the inhabitants of each town, headed by the Mayor of the former, and Messrs. Foster and Westlake from the latter, repaired to the spot [some four miles from each town] with their engines. The flames by this time raged with such violence, that in spite of the most active and laborious exertions, the whole of the building, except the servants' apartments, the kitchen, offices and cellars, is destroyed . . . The greatest praise is due to the gentlemen and inhabitants who attended with engines from Bodmin and Lostwithiel; particularly to Capt. Semple with the staff of the Cornwall Militia, who were the first on the spot.

3 December 1819

CLOSE SEASON FOR SALMON

Notice is hereby given, that in pursuance of an Act passed in the 58th year of the reign of his present Majesty, chapter 43, intitled, "An Act for preventing the destruction of the breed of salmon, and fish of salmon kind in the rivers of England"; I intend to make an application at the next general Quarter Sessions of the Peace, to be holden for this county, to fix certain days, not exceeding one hundred and fifty days in the year, to be fence days, for the River Camel or Allen, commencing from the bar at the mouth of the said river upwards, and all streams communicating therewith. A. O. Molesworth, Pencarrow. 7 January 1820

STANNARIES OF CORNWALL

Notice is hereby given, that the courts for the several stannaries, will be holden at the under-mentioned times and places—viz.

For the stannary of Tywarnhaile, at the Red Lion, Truro, on Thursday the 3rd of February next.

For the stannary of Penwith and Kirrier, at the King's Arms, Penryn, on Friday, the 4th of February next.

For the stannary of Blackmore, at the George and Dragon, St. Clement, on Monday the 7th of February next.

For the stannary of Foymore, at the King's Arms, Liskeard, on Saturday the 12th of February next.

And that the said courts will be respectively holden in future from three weeks to three weeks. 21 January 1820

[The stannary courts, held usually every three weeks, dealt with offences against the laws of the Stannaries, the ancient divisions of the mining districts of Cornwall. Cases were tried before a jury normally of six tinners, and a steward appointed by the Lord Warden of the Stannaries].

DESIRABLE VESSELS

To be sold by private contract, the good brig *Ann*, of the port of Gweek, Wm. Williams, master, burthen per register 156 tons, sails well and amply found in stores, now lying at Penzance pier, where she has delivered a cargo of timber from America. Also the good schooner *Mary*, of the said port of Gweek, Joseph Saunders, master, burthen per register, 66 tons, faithfully built at Appledore, sails fast, and well found now lying in the River Helford. The above are desirable vessels for the fruit or Mediterranean trades. For particulars apply at the Counting-house, at Gweek aforesaid . . . 4 February 1820

PROCLAMATION OF THE KING

On Saturday last, the ceremony of proclaiming his present Majesty George IV, took place at Truro . . . When the whole [procession] was arranged, the proclamation issued by the Privy Council was read by John Edwards, Esq., the Town Clerk, after which the procession moved to the eastern end of the town, in the following order: Officers' Guard of his Majesty's 4th Regiment of Light Dragoons; Killigrew Yeomanry Cavalry; Dragoons and Yeomanry—dismounted; Constables with long staves; Phoenix Lodge of Free and Accepted Masons; Sailors, bearing the Union flag; naval and military officers; staff of the Royal Miners; band of music; constables at Mace; The Mayor; deputy recorder; aldermen; capital burgesses; town steward; constables; churchwardens; clergy; principal inhabitants of the town and neighbourhood; yeomanry—dismounted; officers' guard of the Penwith Yeomanry cavalry. The whole then moved to the High-cross; the West-bridge; Lemon-street, and back to the Town-hall. The proclamation was read six times in different parts of the borough and the adjacent streets. On each occasion the assembled multitude gave three cheers, and the band struck up the national air, "God Save the King".

18 February 1820

TRURO ASSEMBLY ROOMS

On Friday last, Sir H. Vivian and Col. Gosset gave a ball and supper at the Assembly-rooms, to the gentry of the town of Truro and its neighbourhood. The ball room [floor] was handsomely chalked, having the town arms in the centre, and the crest of General Vivian at the top, and that of Colonel Gosset at the bottom. The room was brilliantly lighted, and most tastefully decorated with laurel, military trophies, &c. An excellent band from Bodmin was also provided, in addition to the usual musicians engaged at the assemblies in this neighbourhood. About ten o'clock the ball was opened by General Vivian and Mrs. Thos. Daniell. The company was numerous; and quadrills and country dances were performed in fine style. About one o'clock the company sat down to a supper provided by Mr. and Mrs. Stevens, of the Red Lion Hotel, which equalled anything of the kind ever remembered in this county, and in which every delicacy of the season was displayed in profusion. The wines were of the very best quality. After supper the dancing was resumed, and continued until Aurora hailed the apparent morn, when the company departed highly delighted with the festivities of the night. 24 March 1820

THE KING'S BIRTHDAY

At St. Columb, [the birthday of George IV] was ushered in by the ringing of bells; and in the course of the morning, the new Yeomanry Regiment, the North Cornwall Hussars mustered in the street. There were 32 from St. Columb, 25 from Grampound, and about 15 from St. Enoder; making 72 in the whole. After the regiment had been on parade about an hour, Colonel Vyvyan arrived and marched them to his seat at Truan, where they fired three feu-de-joies. They then returned to St. Columb, where a barrel of porter was provided by the Colonel for the refreshment of the privates, who went home in good order. We are sorry to learn that this was not altogether the case with some of the officers. 28 April 1820

A DEATH AT DOLCOATH

On Saturday a boy named Hosking, being in one of the levels of Dolcoath mine, where a person was preparing to blast a hole in a damp part of the rock, he took up part of a tin tube used as a fuse in such cases, and not observing that it contained powder, attempted to look at the candle through it, when approaching too near, the powder exploded, and the tube being driven through his eye into his head, he was killed on the spot.

28 April 1820

A PUBLIC SUBSCRIPTION

At a meeting held this 3rd day of May, 1820, at the Queen's Head, in the borough of Tregony, for the purpose of taking into consideration the great loss sustained by Mr. Nicholas Boase, of Trebollock, in the parish of Lamorran, on the 24th of April last, by having his dwelling-house, barn, stables, and all his out-houses burnt to the ground, together with about 50 bushels of wheat, 30 bushels of barley, a threshing-machine, a small quantity of hay, a quantity of reed, implements of husbandry, and a quantity of timber. A considerable part of his household furniture was also burnt or destroyed, making altogether a loss of between three and four hundred pounds, besides the great injury and inconvenience he is sustaining in being obliged to reside at a distance from his farm, in carrying on his business. John Penhallow Peters, Esq. in the chair. Resolved—that the under-mentioned respectable persons be requested to solicit contributions within their respective neighbourhoods, and that printed particulars and forms be sent to each for that purpose. 5 May 1820

[Boase's insurance on the property had just expired, and he had not thought a renewal necessary. Altogether thirty-eight parishes, ranging from Mevagissey to St. Columb and Perranzabuloe, together with their representatives, were listed in the above notice.]

A RELIGIOUS MINER

On Monday last, as a miner named William Stephens, was descending the engine shaft in Cuddra mine, the ladder being insecurely placed, slipped, and he was precipitated into the water at the bottom, a depth of eight or nine fathoms, where he was drowned before any assistance could be afforded him. Before he fell, he was singing the 90th psalm, and at the moment the ladder slipped was repeating, "Thou turnest man, O Lord, to dust."

5 May 1820

BODMIN FAIR

The crowds which resorted to Bodmin, during the continuance of the fair on Tuesday and Wednesday, were amused with something of the far-famed St. Bartholemew. Feats of horsemanship; exhibitions of wild beasts; wax-work representations of great personages [see below]; puppit-shows; glass-blowing; tight-rope dancing; giants; dwarfs, and jugglers, were announced with a vociferation and din almost realising the uproar of pandemonium itself. 19 May 1820

THE LATE KING'S FUNERAL

Mr. Hathaway, from Fleet-street, London, returns thanks to the nobility and gentry of Truro, for their support, and begs to inform them that his grand European cabinet of wax figures will be open for inspection, this day, Friday, the 25th, and Saturday the 26th; for the last day; it consists of a superb representation of his late Majesty's funeral [George III] most assuredly the grandest piece of workmanship ever exhibited in this country; the richness of the coffin, the grandeur of the canopy, which is supported by the whole of his royal attendants, together with the lining of the room and the escutcheons, is so impressive a scene as to interest the feelings of every beholder; the cabinet consists of all the principle monarchs and commanders of the world, positively the largest and best collection that ever travelled. It will be seen at Penzance fair on Thursday next, and during a short stay in all the principal towns in Cornwall. Open from eleven till nine. Ladies and gentlemen 1s. Servants and children, 6d. Likenesses taken from 1s. to 3s. 26 May 1820

HOLLABURY FARM, BUDE

To be sold (with immediate possession) by public auction, at the White Hart Inn, in the borough of Launceston, on Monday, June the 19th, 1820 . . . that farm called Hollabury . . . The property lies in the parishes of Poughill and Stratton, in Cornwall, in the centre of a most beautiful, rich and romantic country, adjoining the sea, and forming the northern shore of the harbour at Bude, which is already so well known as a watering place, and likely rapidly to increase in importance, from the execution (now placed beyond doubt) of that great work, the Bude canal; and within a mile and a half of the market and port town of Stratton.

The whole estate is so contiguous to the best sea sand, which may be taken up in any quantity, gratis, and to lime kilns, at Bude, and the land is of so good a quality naturally, that it may be improved to an almost indefinite extent; especially as a fine stream of water runs through the property, by which from 15 to 20 acres may be completely irrigated. The whole forms one of the most desirable and improveable properties of its size in the county.

9 June 1820

FUMIGATING THE 'PRINCE ERNEST' PACKET

On Wednesday morning last, whilst four men were employed in fumigating the *Prince Ernest* packet, at Falmouth, with squibs (after the removal of the corpse of Lady Powerscourt), a spark of fire accidentally communicated with the magazine, which was incautiously left open, and in which was about 50 lbs. of gunpowder, which instantly exploded, blowing the deck and cabin, from the mainmast to the stern, to atoms, and shivering the mainmast. One man has his thigh and collar-bone broken, and another had his head severely cut by the accident. The damage the packet has sustained is estimated at from £700 to £800.

9 June 1820

TWO BROWN OXEN

Stolen or strayed, from Advent Common, two brown oxen, five years old, marked with a spade under the near ear, and a half-penny and spade on the further ear. Whoever will give information to Mr. Henry Pethick, of Trevalga, near Camelford, so that the said bullocks may be recovered, shall receive one pound reward. The person in whose possession the said bullocks may be found, after this public notice, will be prosecuted according to law.

16 June 1820

DEATH OF A YOUNG MINER

On Friday last, as a young man named Joseph Roberts was crossing a plank which was laid over a shaft at Bennar [Binner] Downs mine, the plank broke, and he fell into the shaft, which is about 10 fathoms deep, and was so severely injured that he died in two hours after the accident had happened.

30 June 1820

A CAUTION TO FARMERS

A respectable farmer in the neighbourhood of Launceston, lately entered into a compromise with the person to whom he had sold his wool, to prevent the penalty being levied for rolling up a considerable quantity of dirt and tail-locks in his fleeces. The following is an extract of the Act of Parliament relative to the management of wool: 'No man shall make any inwinding within the fleece at the rolling up of his wool, nor put in the same, cod-locks, pelt (or skin wool), tar, pitch, paint, stones, earth, grass, nor any dirt, nor tail-locks, or any other thing whereby the fleece may be more weighty to the loss of the buyer, on pain that the seller shall forfeit and pay the sum of two shillings per fleece, the whole thereof to go to the finder and prover of the said deceit.' 7 July 1820

HARD LABOUR AT LAUNCESTON GAOL

The gaol at Bodmin being crowded with prisoners, several of those sentenced to be kept at hard labour were a short time since transmitted to the gaol at Launceston. In order to keep these persons fully employed, Richard Penwarden, Esq., the Mayor, has commenced clearing away the rubbish which disfigures the green in front of that fine ruin, Launceston castle, and to render it accessible on different sides, by removing the nuisances which, in a great degree, hid the two gateways which remain in a state of tolerable preservation. The green is to be surrounded by a walk, which on one side commands an extensive prospect over the borough of Newport and the adjacent country. The prisoners employed have a pint of beer a day, in addition to the gaol allowance, and are so desirous of being employed in the open air, rather than within the walls of the prison, that a threat of not being allowed to work on the green is found sufficient to keep them in good order. 14 July 1820

A TITHE OF HAY

In the case of Geake v. Jones, at the last Bodmin Assizes, which was an action brought by Mr. Arth. Geake against the Rev. Thomas Jones for not taking away the tithe of hay after it had been duly set out for him, and which the defendant refused to do, for the following alleged reasons.

First, because the plaintiff had cut the field, which only consisted of eight acres, at four cuttings, and had set out the tithe of each cutting separately as the hay became fit to save, which he contended gave the rector unnecessary trouble—secondly, because the cocks were too small, there being 600 on an acre and a half—thirdly, because there was a great deal of rakings, which he contended were titheable—and fourthly because there was not room to take away the tithe without going over the farmer's hay, and subjecting him, the rector, to an action. Mr. Justice Burrough held that, as to the cutting in different pieces, the farmer had a right to do so, if he was prevented from cutting by change of weather, or if the grass was not equally ripe. That the cocks must necessarily be made small when it was intended to preserve the seed; otherwise the seed must be shaken out; and as to the rakings, he held that they were not titheable; and if a servant through negligence or want of skill should not have taken up the hay so clean as he ought to have done, the master is not answerable on that head for a fraud, unless it appeared to be done through a design to defraud the rector. His Lordship said, he thought the clergyman ought to have sufficient room to pass between the farmer's cocks with his waggons without doing damage to the farmer's hay, or else, it would not be a good setting forth of the tithe, unless the farmer gave the clergyman leave to pass over his hay, in removing the tithe. 1 September 1820

[Despite the above verdict, Geake was imprisoned by the Ecclesiastical Court, which declared he had sinned against the Holy Church by incorrectly setting out his tithe. The case was closely followed by the farming fraternity in Cornwall and when eventually Geake was freed in Exeter, he was met at Polson Bridge by crowds of Cornish yeomanry and escorted home.]

ATTEMPTED PLUNDER

On Monday night as the mail-coach was proceeding from Penzance to Falmouth, about two miles from Marazion, on the Helston road, it was nearly overset, by a large waggon wheel which was placed on the road; on proceeding farther, a large gate was discovered in a similar situation; at a short distance, a second gate was found also laid on the road. There can be no doubt that the object of those who placed these things was the obtaining an opportunity of plundering passengers, but fortunately the vigilance of the driver and guard of the coach prevented its accomplishment. 8 September 1820

TRURO ANNUAL SAILING MATCH

The prizes this year were, a handsome silver cup given by the members for the borough; and two sets of silk colours, given by the ladies of Truro. There were only six boats entered, which started from Mopus at half-past ten o'clock yesterday (Thursday) morning; went round the Black-rock, at the entrance to Falmouth harbour, and returned to a boat placed off Truro Quay. About three o'clock the cheers of the assembled multitudes announced the approach of the boats; the *Psyche*, Lieut. Cory, R.N., secured the first prize; the *Chevy Chase*, Mr. T. Bate, gained the second; and the *Cathlin*, Col. Willyams, obtained the third. 8 September 1820

TRURO SPINNING MANUFACTORY

Between three and four o'clock on Tuesday morning, a fire broke out in the spinning manufactory of Messrs. Plummer, in Mill-lane, in this town [Truro], and though the engines were promptly brought to the spot it was found that every effort to save the building in which the fire originated, must be unavailing . . . It appears that the fire originated in the following manner. The late drought having compelled the persons belonging to the factory to work when the accumulation of water in the reservoir was sufficient to set the machinery in motion, some persons were engaged in spinning at a late hour in the night. The foreman left the premises about midnight, when all was safe; but a woman and two girls continued at work, until two o'clock, when it appears they fell asleep, leaving a candle burning which set on fire a part of the machinery, and speedily the whole room was in flames. Those whose carelessness had occasioned the disaster, were only rendered conscious of their dreadful situation by the heat, which had become intolerable, just in time to save themselves from destruction, part of their clothing being scorched. 22 September 1820

FERRY ACROSS THE CAMEL

The ferry from Padstow to St. Minver has lately been much improved by the proprietor, who has erected, on a rock in the middle of those exposed sands, a house and a stable, for the accomodation of passengers and their horses, where a signal is made for the boat. Heretofore, passengers crossing this ferry, were obliged to stand exposed to the inclemency of the weather. 29 September 1820

TRACTS FOR THE PRISONERS

On Saturday next will be published, price nine pence, by Liddell and Sons, Bodmin, an account of Michael Stephens, who was executed at Bodmin, on the 5th of September last, pursuant to his sentence at the preceding Assizes, for sheep-stealing. By Joseph Fayrer, A. M. Chaplain to the County Prison.

This book is printed from a fund raised by the subscriptions of those friends of humanity who wish to encourage the prisoners in reading religious tracts. The chaplain will thankfully receive further contributions for the supply of tracts, as the prisoners read them with attention; and if they are permitted to carry them into their families, on their release from confinement, much good may be done to the community at large, and perhaps this little effort may tend to check the present alarming increase of crime in the county. 6 October 1820

VIOLATION OF THE SABBATH AT CAMELFORD

His Worship, the mayor [of Camelford] stated the existence of a practice in the borough, which was at once a great inconvenience to the inhabitants, at large, an outrage to decency and good morals, and a violation of the Sabbath; he alluded to the practice, adopted by the keepers of the common bake-houses, who draw the ovens on Sunday, before divine-service is concluded, at the church; by which those returning from public worship, are scandalized by meeting persons carrying dishes of meat, &c, through the streets; and many of them had to eat their dinners half-cold, as the meat was often half-an-hour to an hour from the oven before they were ready to sit down to it. The Bench of Aldermen expressed strong disapprobation of the scandalous practice complained of by the Mayor, and his Worship was requested to put the Act of Parliament against violating the Sabbath strictly into force, against all persons who should open an oven or carry meat from a bake-house before the conclusion of divine service. 6 October 1820

CONTRACT FOR CONVEYING PRISONERS

To the worshipful magistrates of the county of Cornwall. The present contract for conveying prisoners from Truro to Bodmin, being nearly expired, I beg to submit to your consideration the terms on which I am ready to contract with your worships, for conveying prisoners (from Truro to Bodmin) for any period of time you may think proper, viz. For conveying one prisoner only, £1.0.0.; for two ditto £1.7.0; for three ditto £1.14.0. And so on in proportion for any greater number. Should your worships approve of the above terms, I am prepared with security for my performance of the contract, I am, gentlemen, your obedient humble servant, Edward Parker Player. 13 October 1820

[Prisoners from areas west of Truro were conveyed to Redruth, Camborne or Helston and thence into Player's hands. It was not unknown for those convicted to be allowed to escape, so that there was a chance of charging for their conveyance a second time.]

SILVER FROM WHEAL ROSE

On Tuesday last a block of silver, worth £1,500, was smelted at Wheal Rose mine, in Newlyn. This mine is the sole property of Sir C. Hawkins, Bart. 13 October 1820

GATHERING LIMPETS AT CHAPEL PORTH

On Saturday last, four children belonging to a poor man named Cowling, who lives in a miserable hut at a place called Chapel-porth, within a mile of St. Agnes, were gathering limpets for a meal; being eager to obtain as many as possible, they did not attend to the progress of the tide which rushed in upon them before they were aware. Three of them effected their escape, but the fourth, a child aged 7 years, was borne off by a wave and drowned. 13 October 1820

FALMOUTH'S FIRST DRY DOCK, 1820

The public are respectfully informed that the undersigned has completed a dry dock in the port of Falmouth, which is now ready for the reception of ships; the dimensions whereof are, length 190 feet, breadth at the gates 42, do. in the middle of the dock 60, depth of water 18. It is acknowledged by competent judges that a more safe and convenient situation, in every respect, for the repair of ships, cannot be found. Richard L. Symons, Little Falmouth. 20 October 1820

REJOICINGS FOR QUEEN CAROLINE

On Saturday evening this village was illuminated, in consequence of the triumph of her Majesty over the authors of the Bill of Pains and Penalties. There was scarcely a window in which lights were not displayed; a brilliant star was exhibited on the engine-house of Chacewater Mine; the effect when viewed from the surrounding hills was very striking. A number of fireworks were let off, and a bonfire lighted, in which the effigies of Majocchi and Demont, with a green bag, were consumed, after having been paraded through the village, by a great concourse of people, and amidst shouts of "Long live Queen Caroline." 1 December 1820

[The object of the Bill of Pains and Penalties was to dethrone Queen Caroline, wife of the profligate George IV, on the grounds of her reputed indiscretions abroad. Most of the country felt so strongly in her favour that eventually the Bill was abandoned, and there was general rejoicing. Evidence against her was contained in the notorious green bag; Majocchi and Demont were witnesses against the Queen in her trial. The former later left Falmouth secretly for Italy.]

THE FOOTPADS' ASSISTANT

About half-past six o'clock on Sunday evening last, as a man named Edward Cock was going from Wadebridge to St. Columb, on the common . . . he heard a singular kind of noise which proceeded from the side of the road, and immediately felt his legs grasped by what he conceived to be an imp from the dominions of his satanic majesty, and which dragged a chain after it. The appearance of the demon was black, and it had a tail which it twisted around his leg, with great force. The poor fellow was dreadfully terrified and cried for help most lustily, but in vain . . .

15 December 1820

[The assailant was in fact a monkey, which footpads had trained to assist them in their activities].

DETERMINED ACTION BY THE MOONSHINE BRIGADE

Whereas it has been represented to the Commissioners of His Majesty's Customs that on the night of Saturday, the 11th ultimo, Sampson Woodcock, chief boatman, and his men, were out on duty in the preventive boat, stationed at Boscastle, in the county of Cornwall, for the prevention of smuggling, and went on shore at a place called Mullhook [Millook Haven], and seized from four to five hundred tubs of foreign rum spirits, and hauled their boat on to the beach and remained to guard their seizure; that soon after a smuggling cutter came into sight and afterwards two armed boats were sent from her, the crews of which, together with the crew of the cutter, commenced firing on the beach, which the preventive men returned until their ammunition was expended; that the smugglers then came on shore and attacked the said Sampson Woodcock and his men, and by superiority of numbers overpowered them, and compelled them to retreat, and after having driven them from the seizure, the said smugglers carried off the six-oared galley belonging to the preventive station and her materials, together with the tubs which the officers had seized and went off to sea.

The said Commissioners, in order to bring to justice the said offenders, are hereby pleased to offer a reward of £200 to any person or persons who shall discover or cause to be discovered any one or more of the said offenders, so that he or they may be apprehended and dealt with according to the law, to be paid by the collector of His Majesty's Customs at the port of Padstow, upon conviction . . .

N.B. The said smuggling cutter had sixteen black ports, eight of a side, bulwarks painted with a broad yellow side and a narrow black streak above, red counter with a yellow moulding, dark gaft topsail, dark fore-sail, white jib, and running bowsprit, and had a topsail yard across.

5 January 1821

TYTHE-FEAST IN PROBUS

On the 3rd instant, according to annual custom, the farmers of the parish of Probus met at what is called a tythe-feast, given by Sir C. Hawkins, Bart. in order to pay their great tithes for the past year. On this occasion, the worthy baronet, with a liberality highly creditable to him, directed that ten per cent should be deducted from the amount of composition entered into between him and the farmers, previously to the last harvest. This act called forth the warmest acknowledgments from the farmers; and after dinner, the health of Sir C. Hawkins was drank with three times three, followed by long-continued cheering . . . On the following evening, about 150 laborers in the employ of Sir C. Hawkins, with their wives and children, sat down in one room at Trewithen, to the annual abundant supper provided for them by his order, after which they were regaled with a liberal supply of excellent punch. 12 January 1821

DIVINE WORSHIP IN GWAVAS LAKE

A public meeting was held at the sailors' chapel, in Newlyn, on Wednesday evening, February 28th, Rev. G. C. Smith, in the chair; when a society was formed, and called "The Sailors' Children's Bethel Union

Society, at Newlyn, in Mounts Bay". The objects of which are, to obtain a Bethel flag, as a signal for divine worship on board ships, wind bound, in Gwavas Lake [that part of Mount's Bay off Newlyn]; and to procure a certain number of the Sailors' Magazines, every month, to be read among the children of the Sunday school. 9 March 1821

WALKS AWKWARD BUT VERY NIMBLE

Absconded from his family, John Dennis, of the parish of Wendron, on Wednesday the 7th March instant. He went off with a woman called Eliz. Johns. He is about 4 feet 6 inches high, 35 years old, fair complexion, flaxen hair, blue eyes, and has a protuberance on his back; he is something short on his left side, and limps on his left leg; walks awkward, but very nimble; he wore away a nankeen short coat, white waistcoat and barragan trowsers; he also carried off other clothes; speaks in a soft manner, can play on the violin, has been accustomed to travel with show-men and Merry Andrews [clowns], generally called by the feminine appellation of "Molly the Horner". Elizabeth Johns is about 30 years of age, something of a sallow complexion, dark hair, black eyes, rather under the common size, and of a genteel appearance. It is supposed the fugitives are gone in a route towards Launceston.

It is earnestly desired that no one will countenance or support them, as he has left a wife, with four small children who are ill of the small pox, so that he may be necessitated to return to his distressed family.

23 March 1821

THE PREVENTIVE MEN OF MEVAGISSEY

During a very heavy gale on Tuesday afternoon, 15 or 16 large fish of the species called grampus were driven on shore at Mevagissey. Several of them measured from 15 to 20 feet in length. A vast number of them appeared in the bay, and being observed by the persons engaged in the preventive service, were mistaken for a raft of kegs of smuggled spirits which the gale had torn from their moorings, at the bottom, and which were floating and driving about on the surface. Under this idea and in the hope of obtaining a rich prize, the boats were manned and put out, regardless of the tremendous seas then going. Having ascertained their mistake, they were on their return, when one of the boats unfortunately upset; and of seven men who were aboard, three, named Johnson, Clarke and Partridge, were unfortunately drowned; the others were picked up by the boats in company. 25 May 1821

PENZANCE DISPENSARY

We have been, as usual favoured with the Annual Report of this most excellent and flourishing charity . . . It appears from the physician's report that the number of patients admitted last year is much greater than on any preceding one, being, exclusive of the cases of vaccination, 639. Of these 347 have been cured, 172 relieved, 13 have been discharged irregular, 18 have died and 90 remain on the books . . .

By far the most important and numerous [diseases] are the distressing complaints which are either immediately or remotely referable to functional derangement of the stomach and other digestive organs . . . The great majority of these occurred in the persons of women, and some in children. In the former class of persons they can in most cases be traced as the effect of imperfect and improper nutriment . . . The daily food of many of these consists, almost entirely, of imperfectly baked barley bread and warm water (misnamed tea). 1 June 1821

CORNISH COPPER

To be sold by auction, on Tuesday the 12th day of June instant, at two o'clock in the afternoon, at the Battery Mills, in St. Erth, an excellent water wheel, about 42 feet in diameter, and 6 feet in the breast. 8 June 1821

[These Battery mills were formerly an adjunct of the copper smelting works at nearby Hayle.]

MASSIVE LEAD SMELTING HOUSE

For sale by private contract, Garras smelting-house [at Idless, near Truro], with all the offices, smith's shop, two handsome dwellings, comprising four rooms and offices in each, completely furnished, and five acres of land, with a capital stream of water equal to working a large water wheel. The premises called the smelting-house is well calculated where room is required, being substantially built of stone and slated roof, and is 300 feet long, by 23 feet wide within. It may be fitted up for dwellings at a trifling expense, and is capable of being divided into twenty-two houses with four commodious rooms in each. 15 June 1821

THREAT TO THE SEANERS

We trust that, as the [pilchard] season advances, effectual methods will be resorted to by the sean owners, to prevent the driving boats from impeding the progress of the shoals of pilchards on their approach to our shores. Generally, during the season, these boats form a regular line for miles, off the prinicipal fishing stations on the coast, and by throwing their nets, disperse the head of the shoal of fish, and give a new direction to the remainder. This, we understand, has been the case for several years in Mount's Bay, the entrance of which is closed during the fishing season, by a continued line of driving boats. Unless the laws be put in force against these obstructions of the sean fishery, that once profitable adventure must be wholly abandoned . . . 13 July 1821

"CORPORATION COAL" AT MARAZION

Mr. Editor, On passing through Marazion yesterday, in my gig, I met with serious inconvenience from a number of piles of coal lying at the doors of different persons in the principal street or thoroughfare, with a decently dressed man standing by each heap, as its owner or guardian. I thought it had an appearance such as I never before saw (nor do I think would be tolerated) in any town this side of London. On my return this day from Penzance, I found the same nuisance continued in an increasing degree. Heaps of coal, each having its attendant guardian; carts discharging their contents in the street, and returning driven, Jehu-like, to be again filled; the asses and pigs (animals I believe very common in this town, for I counted no less than 17 of the latter on going through) flying before them in all directions. The place seemed as if in arms, and the screeching of a number of sea-gulls over my head forcibly reminded me of the confusion at Babel . . . On making inquiry into these transactions, of a gentleman at the head of the town, I was highly amused on being told, that this coal was what is termed the "Corporation coal", or annual cargo of Newport coals, of 14 weys, which the members of that respectable body divide between them at the rate of half a wey each; and that the person standing at the head of the piles was either an alderman or an assistant.

3 August 1821

OVERNIGHT MAIL, 1821

We understand that arrangements have been made by the Post-Office with the contractors of the mail-coaches by which twenty-four hours will be saved on the time now occupied in forwarding the mail from Falmouth to London. In consequence of this arrangement, the times at which letters are now received and dispatched from the different post towns, will be altered throughout the county; the post from London will reach Truro at half-past seven o'clock in the morning, and Falmouth about half-past nine; the post from Falmouth for London will leave at half-past two in the afternoon. 3 August 1821

THE ROYAL SQUADRON OFF LAND'S END

The fine appearance of the Royal squadron, each vessel carrying every stitch of canvas she could crowd, in order to keep up with the leading [Royal] yacht; the men stationed in the tops, in blue jackets and clean white trowsers, and the number of elegant private yachts that accompanied the Royal squadron, making in the whole between twenty and thirty sail, of all sizes, are described as forming a grand spectacle, even to nautical men. The whole went round the rocks at the Land's End, called the Long-ships, with a fine breeze, and stood up St. George's Channel. A number of persons went from Penzance to the Land's End on Sunday morning to see his Majesty pass round that celebrated headland.

10 August 1821

[George IV was *en route* for a three weeks' visit to Ireland.]

WAY-LAID IN GWENNAP

We, the undersigned, having on Sunday evening the 14th instant, about eight o'clock, in a most shameful, disgraceful and cowardly manner, way-laid, attacked, and assaulted Captain John Barrett and his wife, who were peacefully riding on the high-way, near Comfort, in the parish of Gwennap: in consequence of his unmerited forbearance towards us, in stopping proceedings at Law, which were instituted against us, we have agreed to pay the expenses of inserting this article in the two county papers, paying the law-cost, and giving five pounds in bread, to the poor of the parish of Gwennap, on Sunday next, the 28th instant, as witness our hands, this 22nd October, 1821. John Michell, the sign or mark of X John Scoble, the sign or mark X of Martin Pope, the sign or mark of X Jonath. Jennings, the sign or mark of X John Barratt. Witness John Dinnis, Jun.

26 October 1821

THE ASYLUM'S FIRST YEAR

A general statement of the pauper patients admitted and discharged from the opening of the asylum, 25th October, 1820, to the 25th October, 1821. Cured, males 2, females 2; considerably improved, males 3, females 1; improved, males 9, females 3; stationary, males 7, females 5; died, males 2, females 0. Of the above two have been insane 20 yrs, one 14 years, one 12 years, one 11 years, two 10 years, two 9 years, one 8 years, one 7 years, 2 six years, four 5 years, one 4 years, three 3 years, four 2 years, two 1 year and seven less than 1 year. Richard Kingdon M.D., Medical Superintendent.

26 October 1821

CAPTURED IN TRURO RIVER

The preventive boat of Gerrans, on Friday night last, captured a fine boat in Truro River, (formerly Venn's Truro packet), with 112 tubs and 6 ankers of spirit on board. The crew escaped by running the vessel on shore.

2 November 1821

THE EVILS OF WRESTLING: A RELIGIOUS VIEW

The dispensations of Heaven are awful. Miners, in order to procure the necessaries of life, are obliged to work in foul air, and damp places, and to expose themselves to continual dangers. The consequences are sometimes fatal. What numbers, not much past the meridian of life, are now pining away and dying daily, through asthmas, coughs, blindness, maimed or amputated limbs, and emaciated bodies; and what numbers are suddenly called away from the shafts to eternity. And these calamities are brought on them in the prosecution of their lawful business. There is one consideration, and one only that could reconcile us to such a dispensation, and that is, the assurance granted by a merciful God, that these momentary afflictions will work together for the eternal good of every man who does not counteract their gracious tendency by neglecting his salvation. The confirmation of which promise appears in the conversion of many miners, who are men of experimental religion and practical godliness. Let these be consulted, and they will declare, that they could not attend such sports [as wrestling], without violating the dictates of their judgment, without trampling on that sacred command, "Whether therefore ye eat or drink, or whatsoever ye do, do all to the glory of God". 2 November 1821

[This tirade was part of an advertisement designed to persuade wrestlers and those promoting the sport to abandon it for the sake of the spiritual well-being of those who attended such contests, usually miners. As John Wesley had strongly disapproved of such riotous amusements as wrestling and hurling, so did his followers (see p. 129).]

GRAMPOUND STOP-GATE

Whereas the toll-house at the bottom of Grampound Hill, was unroofed on the night of Monday the 29th instant, and the chimney pulled down, and the stop-gate or bar taken up and thrown over Grampound-bridge; the trustees do hereby offer a reward of ten pounds, to any person or persons giving such information to Mr. John Edwards, Attorney-at-Law; or Mr. John Hayward, Surveyor, Truro, as may be the means of convicting the offender or offenders. The same to be paid by the Treasurer on conviction.

2 November 1821

[Turnpike tolls were unpopular, and evasion of payment fairly commonplace. Such deceits as unhitching one horse out of two being used and circumventing the toll-house with it; of turning down a parish road before the gate was in sight—permissible only if less than 100 yards of the turnpike had been used beforehand; or of altering a toll-ticket to appear to be that of another bar, a most serious offence, were all practised.]

NORTHERN COASTERS

The boats to the number of 80, engaged on the herring fishery in our [St. Ives] bay came in this morning, literally laden with the finest and fattest pilchards you ever saw. They brought on shore from 10 to 50,000 per boat, in all about 800 hogsheads, the like was never seen here before with drift-boats, and they sold at 20s. per gurry [large hand-barrows for carrying fish], containing about 1000 fish. What is worthy of remark is, that yesterday morning they had a fine catch of herrings, without any pilchards, and this morning, pilchards without any (or a very few) herrings. It is the general belief, that they fell in with a body of pilchards, which we call northern coasters, which 30 or 40, or more years back, was common at this season, on our coast. A master of a vessel told me this morning, that he fell in yesterday, off Bude, with shoals of fish, of *several miles* in extent; had our seans been at sea, and hewers [look-out men] on the hills yesterday, I have no doubt but the town would have been full of fish, as the greatest quantity of fish, taken by the boats, was early in the night, and very near the shore. 23 November 1821

MURDER

Whereas some villain, or villains, did, on Wednesday the 28th day of November last, about seven o'clock in the evening shoot at and mortally wound Mr. Anthony Rowse, near Whitehall, in the parish of Kenwyn on his return from Truro to Redruth. The principal inhabitants of Redruth, Gwennap and Chacewater and its neighbourhood, do hereby offer a reward of 400 pounds, to any person giving such information as shall convict the offender or offenders.

The magistrates of the district have also made application that any accomplice turning King's evidence, shall receive his Majesty's pardon, and be entitled to the above reward, except the person who actually fired the shot. 7 December 1821

[The killer lay in ambush with a horse pistol among the mine burrows. Rowse's widow and six children were provided for by public subscription.]

A DESERVING CASE

Last week, a pauper 75 years of age in the parish of St. Teath, after receiving his parochial pay went to a public-house to spend his money, and in crossing the church stile on his way home, being in a state of intoxication he fell and had his leg fractured so badly as to render amputation above the ancle necessary. 28 December 1821

THE NEW PIER AT ST. MICHAEL'S MOUNT

On Friday last, this [Mount's] bay was visited by one of the most tremendous storms ever remembered. During its continuance the great advantages attending the new pier at St. Michael's Mount were apparent, as the vessels within it rode with the greatest ease. But towards the evening the wind shifted to the west and threw a most tremendous sea on the addition to the western pier, which was only about half completed, and wanted a considerable quantity of filling. The consequence was that the whole body of water thus pressed on the outside of the pier rose over the outer wall, and falling on the wall on the inside, occasioned it to give way. The outer wall being deprived of its support, also gave way and fell for about sixty feet. Great fears were then entertained for the safety of the vessels in the pier, and one captain scuttled his ship; but his fears were groundless, as two vessels, a brig and a schooner, which were next to him, rode out the storm without sustaining the smallest injury.

4 January 1822

FEVER FROM THE MARSHES

We are concerned to find that an epidemic disorder of the nature of low typhus fever prevails at Penzance and its vicinity. Between two and three hundred persons are, we understand, at present affected by it; there have, however, but few deaths taken place. The disorder, it is supposed has been occasioned by the flooding of the extensive marshes in the neighbourhood.

18 January 1822

[The marshes were those at Marazion, newly drained by Messrs. Bolitho, tin smelters and tanners at Chyandour, and which were inundated during the recent storm (see 4th January).]

TO CORNISH MARINERS

The light-house on the end of the pier at the port of Swansea is now illuminated by sixty gas lamps, appropriately arranged in the form of an anchor.

18 January 1822

WEEKLY SHIPPING LIST

Truro, Jan. 17. Entered inwards, the *Mary*, the *Caroline*, the *Zena* and *Harriet*, the *Gratitude*, all from Wales; and the *Pheasant* from Plymouth.

Cleared outwards, the *Yeoman's Glory*, the *Hero*, the *Happy Couple*, the *Waterloo*, the *Emerald*, the *Dispatch*, the *Good Intent*, the *Mary*, the *Martha*, and the *Hope*, all for Wales; and the *William* for Liverpool.

Charlestown, Jan. 15. Arrived the *Active*, the *Charles* and the *Rashleigh*, all from Swansea; the *Duporth* and the *Fowey*, from Fowey; the *Fame*, the *Charlestown* and the *Lark*, all from Plymouth.

Sailed, the *Pheasant*, and the *Patty* for Swansea; the *Ann* and *Elizabeth* and the *Lark*, for Mevagissey.

Fowey, Jan. 18. Arrived the *Kitty*, the *Salt* from Bideford; the *Fancy* and *Greyhound* cutters, and the *Medina*, from Cowes; the *Ann* and *Elizabeth*, and the *Fowey*, from London; the *Thomas* from Dublin; the *Flower*, from Neath; the *Hero*, from Swansea; the *Industry*, from Newport; the *Sally* from Neath; the *Lucy* and the *Sprightly*, from Newport; the *Jane and Elizabeth* and the *Good Intent*, from Llanelly.

Sailed, the *Revolution*, for Bristol; the *Nicholas* for New Orleans; the *Ann* for Liverpool; the *Active* for Swansea; the *Shakespeare* for Jamaica; the *Mary* and the *William* for St. Michael's; the *Fancy*, *Greyhound* and *Wolf* cutters, and the *Thomas*, for London; the *Marshal Blucher* for St. Michael's; and the *Susanna* for Swansea. 18 January 1822

THE COMPLETION OF TREGOTHNAN

The Earl of Falmouth has liberally distributed a quantity of beef and bread to the poor inhabitants of the parishes of St. Mary's, Truro, and of Kenwyn and St. Michael Penkivell, on the completion of the noble mansion he has erected at Tregothnan. 18 January 1822

COMFITS AT CAMBORNE FAIR

James Holman, Henry Warren, James Lean, Richard Cock, and James Prideaux, all boys, were found guilty of stealing a bag of comfits from the standing of Samuel Lean, at Camborne fair, on the 12th of November last. To be imprisoned for one month, and to be privately whipped.

25 January 1822

ANTIMONY MINE IN ENDELLION

To be sold by private contract, three-16th parts of shares in all that valuable antimony mine or adventure called Wheal Arthur, at Tresungues, in the parish of Endellion, in the county of Cornwall, with the like parts or shares in the ores, tackle, smelting utensils and materials. Also some tons of antimony ore, now at grass [surface]. For further particulars, apply to Captain Joseph Glanvill, at Port Isaac, in the said parish of Endellion. Persons in want of antimony ore, or regulus of antimony, may be supplied, upon application to the said Joseph Glanvill.

8 February 1822

CORNWALL'S COBALT MINE

The working of Wheal Sparnon cobalt mine, which has been for some time suspended, from some repairs being necessary to the engine, &c, will, we understand be shortly resumed. The Cobalt Smelting Company are certainly entitled to every support from the public; as their mine is the only one in England where cobalt is found in abundance, and producing so beautiful a colour; and as it renders us independent of foreigners for this article, which hitherto was supplied by them. We sincerely hope that after so much exertion and expense, the company will be amply rewarded; for the cobalt raised by them stands unrivalled by any other in the market, as can be attested by houses of the first respectability; viz. Messrs. Flight, Barr and Co., Messrs. Chamberlains, Messrs. Spode and Co., and Messrs. Ralph Bourne and Co. 15 February 1822

THE MARKETS AT ST. COLUMB

There is now newly-erected at St. Columb, a butter and poultry market, (adjoining the corn-market), which will prove very advantageous to both the purchaser and the seller. The above having been made at a great expense to the proprietors of the markets, they, therefore, earnestly request that all persons who may have either of the above commodities for sale, may bring the same to the public market, which will be opened on the 14th instant. 15 February 1822

THE POOR IN NORTH CORNWALL

Mr. Editor, The distressed state of agriculture is now, I believe, universally admitted:- but some seem to admit it with reluctance; for a polite correspondent of yours has lately told us, that he thinks more is made of it than the case will fairly bear; that the labouring poor are better off than they were some time ago; and that the poor rates have not, in many instances, been increased in consequence of husbandmen having been thrown out of employ . . . If your correspondent, who seems solicitous to be correctly informed in the subject, would condescend to visit the vestries of St. Kea, Endellion, St. Teath or Lanteglos by Camelford, four adjoining parishes in the hundred of Trigg; at either of these vestries would be found numbers of able and industrious labourers applying, some for work, some for shoes, some for shirts or other garments for themselves or their children, and sometimes for both . . . Let your correspondent accompany the overseers in the collection of rates; he will find the farm-houses crammed with apprentices, and more than half of them unable to raise a pound note . . .but, at the same time, they will endeavour to conceal their poverty by excuses, and promises to pay the overseers when their debtors have paid them. 15 March 1822

AGRICULTURAL DISTRESS

To David Howell, Esq., High Sheriff of the county of Cornwall. We, the undersigned, owners and occupiers of land in the county of Cornwall, labouring under unexampled distress from the unprecedented low price of all agricultural produce, and oppressed by an excessive weight of taxation, which added to the payment of rent, rates, tithes, and an enormously increased poor-rate, has become intolerable, request you to call a meeting of the owners and occupiers of land in this county, to consider the present distress of all classes, and of the agricultural class in particular, and of the best and speediest means of obtaining relief. Also to take into consideration the defective and unequal state of the representation of the people in the Commons' House of Parliament, to which we believe the burthens and privations under which we suffer, are principally to be attributed.

22 March 1822

[There were 482 signatories to this petition, whose agricultural holdings ranged in size from 4250 acres to as little as four. The numerous small holdings of miner-farmers, who were as oppressed as any, were normally even less than the latter.]

A ST. COLUMB WEDDING

At a wedding last week, at St. Columb, the persons present stood in the following relations to each other—two fathers, two brothers, two uncles, two fathers-in-law, two cousins, a husband and wife, and a son and daughter, yet the company consisted of only four persons.

22 March 1822

YOUNG MERRY ANDREW

To cover this season, at Tresillian House, in Newlyn, at one pound each mare, and half-a-crown the groom, Young Merry Andrew, the property of Richard Gully Bennet, Esq. Merry Andrew was got by Merry Andrew, who was got by Plantation, his grand-dam by Herod, great grand-dam by Old Snip, which mare was also grand-dam of Giant, his great grand-dam by the Godolphin Arabian; his great-great-great grand-dam Frampton Whiteneck, who was full sister to Mixbury Galloway, own brother to the dam of Partner. Young Merry Andrew's dam is a strong useful mare, got by the celebrated horse Nimrod, so well known in the western parts of this county as a hunter. If further proves of Merry Andrew's high blood were necessary, we could trace his kindred from the flying Childers, who ran over the Beacon course, four miles, one furlong, one hundred and thirty-eight yards, in seven minutes and thirty seconds, covering at each bound a space of twenty-five feet, and is allowed by the best judges to be the most perfect stallion in the county.

29 March 1822

AT BOILING WATER MINE

Cornwall Lent Assizes. William Lanyon was indicted for stealing a quantity of rope, the property of Thomas Pearse and others, his co-adventurers, in Boiling-water mine, in the parish of Wendron. It appeared from the evidence adduced, that the mine had not been worked for some time; that several articles of brass work, lead, rope, &c. had been missed by Mr. Pearse, who had care of the materials; that in consequence, two persons were set to watch on the mine, on the nights of the 27th and 28th of February last. On the latter night, about half-past nine o'clock, they saw the prisoner break open the door of the powder-house, and take out a piece of rope, which he was preparing to carry off, when they rushed upon him and took him into custody. Guilty; to be transported for seven years. 29 March 1822

AFFRAY IN ST. DENNIS

Cornwall Assizes. The King v. Martin and three others. The defendants were indicted for assaulting George Fleming, an excise-officer, and W. Truscott, a constable of St. Dennis, in the exercise of their duty. It appeared from the evidence, that in July last, Flemming went from St. Columb to St. Dinnis to look after the unlicensed people who *sold* cakes and *gave away* beer. He called at a public-house kept by Wm. Kent, in which the anniversary of a friendly society was held. He saw Martyn, who grossly abused him; a quarrel ensued and blows were given. Truscott, the constable, interferred to keep the peace, but was knocked down by the members of this friendly society, and very ill-used.

Martin, in his defence, said that there was nothing in the case that could be construed into an obstruction of Flemming in his duty. Instead of searching for ale, which it might be his duty to do, this worthy member of the Excise took a fancy to a slice of the Society's beef, over which his duty certainly gave him no control, and the rude manner in which he performed the operation of cutting it off, was the real cause of irritation. He took it upon him also to interfere with the musicians, who were paid by the Society, commanding them to play him a tune, and he thought this was carrying the Excise laws a little too far. 5 April 1822

THE RUSSIAN VICE-CONSUL

In compliance with an order which I have just received from the Department of Foreign Trade at Petersburgh, I hereby give notice to all whom it may concern, that the new Russian tariff is now in my possession and may be seen at my office. I am ordered by the Minister of Finance to give him regular information on the following five points, and to request all persons sending vessels or goods from the ports of Falmouth, Gweek, Penzance, Scilly, St. Ives and Padstow, to any port in Russia, to furnish me with the desired information which the Minister informs me it is their interest to give. 1st. The names of all vessels bound to Russia and of their masters. 2nd. Particulars of the cargo, if any. 3rd. The shippers and consigners. 4th. The ports of destination. 5th. The day of sailing. Alfred Fox, Russian Vice-Consul, Falmouth. 24 May 1822

WAITING FOR THE SURGEON

Last week a man in the employment of Mr. Stephen Wade, of the parish of Tintagel, was attending to a threshing-machine, the sleeve of his shirt got entangled in the machinery, by which his arm was drawn in and so dreadfully mangled as to render amputation near the shoulder necessary. The operation was skilfully performed by Mr. Avery, from Boscastle, and Mr. Herring, from Camelford, who were sent for on the occasion; the poor fellow is likely to do well. 31 May 1822

CUSTOMS HOUSE AT HELFORD

We understand that a representation having been made to the Board of Customs respecting the great inconvenience sustained by the masters of vessels trading to the port of Gweek, by the custom house being at Helston, the Board have ordered that the custom house be removed from the borough of Helston to Helford, which being near the mouth of the harbour, will afford the desired convenience. 14 June 1822

VAN DIEMEN'S LAND

This fertile and beautiful island has already so far outrun the most sanguine expectations that could have been entertained on its first settlement, as to have nearly doubled its population and produce within two years. To the farmer and the small landholder, who, from the exaction of high war rents, the depression of the agricultural produce, improvident speculation, or any other causes, may incline to emigrate from the land of their fathers.—to the artificer, and indeed to all who command a little capital and a good stock of labour, it will be found a land flowing with milk and honey . . . Of the two rivers whose sources are about the centre of the Island, and whose streams run in opposite directions, the northern one has been called the Tamar, and the southern the Derwent; and the northern half of the island watered by the former is distinguished by the name of Cornwall . . . Iron is said to be most abundant near Launceston, on the Tamar, where there are entire mountains of this ore, and so rich as to have yielded 70 per cent of pure metal. 26 July 1822

[In 1822 for the first time those wishing to settle in New South Wales or Van Diemen's Land were required to have Government permission, good character references and at least £500 in capital. No such conditions were attached to emigration to other British colonies.]

A BALLAD SELLER

On Sunday last a Coroner's inquest was held on the body of a young man who was seen on the road between Wadebridge and St. Columb, in a very exhausted state, the evening before, and who died while he was being conveyed to the poor-house of the parish in which he was found.

It appears the deceased had been in the neighbourhood a few days before he died, selling ballads; he called himself Henry Johns, and said that he was born in Buryan . . . The jury found that he died by the visitation of God. The body was interred in St. Issey church-yard. 23 August 1822

TREAD-WHEEL FOR BODMIN

The Justices at the Quarter Sessions, have ordered that a tread-wheel be immediately erected in the bridewell-yard, at Bodmin, for the employment of the prisoners liable to be kept at hard labour.

18 October 1822

[The tread-mill, installed within an enclosure of iron railings, cost £134. The average healthy prisoner spent from three to five hours every other day on this contraption, working at a rate of about 50 steps a minute. Many of them were ruptured as a result. Where a capstan was available this was used on the intervening days, as well as for the old or the sick (see also p. 162).]

LOST ON THE AUGUST ROCKS

The shore of Mount's Bay, near Marazion, presented a melancholy sight yesterday morning. A smuggling vessel was lost on the August Rocks [immediately west of the Mount pier] during Wednesday night, and all on board perished. The beach was covered with fragments of the wreck, and kegs of spirits. The stern of the vessel has been washed on shore with the words "*Rose*, James Richards, Gweek", painted on it. The bodies of two men have been picked up. A watch found upon one, is marked "James Gilbert". 25 October 1822

THE TURNPIKE ROADS

The turnpike roads in the vicinity of Truro are certainly kept in a much better state of repair than those in any other part of the county; this is the result of the uniform attention paid by the trustees, and the surveyor of the said roads, to the duties of their office, as well as to their perseverance in the practice of breaking the stones employed for the purpose of repairing the roads, to a much smaller size, than heretofore; by which means, the surface is more equal and safe, and also more durable than where large stones are made use of. The operation is necessarily tedious, and, in the first instance, expensive; and is rendered still more so, by the extreme hardness of the stone broken for the purpose.

8 November 1822

MOONLIGHT REMOVAL

On Tuesday last was committed to the House of Correction, at Bodmin, for six months to hard labour, by J. F. Devonshire, Esq. and the Rev. T. Carlyon, magistrates for this county, James Taylor, for removing his furniture by night, with intent to defraud his landlord of the rent.

22 November 1822

CHANGE IN THE PACKET SERVICE

The Lords Commissioners of His Majesty's Treasury have determined on the expediency of transferring the superintendence of the Falmouth Post-office packets, to the Board of Admiralty but that no alteration will be made in regard to the station from which the packets now sail. That the ordinary refitting of the packets at Falmouth will continue as heretofore, and that the Navy Board will adopt all the present contracts and will continue the persons now employed. It is understood that the first building of the packets has not heretofore been wholly confined to Falmouth, and in future, it will probably take place (at least in the time of peace,) in the King's Dock Yards. 6 December 1822

[The establishment was not moved from Falmouth, as had been feared, but in the following year was commenced the introduction of Government 10-gun brigs in lieu of the Falmouth-built packets.]

THE RIOT ACT READ IN CAMELFORD

The good people of Camelford and its immediate vicinity, have been lately occupied by a contest which has arisen between the partisans of the two noble lords, who contend for the patronage of that ancient and respectable borough. The Earl of Darlington having purchased the greater part of the houses and lands within the borough, conceives that he has thereby obtained a legitimate right to nominate the members who represent it in Parliament, according to the ancient and laudable usage of the place. This claim, which the law of the land does not exactly recognise, has latterly been disputed by the Marquis of Hertford, who conceives that the right of nomination belongs to the individual who can adduce to the electors the most weighty and satisfactory arguments in support of his claim; and in order to be in a situation the most favourable for giving to his appeals to the *feelings* and *patriotism* of the said electors, the greatest possible effect, the said Marquis has purchased almost all the houses and land within the borough, that do not belong to the Earl of Darlington. In the course of these purchases, he has become possessed of a moiety [half] of a tenement consisting of a house and about six acres of land, called Culloden, the other moiety of which belongs to Lord Darlington. The tenant in possession of this valuable spot, was induced by some means or other, which must remain unexplained, to surrender the premises to the friends of the Earl, on the night of the 22nd of last month. As soon as this important event came to the knowledge of the friends of the Marquis, they mustered in considerable force, in order to oust the intruders, by force of arms. For this purpose, they commenced an attack upon the outer gate with hatchets, &c. in order to force an entrance;—the retainers of the *legitimate* patron flew to arms, made a sortie, and a furious conflict ensued. There is no knowing what damage might have been sustained in life and limb, amongst the redoubtable champions of *legitimacy*, on the one hand, and of *popular rights* on the other, had not the Mayor of the borough, as in duty bound hastened to the spot, and [read] the Riot Act. 3 January 1823

[In October the Marquis of Hertford erected a house in a large garden in Camelford, the purpose of which was to accommodate several of his supporters threatened with ejection from their existing dwellings by the rival Earl. As soon as the house was roofed, a party of miners commenced sinking a shaft not far away as part of what they christened the Kennel Mine; they then found it necessary to drive an adit under the building, at which point harder rock was unfortunately encountered and gunpowder had to be employed. The house was reduced to a heap of ruins. A second house was later undermined, and it transpired that the Mayor was in charge of the team of eleven miners.]

TIN AND COBALT IN MOUNT'S BAY

New Wherry mine, near Penzance. A few shares to be disposed of by private contract, any time between this and March next, when it is intended to begin working again. It is thought to be a very promising concern, as the last fathom's sinking yielded between £20 and £30 worth of very good tin, on a new lode, a little distance from the Old Wherry, once so famous for its great profits in tin and cobalt. It is only 14 feet deep from the surface of the rock, and a very extensive set. 3 January, 1823

NEAR SHALLOW ADIT

Whereas, in the night of Saturday the 4th instant, the lamp at the Redruth turnpike-gate, was wilfully and maliciously broken, and the door of the turn-pike house, near Shallow Adit, on the same road, also broken and carried off, the toll-board torn down, and the turnpike bar broken into two parts. A reward of ten guineas is hereby offered to such person or persons as will give such information as may lead to the conviction of the offender or offenders. 10 January 1823

FLOODING IN WHEAL SPEED

On Saturday, an inquest was held at Lelant, before Mr. Pearce Rogers, one of the coroners for this county, on the body of William Uren, who met his death at Wheal Speed mine, in that neighbourhood, under the following circumstances. The deceased, his father, his brother, and another man were at work together in the mine, when a dam which kept back a considerable body of water suddenly gave way, and the torrent rushed down upon them with resistless fury. An alarm being made, assistance was speedily procured, when it was found that the deceased had been instantly drowned; the others were got out alive, after having been several times immersed in water, a quantity of which mixed with gravel they had swallowed. Every proper means were resorted to in order to free their stomachs from the gravel they had taken in, but they have been so severely affected by it, that it is apprehended they cannot long survive.

10 January 1823

BURIED ON CASTLE DENNIS

On Thursday last, died suddenly, at his house in the parish of Ludgvan, Mr. James Hosken, a farmer who was possessed of some property, but of singular opinions and eccentric conduct. Several years since, he parted from his wife, in a fit of jealousy, occasioned by her allowing of a salute from a relative who was taking leave on going abroad. The quarrel was never made up, and he afterwards lived with different women. He evidenced little respect for the forms of religion, and in consequence of a dispute with the clergy-man of the parish, declared that he should not be interred in the church-yard. In consequence of this determination, he fixed on a spot as the resting place of his mortal remains, on a hill near the ruins of an ancient tower called Castle Dennis [Castle-an-Dinas], from which there is a view of both channels. Here he enclosed a small piece of ground with a wall, and at each end fixed a tablet; on the one is engraved, "Custom is the idol of fools", on the other "Virtue only consecrates the ground". In this spot his remains were deposited, on Monday last, agreeably to the directions of his will. A concourse of between 5000 and 6000 persons attended, to whom the Rev. G. S. Smith, Baptist Minister of Penzance, delivered a discourse on the occasion.

17 January 1823

SKAITING ON SWAN-POOL

The admirers of skaiting at Falmouth, were gratified on Saturday last by several gentlemen who displayed their skill on the Swan-pool in the neighbourhood of that town. The middle of the pool was quite a promenade for the ladies, who were so delighted with the ease and elegance with which the gentlemen appeared to move as to forget their fair forms on the slippery ice. On Sunday there were more than a hundred on the ice together.

24 January 1823

AN ENGINE-HOUSE TO BUILD

On Monday, the 10th of February next, by two o'clock in the afternoon, a survey will be held at Wheal Vor mine, in the parish of Breage, for setting an engine-house and boiler-house to build, for an 80-inch cylinder. The taker to cut the stone for the same, and finish it in a proper manner.

24 January 1823

THE LOSS OF THE BUDE PILOT BOAT

On Friday se'nnight the pilot boat belonging to the harbour of Bude brake from her moorings and was drifting out to sea, when the men belonging to the preventive service at that place went off in their boat, in which they took four other persons, in order to recover her. Having got alongside the pilot boat, they put on board the four men . . . The state of the weather was very unfavourable, the wind blew off the shore, the sea ran very high, and the cold was intense. The preventive boat with great difficulty reached the harbour, but the pilot boat was driven off, and when last seen, was about four miles from the harbour, the men pulling to the westward. As no account has since been received of them, it is supposed the unfortunate men becoming benumed and worn down with fatigue, were compelled to resign the struggle with the elements. The following are the names of these poor fellows, with a description of the persons and dress:—W. Wilson, a young man aged about 24 years, had on a light fustian jacket and trowsers, a yellow striped waistcoat, and had about him an order for six pounds and a letter addressed to Mr. Waddington, from G. Phillips; R. Cornish, a man about 28 years old, had on a Devon brown round jacket, sail cloth trowsers, and a leather and fur cap; J. Hennings, a young man about 26 years, had on a duck round jacket tied with strings, duck trowsers, and a leather and fur cap; W. Pooley, a sailor, aged about 32 years, had on a pair of blue trowsers, a dark flannel frock and blue waistcoat. Cornish and Pooley have left wives and several children each.

7 February 1823

NOXIOUS VAPOUR

Sir, Having been gratified by seeing a paragraph in your last week's paper, which announces to the public the successful results on the experiments made for destroying the copper smoke at the Swansea works [of John Vivian, the Cornish copper smelter at Hafod]—and having myself taken some pains on the subject, and sent my plan to Mr. Henry Bath, for examination; I shall feel obliged, as a Cornish miner, to any gentleman who will have the goodness to publish, in your excellent paper, a particular account of the method adopted; as the noxious vapour arising from tin burning, in Cornwall, is too often a just ground of complaint by farmers who happen to live in the neighbourhood of the burning-houses; their cattle being sometimes killed, and the vegetation totally destroyed. I am, sir, your most obedient servant, Henry Budge. 21 February 1823

[In addition to Vivian's experiments a subscription fund had been opened in Swansea to remunerate any person able to suggest a means of obviating the injurious effects of smoke produced during copper smelting, which comprised arsenious and other harmful vapours. The methods arrived at were similar to those eventually used in Cornwall where tin-burning (arsenic production) had similar deleterious effects.]

SMOKED BUTTER

Sir . . . I must remark on the very objectionable smoky taste our butter often acquires from the milk being scalded over a furze or turf fire; and though much of this taste goes off when the butter is salted, yet I believe it is more for the interest of the dairy-man to churn than scald. I will not pronounce absolutely that a greater quantity of butter is produced from the same milk by churning, though I am led to think so, and the dried pellicle on the surface of scalded cream, shewing there has been great evaporation, would seem to prove it; but churning would have other good effects, it would save fuel, now become very scarce, and the butter will keep better than when made from scalded cream; but above all, by meeting the taste of his customers, the dairy-man would get a better price.

21 March 1823

BARREN LAND IN SENNEN

Cornwall Lent Assizes. Paynter and others against Permewan. This was an action brought by John Paynter, John Scobell and Uriah Tonkin, Esqrs., lessees of the tithes of the deanery of Buryan, in the western part of this county, against Mr. Permewan, a respectable farmer, holding lands in the parishes of Sennen and Buryan, both in the deanery aforesaid, for not having set out his tithes of wheat, hay, turnips, potatoes, &c. The defendant pleaded, that there is a modus [money payment in lieu of tithe] in the parish for turnips, and that the land from which the tithes were claimed was barren land, and came under the statute of the 6th, of Edward III, which provides that all such barren, heath, and waste land as have heretofore paid no tithes by reason of such barrenness, shall be exempt from paying tithes of corn and hay for seven years after the same shall be so improved.

For the defendent, several witnesses . . . were called, in order to prove . . . that it had not been tilled in the memory of any person living before it was broken up [by blasting with gunpowder] in 1819, when poor persons were allowed to plant potatoes in it without paying rent. That it produced half a crop of potatoes fit for pigs only. That in 1820 a quantity of clay was brought from a distance of a quarter of a mile, and sea-weed from a distance of two miles, to manure it for wheat, but that it did not produce above half a crop of inferior quality. That the ensuing year it was again dressed and sown with oats, but it did not produce half a crop. That in 1822 it was dressed with sea-weed and sown with pellaws [a grain produced solely on the moors of the far west, wherever the soil was exhausted by other crops, and fed to pigs and poultry], of which there were about four bushels to an acre, and that the land is now left fallow, and is never likely to be tilled again, the soil being so shallow and stony as to require being broken up by hacking, instead of the plough. 1 April 1823

[The jury found the land to be barren, and exempt from tithes for seven years, under the Statute of Edward III.]

WELCOME CHRISTMAS AND BOB-ENGINE

To be sold by auction, on Tuesday, the 6th day of May next at three o'clock in the afternoon, at the Queen's Head Inn, St. Austell . . . two-thirds of the tin stream work called Welcome Christmas, in the parish of St. Austell, and one-eighth part of several pairs of tin bounds, including the bounds wherein the work is situated, and twenty-two 96ths of the tin stream work called Bob-engine, in St. Austell, and in several tin bounds adjoining. 25 April 1823

A COMMODIOUS BATHING MACHINE

John Hugh begs leave to inform the nobility and gentry of Cornwall, and the public in general, that he has recently fitted up a commodious bathing machine, which will be kept out, during the season, on the beach, near Penzance, and for which he respectfully solicits their patronage.

2 May 1823

THE METHODISTS AGAINST THE HURLERS

The annual feast of Germoe, in the western part of this county, was held last week. This feast is the only one at which the ancient Cornish sport of hurling is kept up. The sport consists of a contest between two parties for the possession of a large ball, which is thrown up at an equal distance from two goals, and which each party endeavours to carry to that appropriated to it. On the present occasion, a body of Brianites, a sect lately sprung up from amongst the Weslyan Methodists, made their appearance at the time of the hurling, and attempted to put a stop to the diversion by commencing their devotional exercises, but without success.

9 May 1823

BORN IN THE OPEN FIELD

On Saturday last, an inquest was held at Breage, by Mr. P. Rogers, one of the coroners for this county, on the body of a female infant that had been found two days before in a field adjoining the house of William Quick, near Tregonning Mill. It is remarkable, that the mother of the child, who is about forty years of age, her two sisters and two brothers, who were all at home at the time of her being delivered, are all deaf and dumb. In consequence of the absence of any evidence as to the infant's being born alive, the jury returned a verdict of—"Found dead without any marks of violence appearing on the person". When the child was found, there was every appearance of the mother having delivered herself in the open field; and she afterwards attended to her household affairs for several hours, before she took to bed. 16 May 1823

A POLDICE BALL-MAIDEN

On Thursday last, a young woman of Gwennap, about 17 years of age, met an untimely death in consequence of retiring to a stamp shed, in Poldice mine, at the hour of refreshment; when by going too near the axle by which the stamps [for crushing tin ore] are set in motion, her clothes were caught by one of the caps, and she was drawn in between the stamps and the wall, and crushed to death. 16 May 1823

DROWNED IN LOOE ROADS

On Wednesday last, four men went in two small boats, from Looe, to convey potatoes on board a vessel in the roads, and which they reached. The boats were made fast to the vessel, when the wind shifted, which filled the sails, and she got under weigh; the boats were immediately pressed down and upset, by which accident, Edward Galsworthy, an elderly man, was drowned; the other three persons on board the boats were saved when at the last extremity. 23 May 1823

EXPLORING GREAT SEAL HOLE

Perhaps it is not generally known, even to our Cornish readers, that one of the sublimest scenes in the county, is the cavern from which the adventurers of Great Seal Hole mine, in the parish of St. Agnes, commenced their adit . . . This cavern which runs inland from the base of the cliff, upwards of 50 fathoms, was first explored, about 50 years ago, by the late Captain Thomas Stephens, father of the present Capt. Thomas Stephens, who nearly forfeiting his life for the indulgence of his curiosity. It appears that on a calm day, at low water, he managed, by the assistance of two able miners, to land from a boat at the mouth of the cave, and leaving them on the outside, proceeded to explore the interior. Having inadvertently remained until the sea had risen above the top of the entrance, all hope of escape appeared to be precluded, when one of the men who waited for him, heroically ventured his life for the chance of rescuing the captain from his fearful situation. Taking a rope in his hand, he dived through the aperture, which is very small, and found Captain Stephens on his knees on the highest rock he could discover, calmly awaiting his fate. The miner succeeded in fastening the rope around the captain, and making his way through the waves which were roaring over the entrance, he and his companion succeeded in getting him in safety into the boat.

23 May 1823

DANGERS OF THE OPEN FIRE

Last week, the wife of a man named Bassett, who resides at St. Stephens by Launceston, having occasion to go from home, left in the house her daughter, a child of about six years of age, whom, for greater security, she locked in. Soon after the mother's departure, the child in putting some fuel on the fire, had her clothes caught on a blaze. The cries of the poor sufferer at length alarmed some persons who were near, who broke open the door and extinguished the flames, but too late to save the child's life, as she expired in a few hours. This is the second child the same parents have lost in consequence of their clothes taking fire; and it is rather remarkable that the father has two brothers who have each had a child burnt to death. 4 July 1823

[Nearly every issue of *The West Briton* contained a report similar to this, and equal numbers of children met their ends by drinking scalding water or milk from pans hanging over open fires.]

SALT FOR THE HAY RICK

As the hay harvest has become general, we recommend, to our agricultural friends, should the present 'dropping weather' continue, the utility of salt in improving the quality of the hay (whether well made or otherwise), if used when the ricks or mows are constructed. From the best authorities, we can assert, hay so treated will be highly relished by every description of cattle, and its fattening quality will be increased. The late removal of the heavy duty on salts has rendered it available to agricultural purposes, and we hope a fair trial will be given of its effects. When the rick is made, on each layer of hay about a quarter of a peck of salt ought to be equally scattered; on this plan, we believe, four bushels of salt will be required to twenty loads . . . It is a fact that cattle will prefer damaged hay to which salt has been added, to the best hay without it; and in cases where straw was mixed with the hay so salted, they eat with avidity, leaving the primest provender which was put before them at the same time untouched. Salt is equally beneficial when used with clover. Salted hay is also excellent for sheep when put on turnips early in the season.

18 July 1823

ST. DAY SHOW FAIR

St. Day Show Fair will be held on Tuesday the 29th of July instant, when free ground and every other accommodation will be given to those who may bring cattle; and the following prizes, awarded by just umpires; —For the two best fed oxen, £2. 2. 0.; for the two best working oxen, £1. 1. 0.; for the best bull, £1. 1. 0.; for the best fat cow, £1. 1. 0.; for the best cow and calf, £1. 1. 0.; for the best five-years-old saddle horse, £1. 1. 0.; for the best three-years-old colt, £1. 1. 0.; for the best half score sheep, £1. 1. 0.; for the best ram, 0. 10. 6. The above must have been in the possession of the owners, for the space of two months. No inhabitant of St. Day or Gwennap will be allowed any prize, which is done solely to encourage strangers, and it is sincerely hoped that no inhabitant will feel offended, the intention being pure. 25 July 1823

POLGOOTH MINE RESTARTED

Last week, the powerful steam-engine at Polgooth, near St. Austell, commenced its task of clearing that extensive and ancient tin mine of the water which had, for a series of years, been accumulating in its lower levels. The engine has an 80-inch cylinder, and draws 1000 gallons of water per minute. Though assisted by a water engine of considerable power, the progress at present made in the reduction of the water is trifling; but there is no doubt that the object will be ultimately accomplished. By means of a forcing pump, which is also completed, a stream of water will be conveyed to the summit of a hill of above 200 feet perpendicular height (within which the chief riches of the mine are presumed to lie), for the purpose of supplying a smaller steam-engine to be erected on its summit for drawing ore, &c.; the water will then be conveyed down an inclined plane to the foot of the hill, where another steam-engine is in the course of erection for the breaking and pulverizing of tin-stuff by stamps.

8 August 1823

LAUNCESTON MARKET

On Saturday morning last, some hundreds of the following hand-bills were circulated at Launceston:

"A caution to butchers frequenting Launceston Market. The principal inhabitants of Launceston, having often observed, with disgust, the extreme *filthy* conditions of some who are employed as their slaughter-men and carriers, hereby inform them by this friendly hint, that in future they shall decline dealing with them, except the cause is removed by a great improvement in the appearance of the persons alluded to, or that they procure more decent persons for those purposes." 22 August 1823

LAUNCH OF A FALMOUTH PACKET

A packet, named the *Lord Melville*, was launched from the yard of Mr. R. Symons, opposite Falmouth, on Saturday last. This is the first packet launched since the Establishment has been placed under the direction of the Admiralty; she is to be commanded by Captain Furze, late commander of the *Chesterfield*. 26 September 1823

GANNETS SEEN FROM THE HILLS

On Tuesday night, it blew a severe gale, from the N.E. to N.N.W. but several boats ventured out, and some of them took from two to six hogsheads each; such of them as did not return by 11 p.m. were compelled to keep the sea all night and the ensuing day, it being impossible for them to approach the shore. Notwithstanding it continued to blow very hard several boats went to sea on Wednesday night. The fishermen there say, there are large shoals of fish in deep water. The gannets can be seen from the hills, darting into the sea from a height above, with the rapidity of a falling stone, in order to prey on the fish; this being a sure indication of the continuance of shoals of pilchards off the coast, it is still hoped that if the weather should become moderate, the seans may be used with effect.

3 October 1823

SHOT FOR SALE AT PENDENNIS

To be sold by sealed tenders, to be sent to Mr. Hall, Deputy Ordnance Store-keeper, at his office, Pendennis Castle, on or before the 8th of November next, several tons of cast-iron shot, viz. round, double-headed and case. Also a quantity of Langridge shot; composed of bushel iron, with some small quantities of cast-iron intermixed. A considerable number of double-headed shot may be seen at Milor, at the King's cooperage, at that place; and the round, case and Langridge, with a few double-headed, at Pendennis Castle. 31 October 1823

A WORKING POTTER

Wanted immediately, a man who understands the working part of the pottery business, in all its various branches, and who has been in the habit of using coals for burning the ware instead of furze.

7 November 1823

A WHITE SQUALL ON SCILLY

Last week we experienced one of the most heavy gales that has been remembered by some of the oldest islanders. It commenced on Thursday afternoon, with what is called a white squall, which, in its violence and effects resembled a hurricane, whirling up light substances (such as dry ore-weed, straw, &c) to a great elevation in the air. In a short time the roofs of the houses began to be disturbed, and not only thatch, but slate and tiles, were seen flying about in every direction. Many cottages, &c. were completely peeled of their covering in less than a quarter of an hour, the straw in its ascent resembling a thick cloud of smoke. Towards the evening, the terrors of the shivering inmates of these dwellings were increased by a fall of rain resembling a torrent, and which continued, without any considerable intermission, the whole night. Most of the houses were shaken violently; some chimneys were blown down; and so great was the consternation excited, that several people remained watching throughout the night.

7 November 1823

LIME AND COAL BUSINESS

To be disposed of, by private contract, a respectable business, in the above line, at Pendower Beach, in the parish of Philleigh; where the trade in lime and coal has been for some years established, and is now carried on to a considerable extent.

19 December 1823

A HUSBAND DESERTED

Whereas I, James Skinner, of the parish of Camborne, in the county of Cornwall, was separated from my wife Jane Skinner, on the 5th day of September, 1822, by the means of Captain William Michell, and his wife Jane Michell, my said wife's parents. My said wife leaving behind her, at the time she went from my house, two infant children, the one eighteen months old, and the other, who was at the time suckled by her, five months. Now, I do hereby give notice that I will not be answerable for any debts my said wife may contract, in my name, she being wholly separated from me, without my consent. Treswithen, near Camborne. Dec. 28 1823.

2 January 1824

TRURO GAS COMPANY

Sir, Many complaints have been made of the manner in which the contract for lighting the streets of Truro with gas has been carried into effect. On many dark evenings, before the rising of the moon, the lamps are not lighted, and the passengers are left to groupe their way, whilst the inhabitants pay a heavy tax for light. This great omission has, by many, been attributed to the Gas Company, and has been stated to rise from their desire to make the most of their contract, regardless of the inconvenience, not to say, the danger to which they expose their fellow town's-people. But the inhabitants may rest assured that this is not the cause of the neglect complained of; the Gas Company, in lighting the streets, are entirely guided by the Clerk of the Commissioners for Paving and Lighting, and if the streets are left in darkness at the times before-mentioned, it is because the Commissioners have ordered them to be so. 23 January 1824

[The lights were also extinguished long before dawn, and gave ample opportunity for frequent robberies in the town, while the citizens were still sleeping.]

TREBARWITH SANDING ROAD

The public are requested to take notice that a meeting will be held at the town-hall, within the borough of Camelford, in the county of Cornwall, on Friday, the 6th day of February next, precisely by twelve o'clock in the forenoon, for the purpose of considering the best and most effectual plan for driving and making a new sanding road, from Trebarwith beach, in the parish of Tintagel, to Condolden-bridge, in the parish of Minver, in the said county. 30 January 1824

[Sand and sea-weed for manure were at this date "brought over very steep cliffs, at great expense, on horseback." The new road cost £2000, raised by the issue of shares, and recouped by the erection of a toll-gate at the entrance.]

PLAYING TOSS-PENNY

At a petty session last week, held at the Guild-hall, Helston . . . four boys of Helston were fined three shillings and four-pence each, for playing at toss-penny on a Sunday. 27 February 1824

SALMON SPEARS

Many persons in the eastern part of this county, have lately been entrapped by a man who goes about the county, in the neighbourhood of the rivers where salmon are found, inquiring for salmon spears. Should the unwary produce an instrument of this description, it is immediately seized, and the owner is summoned to appear before a magistrate, by whom he is, of course, fined for having it in his possession.

5 March 1824

[Salmon poaching was carried on at night usually by two people, one of whom held a blazing torch to attract the fish, the other a three-pronged spear, or trident.]

TURNPIKES ON THE SABBATH

On Tuesday last, Richard Kingdon, one of the turnpike-gate keepers in the neighbourhood of Launceston, appeared before a bench of magistrates at that place, on a summons granted to Mr. Langman, a respectable farmer, whom Kingdon had compelled to pay a toll on a Sunday, when on his way to a place of worship. The magistrates decided that the toll was illegally extorted, and Kingdon was ordered to refund it, and pay the costs of the proceeding.

5 March 1824

A BED OF STRAW

Last week, a poor man, 87 years of age, who was for many years supported as a pauper by the parish of Ludgvan, was found dead in his bed in a small cot, of which he was the sole inhabitant for nearly 20 years, in Lelant. He was regularly attended by a woman, who left him the evening before, when he complained of being unwell; when she came in the morning to prepare his breakfast, she found him dead on his bed of straw.

12 March 1824

CORNISH MINERS FOR MEXICO

We understand that two Mexican mining companies have engaged some of the most active and best practical miners in this county, to proceed across the Atlantic to superintend the working of their mines in that country. These persons consist principally of young men, who are to act as mine captains, draughtsmen, and accountants. Some of the ablest working miners are also engaged to act as superintendants of pitches, [working areas allocated to groups of miners]. The salaries we hear are liberal, and the engagements are for three years. A vessel will touch at Falmouth for the second party, the first, we believe, is on its way to its destination.

26 March 1824

TIN SMELTING IN TRURO

The assay-office in Fair-mantle-street, Truro, formerly occupied by Mr. Provis, is open to receive stream and mine tin for Trethellan tin smelting house, which is now erecting in Roper's Moor. [near the head of Truro River].

9 April 1824

A LIGHT IN THE OFFING

The King against Pitts. This was a prosecution instituted by the Attorney-General against the defendant, a fisherman of Mevagissey, for striking a light, by way of signal to smugglers. . . . It appeared from the evidence given by Mr. Vallack, chief officer of the preventive boat stationed at Mevagissey, that on the night of the 20th of December, he boarded a boat off Chapel Point, in which was the defendant and another person; but that not finding any contraband articles on board, he left her; when he got about 100 yards from the boat, he saw a light made from her, which was immediately answered by a light in the offing, and another from the shore. On seeing this he returned and took the defendant and his companion into custody, who said they had struck the fire to light their pipes.

9 April 1824

THE LOGAN STONE

"I have visited this rock at times with my friends, and have found on the approach of visitors, men, women, and children anxiously striving for what little pittance they could obtain; instead of attending to a more substantial mode of seeking their livelihood." 30 April 1824

[In April, the Logan Stone near the Land's End, a giant block of granite so poised as to rock at the slightest touch, had been brought down as a prank by a party of sailors from the *Nimble* revenue cutter, then lying off Land's End and commanded by a Lieut. Goldsmith. Later he was compelled to replace it, but the delicate poise was not recovered, and the inhabitants of Treen nearby were as a result deprived of their previous livelihood.]

THE FRAIL SISTERHOOD AT PENZANCE

It is the established practice amongst the frail sisterhood at Penzance, when one of the fraternity finds herself likely to become a mother, to extort money from all who are likely to be intimidated by the threat of being brought before the public as the father of the expected stranger. We understand that one woman lately obtained no less a sum than £100 by this mode of proceeding. 30 April 1824

A NIGHT IN OLD PINK MINE

On the night of Thursday last a miner named Thomas Prout, belonging to the Friendly mines, St. Agnes, was returning home from St. Agnes church town, and took the cliff path, as he conceived he should have better light in that direction than in the other. As he was passing over the site of a deserted mine, called Old Pink, he felt as if he had made a false step and immediately was precipitated into a shaft at the bottom of which is a large quantity of water. He was not so stupefied by his fall as to be deprived of recollection, and felt himself sink through the water, he rose to the surface and being a good swimmer, kept himself from sinking, whilst he felt about the sides of the shaft for a resting place; he found however that this was impossible, and he had no resource but to fix his back against one of the sides whilst he placed his feet against the other . . . About seven o'clock [in the morning] a boy passing to work heard his voice, and to his great joy approached the shaft. 28 May 1824

[Prout was rescued almost unhurt, but badly grazed by his movements against the shaft walls during the night. It is recorded that he walked home, slept an hour or two, and went back to work.]

THE FAIR AT TRURO

The usual amusements of the holiday folk in the vicinity of Truro, at the fair on Wednesday last, were greatly marred by the heavy rain that fell in the after-part of the day. The exhibitions were limited to dwarfs and gigantic children, dancing bears and monkies. The genial showers, however, were beneficial to the innkeepers as well as to vegetation, as they compelled the lads and lasses to take shelter where they could obtain it; how far good morals were promoted by the potations that were swallowed, it is scarcely necessary to say. There was a full proportion of the light-fingered tribe in attendance; but the activity of the police rather impeded their operations. Several of these professors, with some individuals who exhibited gambling tables, were taken into custody, and seven were the next day sent to the county gaol, some for trial, and some to enjoy the beneficial exercise of the treadmill. 11 June 1824

ANCIENT DIVERSION

Yesterday the bounds of this borough [Truro] were viewed by the Mayor, Town-clerk, and some other members of the corporation, attended by a band of music, and a vast concourse of both sexes. Early in the morning, the ancient diversion of drenching with water from the fire-engines, buckets, &c. all not born in the borough, commenced with great spirit, to the no small annoyance of those who found it necessary to leave their houses. 11 June 1824

A WANDERER SOUGHT

Left his home, in a deranged state of mind, on Wednesday the 2d. instant, John Harpur, son of Stephen Harpur, of Greenbottom, in the parish of Kenwyn, near Chacewater. On the same day he was seen on the road between Truro and Bodmin, proceeding towards the latter place. He is about 5 feet 4 inches in height, stout made, dark complexion, and about 32 years of age: he had on when he left home a fustian working jacket, a black waistcoat, and a dark velveteen trowsers; he is perfectly inoffensive in his conduct, nor is it supposed that he will ask for food. The overseers of any parish in which he may be found will please to detain him, and transmit an account to his afflicted family, directed to Mr. Matthew Moyle, Chacewater. 11 June 1824

A REVIVAL OF THE KELP INDUSTRY

Hopes are entertained that the manufacture of kelp [calcined ashes of seaweed containing soda and used in soap or glass manufacture] may be revived this year at Scilly, which, if properly conducted, would be a great advantage to the islanders. Fifty shillings per ton have already been offered on the spot, but as it is understood on all sides that the article is to be prepared in a superior manner to what has hitherto been followed, it may be worth the attention of the merchants in England, by direct interference, to offer such a price as shall insure the excellency of the kelp. The ore-weed being now of two years' growth, promises much for the fineness of the article.

18 June 1824

THE MOST POWERFUL ENGINE IN EUROPE

On Tuesday the 15th instant, the second steam-engine lately erected on Wheal Alfred mine was put in motion, in presence of an unprecedented number of spectators, among whom science had many votaries, assembled to witness this exhibition of improvement in a popular branch of mechanics, so interesting to the county, as a mining district. The engine, the most powerful yet erected in Europe, is on Wolf's [Woolf's] patent; and for exactness of movement, simplicity of action, and all the requisite qualities, for which machinery of this description can be applied to the intended purposes, this engine is said to stand unequalled. The castings were chiefly effected at Hayle, and has done infinite credit to Mr. Harvey the founder. Fire-works of a splendid description, including the burning of nearly twenty tar-barrels, were skilfully managed under the superintendence of Mr. Gregory Nicholls, surgeon, and the company retired late in the evening, highly gratified with the hilarity of a day to be recorded as most congenial to the best interests of the neighbourhood.

18 June 1824

A CELEBRATED WIZARD

A man named French, who resides in the parish of Davidstow, within 3 miles of Camelford, and who maintained a large family by working for hire, with a team of horses, was reduced to great distress about three months since, by the sudden death of his four horses, which expired in great apparent agony, in the same day, and for which disaster no cause could be assigned. The calamity, was however, in some degree, alleviated by the liberality of his more opulent neighbours, by whose aid he was enabled to purchase two horses, and he resumed his occupation. Shortly after, these animals shared the fate of the former ones, and the poor fellow was driven to despair. His acquaintance being unable to account for the disasters that had befallen him, sagely concluded that it was the effect of a supernatural agency. Full of this idea, French went to consult a celebrated wizard who resides in the north of Devon, and by whom he was assured that his conjectures as to the cause of the death of his horses was correct; a very particular description of the witch—of course, an old woman—by whom these deeds were perpetrated, was also given, and the dupe returned fully persuaded of the truth of the story and with a resolution to search in the neighbourhood for the person so accurately described . . . 25 June 1824

[Before the witch was found French, having no horses, sold his hay to a clergyman, whose three horses ate it and also died. On analysis it was found to have been mixed with arsenic.]

HORSES LADEN WITH SMALL CASKS

In the night of Saturday the 29th ultimo, James Sturgess, Chief Officer, James Farrow and George Kingston, boatmen all belonging to the preventive boat in the service of the Customs, stationed at Polperro, in the county of Cornwall, were out on duty for the prevention of smuggling and saw near Trelawney Gate, in the parish of Pelynt, in the said county, five or six horses laden with small casks, and guarded by several smugglers, upon which the said boatmen immediately made towards them, and upon one of them coming up to them, he was struck a violent blow on the head with a stick, by one of the said party of smugglers, but succeeded in seizing and securing from them two casks of foreign rum spirits; that the said smugglers threatened further violence, but on the other two boatmen coming up, they galloped off and made their escape. 2 July 1824

LARGE FAMILIES

Penwith Agricultural Society. The first meeting of this society took place at Camborne on Monday last, and was very respectably attended. The ploughing and sheep-shearing were in the very best style, and the shew of cattle reflected great credit on the farmers of that confined district . . . The following prizes were adjudged . . . To William Retallack, Illogan, as a labouring man who has maintained the largest number of children (19) without parochial relief, £2 2s.; and to John West, Camborne, as maintaining the 2nd largest ditto (15) ditto ditto, £1 1s.

2 July 1824

BODMIN RIDING

We are informed that the ancient festival of Bodmin Riding, which for some time past has been on the decline, will this year be revived with all the spirit of former days. The games, including wrestling, ringing, &c. &c. will be on an unusually extensive scale; the wrestling, it is supposed, will afford the best sport which has been witnessed in this county for many years, there being *ten sovereigns* for the best man, and *five shillings* for every standard [wrestlers who have thrown two men during the contest, or thrown one and stood a limited time with another], with other prizes in proportion. 2 July 1824

COMMITTED TO THE TREAD-MILL

Two disorderly women, named Cleave and Seccombe, were committed by Wm. Paul, Esq., the Mayor of Truro, at his petty sessions, on Thursday last, to hard labour at the tread-mill for one month; and a man called Robertson was committed for two months to the tread-mill, for endeavouring to impose upon the overseers of the parish of St. Mary, Truro, by false representations, with a view to obtaining relief as a pauper.

9 July 1824

A FIRE-ENGINE FROM LOOE

Early on the morning of Wednesday, an alarming fire broke out on the farm of Mr. John Tuckett, of Langos, in the parish of St. Martin's, near Looe. The disaster was occasioned by a quantity of flax placed on a kiln to dry, taking fire. The flames quickly communicated to the outhouses and threatened the dwelling-house with destruction, when they were happily arrested by the vigorous efforts of the neighbouring inhabitants; aided by the opportune arrival of an engine from Looe. 9 July 1824

RABID DOGS IN THE STREETS

The most afflicting accounts every day reach us, through the public papers, of the lamentable consequences which have attended the bite of dogs, during the present summer. Numbers in various parts of the country, have lost their lives under all the horrors attendant on that most deplorable of maladies, hydrophobia. Precautions have been taken by the magistrates in different towns, to prevent disasters from rabid animals, and directions have been given that, after public notice, all dogs found at large, unmuzzled, should be killed by persons appointed for that purpose. But we have not as yet heard that the magistrates in any of the towns of Cornwall have judged it necessary to bestir themselves, in order to guard the public against this most direful of human calamities. The Mayor of Truro, we know, cannot be blamed, for he is absent, but we suppose he has delegated his authority and the superintendence of the police of the town to some suitable person, during his absence; who, we should suppose, cannot fail to observe the great number of dogs, which have no legal owners, that roam through the streets by day, to the no small alarm of the inhabitants, whose rest is frequently disturbed by their howls and contests during the night.

13 August 1824

[Rabid dogs ranging loose were quite common in the county, and this despite instances of the deaths of animals or persons bitten by them, as well as the fact that the only known remedy was that of immediately cutting out the whole wound. The above comment had a most salutary effect, however, for an order was immediately issued in Truro that all dogs must be muzzled, unless confined.]

A MULATTO AT PERRAN

Cornwall Assizes. William Coss, (19) a mulatto, was indicted for stealing from Thomas Keskeys, twelve shillings, at Perran, on the 6th of the present month. The prosecutor, was engaged at Perran [Perranuthnoe] fair in assisting farmers in taking care of their cattle; and the produce of his day's exertions, about 12 shillings, being securely deposited in his pocket, he, at a late hour, sought some repose from his toils, on the floor of the cellar chamber of a public-house at Perran. At this time, the prisoner and a person named Jones were also in the chamber; after having enjoyed about an hour's sleep . . . he discovered that his trowsers and pocket were cut through, and all his money abstracted . . . Jones, who was now the only person present, told the almost distracted attendant on cattle, that whilst he was asleep, the prisoner had been fumbling about his person; that he (Jones) had heard what he thought was the clinking of money, and that the prisoner had immediately left the room. This was proof positive, and therefore the prosecutor and Jones sallied forth in search of the delinquent, whom they found in bed at the mumper's-inn [a lodging house for vagrants, and beggars or mumpers] at Marazion, about a mile and a half from Perran . . . The prisoner is well known to the conservators of the peace, throughout the county, as a keeper of a gaming table at fairs, where, in imitation of their betters, country lads and lasses are indulged in the fashionable amusement of throwing dice for various prizes, and who had more than once felt the rough grasp of authority . . . To be transported for life.

27 August 1824

TRURO RACES

These races took place on a spot about two miles from Truro, on the Bodmin road, on Tuesday last. Notwithstanding the threatening aspect of the day, and the discouraging state of the roads, persons of all classes, some on foot, some on horse-back, and others in almost every species of carriage known in this county from the gay barouche to the dung-cart, were seen hastening to the spot, in every direction. When collected, the assemblage presented as varied an appearance as can well be conceived; carriages filled with ladies elegantly attired; dashing equestrians sporting their bits of blood; respectable farmers, mine-captains, tradesmen, &c. with their wives and daughters in gigs, taxed-carts, or on horseback; plough boys, seated bare-ridged on sober cart-horses, and buddle boys [employed in tin dressing operations] on humble donkeys, grinning delighted as they surveyed the novel scene. The spot selected was tolerably well adapted for the purpose, except that one of the corners of the field forms an acute angle, with a stiff descent, which required great caution in the riders, and was unfortunately the occasion of a very serious accident in the course of the day. 8 October 1824

[Bodmin Races had recently been discontinued, and the gentlemen of Truro resolved to get up races on a more limited scale, of which this was the first. Later, a more permanent course was laid out at Trevellan, near Shortlanesend.]

WINDMILL ON A MINE

A correspondent at St. Agnes informs us, that it is the intention of some mining speculators there, to attempt to draw water from their works by a windmill, which is already in a state of forwardness!!

19 November 1824

CONVICTS BOUND FOR AUSTRALIA

The *Lady East*, now lying in Falmouth harbour, has on board 210 convicts bound for New South Wales. A number of these ruffians, formed the project of overpowering the crew, liberating their fellows, and after running the vessel on shore, making their escape. On Wednesday night, about 40 of the most desperate contrived to saw off their irons, and made towards the place where the arms are deposited. Fortunately, the watch heard the bustle they made and gave an alarm and the villains were prevented from executing their purpose, and secured. The discovery was made most opportunely; for a few minutes more would have put them in possession of arms, when there is no doubt they would have butchered the whole crew. The ringleaders were flogged on Thursday, and every precaution has been taken to guard against a similar attempt.

17 December 1824

RAISING LANYON QUOIT

The celebrated cromlech or quoit, at Lanyon, which had been blown from its ancient position during a tremendous gale of wind, on the 19th of October 1815, has been re-placed by the united exertions of Lieut. Goldsmith and Capt. Giddy, by the use of machinery lent from the Plymouth naval-yard, to re-place the Logan Stone [see p. 137]. The cromlech weighs about 19 tons. 31 December 1824

[According to a letter in the same issue the collapse of the quoit was caused by persons digging there in the hope of discovering the giant of St. Michael's Mount and his treasure, supposedly buried beneath the structure. The legend was based on the fact that human bones of a large size were reputed to have been discovered interred in the same spot.]

WAGGONS WITHOUT BELLS

Sir . . . I beg to call your attention to . . . the inattention that has been and I much fear, still is paid to lights in post chaises, and other vehicles, and of bells to all waggons travelling in this county. Not a great while since, (in a dark and dreary winter's night) a very serious accident happened to a waggoner, in consequence of his team coming into contact with a post-chaise; the former not being supplied with bells, and the latter being destitute of lights. 7 January 1825

BUSTLE AT FALMOUTH

The streets of Falmouth are at this time quite thronged, in addition to the usual bustle of packet passengers and other strangers, there is an influx of the agents and others engaged for the different mining speculations abroad, and who are about to sail for their various destinations. The principal inns are consequently thronged, and the streets, which generally have a Cheapside character, are now more than usually crowded; at the same time, every species of provision is comparatively cheap.

18 February 1825

HUSBANDRY AFTER WORK

Last week, an inquest was held at Crowan, on the body of Thomas Rodda, a young man of about 20 years of age, who was killed in the act of blasting a rock in his field, which he was clearing for the purpose of cultivating. It being dark when he began his work, it is supposed he applied the fire to the touch paper too near the hole. 4 March 1825

THEFT AT THE ANGEL INN

Cornwall Sessions. Richard Dennis was found guilty of stealing two half pounds of butter, some cream, and a piece of pork, belonging to William Behenna, a publican at Truro [of the Angel Inn, St. Mary's Street], on the 16th of Feb. The prisoner came to the house of the prosecutor and called for a pint of beer which he sat drinking for some time, until he saw an opportunity of slipping into the dairy, where he devoured a quantity of cream, broke a pan, and took away two half pounds of butter and a piece of pork; but being heard in the dairy, an alarm was made, when he escaped into the yard and threw the butter and pork into the cess-pool. To be imprisoned for one month at hard labour. 15 April 1825

RENAMING COPPERHOUSE

It is the intention of the inhabitants of Copperhouse in the harbour of Hayle, to imitate the good people of Devonport, and discard the present name of their popular and overgrown village, and to substitute a more appropriate one; Mining Port has been suggested, but the name will be determined on, at a meeting which will be convened for that purpose, due notice of which will be given in this paper. 15 April 1825

IN A STATE OF INTOXICATION

On Monday night, at St. Austell, a miner, in a state of intoxication, to prove the strength of some gunpowder of which he had a considerable quantity in a bag, enclosed a little in paper, and held it to a candle, leaving the open bag close at hand. As might have been expected, the smaller quantity ignited the larger; which exploding, burst out the window of the room, shattered and threw down a partition which separated that apartment from the next, and otherwise damaged the premises. The man, his wife, and child are dreadfully burnt, but their lives are not considered to be in danger. 6 May 1825

SEA WATER BATHS, 1825

To be sold, by sealed tender, for the remainder of a term of 1000 years, subject to a yearly rent of £3, the sea water baths, lately erected at Penzance at the end of Jennings' Street, close to the sea. Together with all the furniture belonging thereto, which consists of everything useful and convenient for the accomodation of ladies and gentlemen bathing. The house consists of two excellent warm baths, a cold bath, a pump room, and a handsome spacious waiting room over the baths, which commands a delightful view of Mount's Bay. The baths were built a few years since at the expense of upwards of £600, and are now in complete repair and good condition. 17 June 1825

LIEUT. GOLDSMITH'S CUTTER

The buoy sent by the Trinity House, to be placed near the Rundlestone [off the southern tip of the Land's End peninsula], has been laid down by Lieut. Goldsmith, of H.M. cutter, *Nimble*. Since Lieut. Goldsmith's feats, in overthrowing and replacing the celebrated logan-stone, the cutter he commands is called by that name only; the Lieut. has had the words *Logan-Stone*, painted on her stern. 15 July 1825

LISKEARD AND LOOE CANAL

The first general meeting of the Liskeard and Looe Canal Company took place on Tuesday last. At five o'clock in the morning, a numerous body of shareholders assembled on the west parade, and preceded by the Liskeard band of musicians, about twenty in number, proceeded along the line of the intended canal, to Tarras Pill, where they were met by a large party of shareholders, &c. from East and West Looe, who came from that place in boats elegantly decorated. On the meeting of the two parties, the band struck up the National Anthem—God Save the King—in which all present joined. After congratulating each other on the success of their efforts, in obtaining the sanction of the Legislature to their beneficial project, Mr. Glubb, the secretary of the company, proceeded to turn up some turf, as a commencement of the undertaking. After which the company returned through Sand-place, to St. Keyne's Well, where three hogsheads of cider were distributed to the crowd; and which proved a most seasonable refreshment, as the heat of the weather was intense.

22 July 1825

FROM FALMOUTH FOR VALPARAISO

On Sunday evening the 17th instant, that beautiful and handsomely fitted ship the *Auriga*, of London, Thomas Walford commander, sailed from Falmouth for Valparaiso, laden with mining materials and apparatus, and having on board T. M. Bagnold, Esq., commissioner, Robert Ewer, Esq. secretary, James Gilbert, and G. M. Lewis, Esqrs. chief engineers, with Dr. Ryan and suite, and 40 Welch and Cornish miners, navigators, &c. appertaining to that respectable company the Chilian and Peruvian Mining Association. The cabin passengers embarked at seven p.m. under a salute from the ship, and three hearty cheers from the miners and crew, when the anchor was immediately weighed, and she proceeded to sea with a fair wind and fine weather. 22 July 1825

A TONGUE IN HIS HEAD

A fellow who has lost a leg and an eye, and who pretended that he was thus mutilated and also had his tongue cut out by the Algerines [see p.72], was last week examined at Liskeard, where he had been begging, when the latter part of his tale was found to be false, as he was induced to resume the use of the organ of speech; after which discovery he left the place and directed his course westward, where he doubtless intends to levy contributions on the credulous and compassionate. 29 July 1825

A CELEBRATED VESSEL AT FALMOUTH

The *Enterprize*, steam-vessel, from London, for Calcutta, respecting which so much has been said in the London papers, arrived at Falmouth, on Friday last, and sailed for her destination on Tuesday. She is a fine vessel, and is completely and elegantly fitted up for passengers, several of whom are on board. 19 August 1825

[The *Enterprize*, 479 tons, aroused national interest as the first steamship to reach India from England. 122 feet long, and with an engine of

120 horse-power, she made the journey in 113 days, at an average speed of about 6 knots. On arrival she won a 100,000 rupee prize for the feat from the Government of India, which purchased her as a ship of war.]

HALF-WAY OVER HAYLE SANDS

A woman afflicted with the disease called the King's Evil [scrofula], set out in a car, from her home, in the neighbourhood of St. Ives, on Sunday morning, for Redruth, in order to obtain the benefit of a conjuror's skill who resides at that place, and who is supposed to cure all the diseases to which humanity is incident, by virtue of certain charms. The woman in question was accompanied by two female neighbours and a child; and when they got about half-way over Hayle sands, the driver of the car, having no faith in the efficacy of conjuration, told the party he thought a dip would do as well as a charm, and brutally threw the patient and one of her companions into a stream which crosses the sands, but which is not sufficently deep to do more than give them a complete wetting. 26 August 1825

TRURO LOCK-UP

When a person is charged with an offence (suppose in a distant part of the county) and the magistrate thinks it proper to commit him, he is transferred to Bodmin; then if the next Quarter Sessions be held at Truro, he is conveyed with a motley group of various characters, well secured, to be deposited in the small lock-up place called Truro town-gaol. Having recently visited this prison, I can describe it. It contains two small rooms upstairs, and a strong room below, strewed with straw, with a block in the centre, to which the refractory are chained. As there is no privy, and the rooms have no ventilators, the air was found exceedingly close and offensive. I know not how it is with the Lostwithiel prison; but these places being intended only as lock-up houses or cages, there can be no doubt that they all must be very unfit for the reception (even temporary) of a number of persons, unconvicted, several of whom may and are often found 'not guilty' of the offence charged to them. 16 September 1825

[It had been proposed that the Quarter Sessions be held henceforward in Bodmin, in which town those committed by magistrates were held until their trial, and to which they were returned if found guilty, to serve their sentences in the gaol or house of correction. The Sessions hitherto had been held at Truro and Lostwithiel, involving the expense of removal of prisoners to and from either town and Bodmin, as well as the humiliation and discomfort of the innocent. Eventually it was decided to continue to hold Sessions at Lostwithiel and Truro, on condition that a new gaol be built in the last named town.]

A WEDDING AT GWITHIAN

An extraordinary scene was witnessed at Gwithian on Monday last, in consequence of a wedding which took place there, between two persons who have for many years been inmates of the parish poor-house. The bride-groom, Benedict Hammill, is a most decrepid object, aged 68 years; the bride, who is in her 49th year, is the mother of a numerous progeny, though she never before submitted to the trammels of matrimony. The report of their intended union collected a great crowd round the church, who became so clamorous for admittance, that the clergyman, fearing that they would force an entrance, suspended the service and went in quest of constables to disperse the mob, leaving directions to keep the doors locked until his return. After some time he came back accompanied by the village conservators of the peace, who succeeded in getting the mob to a respectful distance from the sacred edifice, which it was at one time feared they would have profaned; but when his reverence was about to resume the service, the bride was not to be found. The greatest confusion now prevailed, and messengers were dispatched in search of the truant, who was shortly seen emerging from the village inn, leaning on the arm of the aged sexton, who had been prevailed on by her entreaties during the absence of the clergyman, to let her out at a side door, in order that by an application to the gin bottle, she might exhilarate her spirits, which were greatly agitated by the unexpected events of the day. The sexton, who has no objection to a cheerful glass, took the opportunity of indulging in a similar libation, and thus interestingly employed, the friendly couple forgot the lapse of time, until they were alarmed by the hue and cry raised after the bride. Order being restored, the sacred rite was performed, and the happy couple returned to the poor-house amidst the shouts, hootings and groans of the assembled multitude. 21 October 1825

A REWARD OF FIVE GUINEAS

Robert Oliver, (the noted wrestler), carpenter, of the parish of Kenwyn, escaped from the prison of E. P. Player [see p. 108], of Truro, last night or early this morning. He is about 5 feet 9 inches high, dark complexion, and dark hair, stoops in walking, and is supposed to be about 40 years of age, had on a green coat, and velvetteen trowsers. A reward of five guineas is hereby offered to any person who may lodge him in any of his Majesty's gaols, by the said E. P. Player. 18 November 1825

A PINT AND A HALF OF GIN

One of the lads employed in a mine near Chacewater, last week found a counterfeit half-crown piece on the road, where it had probably been cast by some person on whom it had been imposed, but who finding it too much defaced for being again put into circulation, threw it away. The lad shewed his prize to a companion, who speedily devised a mode of turning it to account. He procured two bottles, one of which he filled with spring water and then corked, the other being empty; he put one in each pocket, and set off to a public-house, where he boldly desired the landlady to give him a pint and a half of gin. This was soon put into the empty bottle and being corked was thrust into his pocket, after which he offered his base half-crown in payment. As he expected, it was refused, whilst he, loudly exclaiming against those who had sent him on a fool's errand, very deliberately took the bottle of water from his pocket and handed it to the good woman, who unsuspicious of the cheat, poured the contents into the gin-barrel, and returned the bottle, with which, and the prize he had obtained by the trick, the fellow walked deliberately off. The liquor was soon quaffed by this youthful trickster and his companions, who then loudly boasted of having so cleverly *done* the landlady. 20 January 1826

DISTURBING A CONGREGATION

Whereas Paul Hodge, Richard Johns, Henry James, Edward Arthur, and John Johns, were brought before George Thomas, Esq. Mayor of Truro, on this day, upon a charge preferred against them of having disturbed a congregation assembled for religious worship, in a chapel, duly registered, and which is situate in St. Clement-street, Truro, on the evening of Thursday, the 19th of January instant, by outrageous conduct, and making violent noises; singing songs, &c. And being duly convicted of the said offence, they were fined eight shillings each; which the four first named paid, and in default of paying which John Johns was committed to the borough prison. It is hoped that this conviction will deter evil disposed persons from committing such outrages in future, as the congregation assembled at the said chapel are resolved to prosecute all who may hereafter offend in a like manner. 27 January 1826

AN OLD OFFENDER

James Ernold, a labouring man, was this week committed to the house of correction, at Bodmin, by the magistrates at Camelford, in order to his being kept at work on the tread-mill, for a month, in consequence of his having refused to work at the employment provided for him by the parish overseers, leaving his family chargeable to the parish; Ernold is an old offender in this way, having heretofore given the overseers and magistrates much trouble. 3 February 1826

FRENCH SLAVER AT ST. IVES

The French slave vessel, which was forced into St. Ives, by stress of weather, was taken possession of by Lieut. G. H. Rye, and his party of seamen belonging to the coastguard service. She is pierced for 20 guns, has six on board; her main booms are fitted with boarding spikes, and her cabin with cutlasses and loaded fire arms; she has also an implement for turning red-hot shot from the furnace into her guns (which are 12 pounders). She had made 14 slave voyages in the last eight years since she was built. Lieut. Rye gave a poor negro child his freedom, by taking him from his cruel master's grasp, and carrying him home to his own five motherless young children. The master of the vessel, as may well be imagined, is described as one of the most brutal hardhearted monsters on the face of the earth. The vessel still lies at St. Ives under detention.

3 February 1826

[In March 1815 Napoleon ended French participation in the slave trade, but little was done to enforce the law after his defeat at Waterloo later in the same year. The slavers were based on the Breton ports and Nantes, and it was not until 1827 that a French national faced banishment for trading in slaves.]

POWDER MILLS IN KENNALL VALE

We regret to state that an accident which has been attended with melancholy results, occurred at the powder mills near Ponsanooth, on Friday last. About half-past twelve o'clock on that day, an explosion took place in the mixing-house (as it is termed), in which were four persons—three men and an old woman—at their usual employment. Two of the men escaped with comparatively little injury, but the woman, whose name was Elizabeth Rutter, was so dreadfully scorched that she died on Friday night; the third man, whose name was Weeks, survived until Sunday morning, without suffering much pain, when he also expired. Although it is generally difficult to account for accidents which occur at powder mills, in the present instant it has been ascertained that the fatal event was occasioned by the negligence of the old woman, who fell a victim to her own want of caution. She had been roasting potatoes in a house at a considerable distance from the works, and had unconsciously carried a small spark of fire on her clothes from thence to the mill. This was seen almost immediately on her entrance, but before it could be prevented, it fell, and the explosion instantly followed.

24 February 1826

TIN BOUNDS NEAR ST. AUSTELL

To be sold by auction . . . part or shares in several pair of tin bounds, called Polgooth, Hewas, St. Margaret's, Colscarne, Boskelling, Poldest, Small Hopes, Good-Friday, Easter-Eve, Baldew-weel, Screed, Come-by-Chance, St. Lawrence, Great Hope, Bonaventure, Shillings-go-by, the Pool, Great Groan, Ployden's Misfortune, Hall-Stennicks, Baldew, Lady

Beam, Come and Welcome, Little Boskelling, Cock's Barrow, New Bounder's Folly, Fear Nothing, the Pleasure Bounds, High Land, Cafflers, Good Fortune, St. George's Day, Welcome in, Good Speed, Justification, Long Sleave, Rusty Hammer, Ream Slip, the Slead and Welcome Fortune.

17 March 1826

REDRUTH MINERS' HOMECOMING

The town of Redruth was enlivened on Tuesday last, by the appearance of two miners who had left for Mexico about eighteen months before; but who have returned on account of ill health. They entered the town in a post-chaise, and were heartily welcomed by their acquaintance, whom they entertained by a relation of their adventures, &c. They left Mexico in company with another miner named Teague, who died on the passage . . . On Wednesday, one of the emigrants named Warren (brother to the celebrated wrestler of that name, who has suffered so severely by assisting the sufferers from the *Kent*, East Indiaman) astonished the natives by appearing in the streets in the dress usually worn by the Mexican miners.

7 April 1826

[The wrestler, Warren, had been on board the *Cambria* bound for Tampico, one of a party of miners engaged by the Anglo-Mexican Mining Company; he was injured in helping survivors from the boats of the sinking *Kent*, which the *Cambria* encountered.]

PLUNDERED ON HAYLE BAR

The French ship *Ocean*, from Campeachy to Havre de Grace, put into St. Ives, in distress some weeks ago; and having undergone a repair which cost about £4,000, she lay at anchor in the bay, waiting for a fair wind. On Wednesday morning, she parted from her cables and drove on shore at Hayle Bar. The pilots and seamen of St. Ives, at the imminent hazard of their lives, rescued the crew . . . We are sorry to state, that on the first intimation of the disaster, a number of persons from the adjacent villages crowded down with the view of plundering the stores; the greater part of these miscreants were women, who carried off whatever they could lay their hands on, and were very dexterous in concealing bottles of wine and other things, so as to elude a search. Some of the men knocked in the heads of three or four casks of wine, into which they dipped their hats and drank what they took up in them. As the day advanced, the plunderers, male and female, became intoxicated, and a variety of contests, some of them of the most ludicrous description, took place. 14 April 1826

FROLICS AT CAMBORNE

On Tuesday the good people of Camborne were not a little surprised at finding nearly all the signs in the place removed from the fronts of the houses, no doubt by some persons who have been paying their respects to Sir John Barleycorn, and having to carry more good liquor than good sense, took the above mode of amusing themselves. They were particularly attentive to the Knights of the Shears, whose signs they cabbaged without compunction. Amongst other frolics, they took down a barber's pole, and placed the party-coloured emblem before the door of a surgeon; thereby showing they were men of reading, and had become acquainted with the ancient union of the two professions designated by the bandaged pole [until 1745, when the surgeons broke away from the barbers to form the College of Surgeons]. Though the tailors were highly displeased, the inhabitants were not disposed to relish the joke at the expense of the son of Aesculapius [the Roman god of Medicine]. 21 April 1826

SLATE OUT OF BOSCASTLE

A vessel from Clovelly, called *The Narrow Escape*, was wrecked last week in one of the creeks near Tintagel, by the sudden rising of a ground-sea, which dashed her to pieces against the rocks; the crew were fortunately enabled to gain the shore in safety. Just before the accident, Messrs. Sloggatt and Co. had completed her loading with slate, at Boscastle.

28 April 1826

[Messrs. Sloggatt and Co (Messrs. Rosevear and Sloggatt) owned the North Delabole or Bowithick slate quarry, as well as a large part of the village of Boscastle, whence their produce was shipped. They were also Lloyd's agents for the coast from Hartland Point in Devon south to Port Isaac, in recognition of their exertions towards the protection of ship-wrecked property in north Cornwall.]

ORE SHIPPED FROM ST. IVES

On Saturday last, a cargo of copper ore, raised in Wheal Trenwith mine, and which was sold on the 11th instant, was shipped on board the *Pulmanter*, Grenfell, master, at St. Ives pier; and on Wednesday a cargo of the same ore was shipped on board the *Betsey*, Tanner, master, at the same place. These, we understand, are the first copper ores ever remembered to have been shipped from that place. 19 May 1826

TWELVE THOUSAND CANDLES

Wanted for the use of the Consolidated Crinnis Mines, in the parish of St. Austell, 1000 dozen of good miners' candles, to be delivered in such quantities as may be required, and paid for at the end of every two month's delivery, by bills on London, at two months date. Sealed tenders for the above, with the words, 'Tenders for Candles' on the outside, will be received at the counting-house of the mines, until twelve o'clock at noon on Thursday 25th instant. 19 May 1826

A WEEKDAY AND SUNDAY SCHOOL

Wanted, a master and mistress to superintend a week day and Sunday school, at St. Enoder, in this county. The joint salary, which will be permanently secured, £25 per annum; with the probability of considerable increase. The candidates to take charge of the boys school, will be expected to write a good hand; and to be well acquainted with arithmetic. The candidates for both situations must produce testimonials of their qualifications and character. Applications to be made (if by letter, post-paid) to Rev. J. Punnett, St. Enoder, Vicarage, Truro, Cornwall.

26 May 1826

SHEEP ON COMMON LAND

At a petty sessions held at Five Lanes, on Monday last, George Jewel was fined forty shillings, and John Harris, twenty shillings, for having depastured sheep infected with the scab on a common in the parish of St. Juliet. An association has been formed in the hundred of Lesnewth, for the purpose of prosecuting persons so offending, with the hope of preventing the spread of this infectious disease mentioned, among sheep. We understand that in consequence of the precautions taken, the whole of the sheep in some parishes in the hundred are now free from the disorder.

9 June 1826

A LIBERAL MEMBER FOR THE COUNTY

The multitude that attended him to Camborne was immense; there could not be less than between 500 and 600 horsemen, in regular order, bearing at intervals, flags, banners, &c. with suitable mottos . . . When the procession advanced to Roskear, a large body of miners made preparations to take the horses from [his] carriage, for the purpose of drawing it into Camborne. This purpose, however, after much intreaty, Mr. Pendarves prevailed upon them to forego. The appearance of this town on the entrance of the procession was very striking. The houses on both sides of the streets, were shaded by large branches of trees, decked with rose-coloured ribbands; triumphal arches, handsomely decorated, were thrown across in several places. One arch, in the centre of the town, was so constructed as to have seats for a band, which continued to play national airs during the advance of the procession, and after its separation gratified the crowds that thronged the streets to a late hour. As the procession moved forward, the cheering of the multitude at intervals; the pealing of the bells, and the inspiriting strains of the numerous instruments produced an effect which those who witnessed it will never forget. 30 June 1826

[The liberal E. W. W. Pendarves, of Pendarves near Camborne, supporter of constitutional reform, was returning home from Lostwithiel, where he had just been elected as one of the two Members for the county (see p. 35), unexpectedly defeating the candidate representative of the Tory aristocracy.]

THE BUDE CANAL

Great complaints have been made of repeated depradations, and considerable damage has been done to the Bude Canal by cutting through the canal banks, opening the sluices at the inclined planes, and letting off the water into the river Tamar and the different mill leets in the neighbourhood of the canal. 21 July 1826

FOR KEEPING THE CAPSTAN AT SENNEN

Cornwall Assizes. The Earl of Falmouth v. Penrose and another. The pleadings were opened by Mr. Carter, and stated that the plaintiff is legally entitled to the second best fish of every cargo landed at Sennen Cove, in this county, and to the worst fish out of every cargo hauled on shore there, in consequence of affording certain accomodation to the fishermen who entered that cove, especially by keeping a capstan and rope there, for their use. 18 August 1826

[During these and subsequent court proceedings, Lord Falmouth's representative stated that his Lordship's family had originally hewn out of the cove, and had enjoyed the right to landing fish (the second best from each boat), for the liberty to land, and hauling fish (the worst from each boat), for the use of the capstan and rope, over a long period of time. They had maintained the rope and capstan, without which boats could not be hauled up from the sea, until recently. Of late, the fishermen had repaired it and, in consequence, contended that they were exempt from toll. The jury found, however, that by ancient right, Lord Falmouth was entitled to the toll on all fish landed at the cove except pilchards, which in early days were not brought in to Sennen.]

UNEQUAL JUSTICE

On Saturday, three farmers were convicted in mitigated penalties, by a bench of magistrates, at the Guild-hall, Helston, for offering wheat for sale at the public market, which was short of measure; and on the same day, two boys were committed to the county prison, at Bodmin, by the Mayor of Helston, for stealing fruit from the garden of the Rev. Mr. Stabback. Some people will be apt to doubt whether equal justice required the sending of two boys (children perhaps) to the tread-mill, for taking fruit from the garden of a Rev. Gentleman, whilst adults, who have defrauded those (probably poor persons) who purchased their corn, of a portion of the food they find it so difficult to procure, are let off on the payment of a mitigated penalty. 1 September 1826

WEIGHTS AND MEASURES

On Saturday last, pursuant to directions from George Thomas, Esq., Mayor of Truro, the constables proceeded to examine the weights and measures used in the market, when 18 gallon measures, used by potatoe sellers, were found to be too small, and were in consequence seized, and adjudged to be burned in the market place. The weights used by 10 butchers were also found to be deficient and were seized, as were 5 scales which were not properly adjusted. Afterwards the different inns and public-houses, of which their are 27 in the town, were visited, and the spirit, beer and corn measures examined, not one of which were found to be deficient in capacity. The weights used in the different shops have also been examined, and a few were seized; the coal, corn, malt, and lime measures were also examined, all of which were found to be correct.

1 September 1826

LAUNCHED AT PADSTOW

There were launched from the yard of Mr. J. Tredwen, ship-builder, Padstow, on Tuesday the 5th instant, amidst a large assemblage of spectators, a schooner named *Delabole*, built for R. Bake, Esq; and a smack named *Affo*, built for Messrs. Rosevear and Sloggat.

8 September 1826

[Robert Bake owned the famous Delabole slate quarry, the produce of which was shipped from Port Isaac and Portgaverne. Messrs. Rosevear and Sloggatt were also slate quarry owners (see p. 152).]

CLOUDBURST AT ST. NEOT

On Thursday, in last week, a fall of rain resembling the bursting of a water-spout, took place at St. Neot, near Dosemary-pool, in this county, and which has caused very serious injury in that neighbourhood. Though the ground slopes very gradually towards the village of St. Neot from the place where the rain fell with the greatest violence, the torrent rushed forward with irresistable force, carrying with it large portions of soil. The flood was perceived approaching the village like an immense wave, which, in an instant, carried away a bridge that was thrown over a rivulet; the water overflowed all the lower part of the village, and entered the house of Captain Sibley so suddenly, that the inmates had scarcely time to save themselves by running up stairs. Several articles of furniture &c.

were carried off by the stream, which burst into Lampen mine with such force as to render the escape of the three miners then at work, a matter of great difficulty. Below the mine, the river has opened for itself a new course. The slate quarries in the neighbourhood were also inundated. Seven men who were at work in them when the water broke in, with much difficulty scrambled to a ledge, fifteen feet above where they had stood, from which they were drawn to the surface by ropes.

8 September 1826

A CARGO OF BARK

The schooner *Sisters*, having landed a cargo of bark at Chyandour, near Penzance, for which purpose she was laid on the beach opposite that place—on being warped off, the stern-fast broke, in consequence of which she swung round and went on shore, in a rather dangerous situation. By the prompt assistance of boats, &c. from Penzance, she was speedily warped into deep water, having sustained but little damage. 22 September 1826

REJOICINGS AT THE MOUNT

On the 16th instant, Sir John St. Aubyn, Bart., visited his ancient castle on St. Michael's Mount, in Mount's-bay, after an absence of twenty-five years. The honorable baronet was received with every demonstration of respect; the ancient standard was displayed on the tower, the guns on the ramparts were fired, and the bells of the chapel steeple were rung. On Wednesday, the inhabitants of the harbour at the Mount were entertained at the castle, where a sumptuous dinner was served in the antique and spacious hall. 29 September 1826

THE MEXICO PACKET

The *Lady Mary Pelham*, Capt. Carey, takes out the first mail for Mexico, St. Domingo, &c. on Saturday. She sails direct [from Falmouth] for Jacquemel, thence to Jamaica, Vera Cruz and Havannah. A packet will sail for the same destination, the third Saturday in every month; the mail will be made up at the General Post Office, on the Wednesday preceding. 20 October 1826

[Representation had been made to the Government early in September on the need for a Mexico packet by merchants trading with that country.]

PROJECTIONS AND OBSTRUCTIONS

The waywardens of the borough and parish of Fowey and others whom it may concern, are hereby requested to take notice, that unless the timber, plank, slabs, offal wood, erections, projections and obstructions, now lying on that part of the public road near to, and adjoining the wall of the shipwright's yard, now occupied by Mr. George Nickels, shipbuilder, within the said borough and parish, be immediately removed and cleared, whereby His Majesty's subjects may be enabled to pass without endangering their lives and property, steps will be taken to enforce a compliance therewith. Richard Lean. N.B. Notwithstanding the very positive way in which a certain Grand Juryman stated "that there was no such thing there on the road on Monday last" it is still visibly to be seen up to this day, just as bad as it has been for many months last past!!!

27 October 1826

THE COUNTY CHAMPIONS MEET

When Cann entered the ring, he went up to Polkinghorne, and the competitors immediately shook hands, when they retired to equip themselves for the contest. Two strong canvas jackets were provided, the one marked C. and the other D. and which they put on; Polkinghorne wore loose trousers, but no shoes; he had on a pair of stockings, over which he buttoned a pair of leather leggins, to shield him as far as possible from the kicks of Cann, and over these he drew on another pair of stockings. Cann, who was aware that kicking forms no part of Cornish play, wore only a single pair of stockings; he had no shoe on his left foot, but on his right foot he put a prepared shoe which weighed nearly four pounds, and which after being steeped in some liquid, was hardened by being placed in an oven partially heated, until it became of the consistence of horn; the sole of this shoe projected, so as to inflict very severe wounds on the legs of the person kicked by the wearer, and it was fastened to the foot by a silk handkerchief bound round the instep. 27 October 1826

[This famous match at Devonport between Cann of Devon and Polkinghorne of Cornwall had been long and eagerly anticipated, negotiations between the wrestlers being continued for about twelve months. Altogether the behaviour of the 8000 spectators during the hours long contest was noisy and unsportsmanlike, but feelings ran very high on that day on account of the intense rivalry between the two counties, and more so because of the different wrestling styles used each side of the Tamar. Cornish wrestlers played without shoes, and grasped each other by the short jacket which was always worn. A man could be "thrust and hugged, and thrown and fallen upon", but kicking in the Devon style was unheard of. This latter, which was claimed to be more ancient, involved the use of a hard shoe, and was sneered at by the Cornish as both cruel and unsportsmanlike. The decision to declare Cann the winner was hotly disputed and eventually the stakes were returned to each party and all bets declared void.]

TOES RATHER TURNED IN

Whereas, John Dyson, of the borough of Penryn, collecting-clerk and agent for Messrs. Collan and James Harvey, of St. Day, stands charged with having feloniously embezzled money, which he had received for them, and having been apprehended under a magistrate's warrant, the said John Dyson did, on the night of Wednesday or early on the morning of Thursday the 14th December instant, effect his escape from the constable who had him in custody; the above reward [of £20] will be paid to any person who will bring the said John Dyson to William Pender Roberts, Esq. of Penryn, the magistrate who granted the warrant for his apprehension.

The said John Dyson is 44 years of age, about five feet four inches high, slight made, has brown hair, prominent nose, which is rather aquiline, his lips protrude a little, and shews his teeth when speaking; walks quick, with his toes rather turned in, and generally with his hands in his trowsers or small-clothes pocket, and stoops a little in walking.

22 November 1826

TOES TURNED OUTWARDS

Whereas John Riches, of the parish of Camborne, late servant to William Penpraze, of Illogan, hath absconded with a sum of money, the property of his master, whoever will apprehend the said John Riches, and lodge him in either of His Majesty's Gaols, shall receive the above reward [Five guineas].

The said John Riches is about 23 years of age, about 5 feet 2 inches high, stout made, has light hair, a pit in his right cheek, very short neck, blue eyes, a little marked in the face, rather pale complexion, walks quick with his toes turned outwards, is a butcher by trade, had on blue clothes, light frieze great coat, and new shoes. 29 December 1826

RUNNING FROM A BARGAIN

We, the undersigned, having quitted the bargains [contracts by miners for certain work to be done] we had undertaken to perform, at Great St. George mine, and thereby occasioned to the adventurers considerable expense and loss of time, have for the said offence subjected ourselves to imprisonment and hard labour in the county gaol at Bodmin. The agents however of the said mine having leniently abstained from putting into force against us the extreme rigour of the law, we do hereby beg pardon for our misbehaviour and acknowledge it to have been very improper and injurious, agreeing, at the same time to pay the cost of the magistrate's warrants which have been issued against us, besides a fine of 10s. each, to the Club of Great St. George mine, and the expense of inserting this advertisement in the West Briton. As witness our hands this 24th day of December, 1826. Henry Roberts, John Sobey, the mark of X Francis Daniell. 5 January 1827

THE TREWEEK FAMILY

So lately as the beginning of November, the family of Christopher Treweek [of the parish of Kea] were attacked with a most dreadful malignant and contagious fever, which raged with such violence, that within the short space of thirty days, death destroyed four of his children, who are consigned to the silent grave. The disease, as if annihilation was its object, attacked one other son and daughter; and to make up the train of misery has also levelled its fury at the poor mother, who had attended her numerous children upon the beds of sickness unto death; and on Saturday last death also mowed down the son, aged 22 years, making five; and it may yet be (though we hope not) the trying task of the father to witness the dissolution of the remaining two. 12 January 1827

[In fact it was the father who died shortly afterwards, leaving his aged wife and two children still stricken with the disease.]

MADE IN HELSTON

Lane's Haemacathartic tincture which is offered to the public as a certain cure for the King's Evil, Leprosy, cancers, white swellings, scurvy, and every disorder arising from impurity of the blood. This invaluable medicine is prepared only by Samuel Drew, chemist and druggist, Helston. 12 January 1827

DEATH OF THE DUKE OF YORK

At Falmouth, the flag at the garrison was displayed half-staff high; the Royal Standard was hoisted half-mast high, on board the *Astrea* frigate [superintendent of the packet service], and the packets and other vessels in the harbour hoisted their colours in the same manner. At 8 o'clock in the morning, the bell of Falmouth church was tolled; and about half-past two, one of the packets commenced firing minute guns, thirty of which were discharged by each of three of these vessels, in succession. The *Astrea* frigate then fired thirty minute guns, and afterwards the same number was fired by the garrison; the firing being so regulated as to conclude by sunset, and at eight o'clock in the evening, the bell of the church was again tolled. 26 January 1827

SOLD FOR THE HOUNDS

A poor man named Pearce, who resides at Perran, had a horse stolen on the night of the 17th ult; and another person named Martyn, had one stolen on the night following. The loss of two horses, neither of which were supposed to be worth taking by a regular horse stealer, appeared rather extraordinary, and an active search being commenced, it was found that the horse of Pearce had been sold for carrion, which it much resembled, at the kennel of the Four Burrow hunt, on the 18th, for three shillings, and that of Martyn, on the day following, for four shillings, by a lad named James Brenton, who was apprehended, and after an examination before William Peters, Esq. one of the magistrates for this county, he was fully committed to Bodmin prison, for trial. The prisoner is in his 17th year.

2 February 1827

A HANDSOME CHARIOT

To be sold, a handsome town-built chariot, (nearly new) painted yellow, and picked out in black, with blue lining, and red Morocco squabs, boot in front, and rumble behind, lamps, &c. complete. Price £60.

16 February 1827

ENDEMIC TYPHUS FEVER

The wretched cob-built cottages [of Cornwall], scattered over the country, have, almost invariably, open catch-pits close to them; and I scarcely know of a single village or church-town, where the same nuisance may not be seen before the very doors and windows of the houses. Nor is the evil by any means confined to the country—our towns are sadly negligent of measures conducive to the health of the inhabitants . . . How then can we be surprised at the perpetual recurrence of typhus fever? The situation of Truro, with a river flowing on either side of it, is remarkably favourable to cleanliness, yet, notwithstanding its fair exterior, it contains, I am sorry to say, dirty, ill-ventilated alleys, and backlets so offensive to health and decency that they are scarcely to be approached without risk of febrile infection. To the east of Truro, we find St. Austell enjoying the peculiar and unenviable privilege of chains of open catch-pits, which, from time immemorial, have been diffusing throughout the neighbourhood, their infectious exhalations, and which, no doubt, have largely contributed towards its frequent visitations of typhus fever. The populous town of Redruth is situated about eight miles to the west of Truro, and, in proportion to its population, is the abundance of liquid stagnant filth which is suffered to accumulate in open pits, or rather reservoirs, even in the immediate neighbourhood of houses remarkable for their neatness of appearance, and inhabited by persons of respectability and opulence.

8 March 1827

MR. PETERS' EXTRAORDINARY HEIFER

Having been fifteen days on her western exhibition, and strange places, strange faces and public admiration giving her more pain than pleasure, this natural curiosity will be relieved by being slaughtered at Truro, on Tuesday the 13th inst. Her carcase will be shewn before cutting up, on that day and the following. Tickets of admittance, 2s.6d. Her beef, 1s. per lb. to be cast lots for on completion. 9 March 1827

INTOXICATED AT THE TIME

Whereas I, Barney McCarthey, hawker, did improperly accuse John Harris, ostler, at the Barley Sheaf Inn, Truro, of robbing me of three pounds. I do hereby make this public apology and beg his pardon, I being intoxicated at the time. Witness my hand this 2d day of March, 1827. Barney McCarthey. 9 March 1827

OCTOGENARIANS AT PERRANWELL

Last week, at Perranwell, a man aged 86 years was shaved by a barber whose age is 85, whilst another who has attained his 84th year, held a candle during the operation. 16 March 1827

BODY STEALING

This practice, so very distressing to the feelings of surviving relatives, has, it seems, commenced in Cornwall. On the night of Monday last, the body of a person named Abraham, which had been interred on the preceding evening, in the parish of St. Veep, near Fowey, was abstracted from the grave. It appears that the interment took place late in the evening, and that the sexton, having partly filled up the grave, intended to complete the operation the next morning. On coming to the spot, however, he found that the grave had been disturbed, and in consequence the coffin was uncovered and examined, when it was found that the body had been carried off. 23 March 1827

[The "resurrection men", as they were called, removed bodies from graves in order to sell them to surgeons for dissection purposes. In *The West Briton* of 22nd June 1827, a surgeon, who had been fined £100 for his part in such a "resurrection", appealed for contributions from those who had benefited from "the art and science of surgery" to help him meet the fine, his argument being that the law required all medical men to practice dissection in order to become proficient in their profession.]

A TROTTING MATCH NEAR LISKEARD

On Tuesday last, a trotting-match took place on the Eastern Turnpike-road at Liskeard, between Mr. Austen's brown horse Bagatelle, and Mr. W. William's grey mare Jenney, for one mile only. Bagatelle broke from the trot once, and was turned round in consequence, but notwithstanding he won the match, in admirable style, by upwards of 100 yards, performing the mile in three minutes and a half. This is the second match he has won during the last week.

23 March 1827

RIOT AT BODMIN GAOL

On Monday last, the prisoners in Bodmin prison, sentenced to hard labour, refused to go upon the tread-mill, and declared they were resolved to resist every attempt to compel them to resume their labour. Two of the visiting magistrates . . . were immediately sent for, and on their arrival they remonstrated with the rioters, but in vain; they tore up the railing that was round the wheel and arming themselves, prepared for resistance. Finding every other means unavailing, the staff of the Cornwall Militia were called together, and being armed and provided with ammunition, were drawn up in the outer yard of the prison. As soon as their arrival was announced to the rioters, they gave three cheers, shouting—"death or victory." . . . The militia men were then directed to enter the inner yard; and as the first file were about to pass the gate, some of the most daring of the rioters attempted to wrest their muskets from them. This attack was spiritedly and successfully resisted without firing, and the rioters retreated, some of them having been knocked down by the butt end of the soldiers' firelocks, and five of the most refractory being secured, and lodged in separate cells, the others then submitted. Sowden, who was convicted at the late Truro Sessions of a violent assault on the constables of Camborne, being the ring-leader, was ordered by the magistrates to ascend the wheel, which he positively refused to do. The magistrates finding it absolutely necessary to shew the prisoners that they were resolved to enforce obedience, and to correct a notion they appear to have entertained, that the magistrates could not inflict corporal punishment on them, orders were given to flog Sowden, which were instantly carried into effect, in a manner that will for some time afford him a *feeling* proof of his error. The other rioters, who beheld the punishment of their leader, were then ordered to ascend the wheel, under pain of a similar infliction, when they wisely chose the lesser evil, and resumed the obnoxious operation and promised obedience.

18 May 1827

MACKAREL FOR BILLING'S-GATE

The weather has been this week very unfavourable to the mackarel fishery; in the preceding week the boats belonging to St. Ives were tolerably successful. Owing to arrangements made for conveying fish from Bristol to London by vans or light carts, the price of mackarel has been kept up to from 20s. to 25s. per hundred. The fish caught on our coasts are taken to Bristol, where they are purchased by regular dealers and sent to London; fish caught on the Cornish coast have been offered for sale at Billing's-gate on the third day from their being taken—the price of mackarel in the London market is stated at 70s. to 90s. per hundred.

1 June 1827

[Several months earlier a vessel carrying fish from St. Ives to Bristol had been wrecked on the Doom Bar at Padstow.]

HAYLE SUNDAY SCHOOL

The anniversary of Hayle Sunday school, including the branch at Angarrack, was held on Whitmonday. At two o'clock, the children of Hayle school assembled in the school room, and shortly after, walked in procession with the two resident Wesleyan ministers at their head, towards the Towen hills [the area of sand-hills seaward of Hayle]. On the way, the children of the Angarrack school fell into the line, and the whole number with their teachers being now between four and five hundred, presented a most interesting spectacle as they ascended these heights. On reaching the appointed place where, in a natural amphitheatre, carpeted with nature's green, a booth was erected for the minister, the children were properly arranged, and a most impressive address was delivered by the Rev. Thomas Martin to the children, their teachers and parents, and a vast concourse of spectators who surrounded the pleasing scene. Appropriate hymns were sung in excellent style by the children; immediately after which they retired in regular procession to the chapel, where tea and cakes were plentifully provided for this large family. 6 June 1827

RABBIT WARREN ADJOINING

To be let, for a term of fourteen years from Michaelmas next, all those tenements, called Higher Reen, Reen Wollas, and Reen Wortha, situate in the parish of Perranzabuloe, consisting of an excellent dwelling house, with convenient stables, out-houses and other buildings, and of about 78 acres or arable and pasture land and inclosed crofts, together with the common adjoining Higher Reen. Also all that rabbit warren adjoining Higher Reen, extending over about 240 acres of land, statute measure, and well stocked with rabbits. 22 June 1827

ST. JOHN'S DAY ON SCILLY

The eve of St. John the Baptist's Day was observed at St. Mary's [Scilly] in the manner which has been practised from time immemorial; but which is not, on that account, the less objectionable to persons of regulated habits. Great numbers of boys paraded the principal thoroughfares, whirling torches from right to left, and darting their fitful glare in every direction; while the air was loaded with the stench of fire-works, which had nothing of either ingenuity or novelty to challenge the attention. No accident occurred, although such practices cannot but be extremely dangerous, and therefore it is to be regretted that they are not wholly abolished, not only at Scilly, but in the more enlightened town of Penzance.

29 June 1827

[The eves of both St. John's and St. Peter's Days were celebrated with the whirling of torches and the letting off of numerous fireworks.]

MERMAIDS AT MAWGAN PORTH

One evening this week, a young man who lives adjoining the beach at Mawgan Porth, had made an appointment to meet another person on the beach to catch sprats with him. He went out about 10 o'clock at night, and coming near a point which runs into the sea, he heard a screeching noise proceeding from a large cavern which is left by the tide at low water, but which has some deep pools in it, and communicating with the sea by another outlet. He thought it was the person he had appointed to meet, and called out to him, but his astonishment is not to be described when on going up he saw something in the shape of a human figure staring at him, with long hair hanging all about it. He then ran away thinking, as he says, that he had seen the devil. The next day, some men being on the cliffs near this place, saw three creatures of this same description. The following day, five were seen. The persons who saw the last five, describe them in this manner. The mermaids were about 40 feet below the men (who stood on the cliff) and were lying on a rock, separated from the land some yards by deep water; two of them were large, about 4½ to 5 feet long, and these appeared to be sleeping on the rock; the other small ones were swimming about, and went off once to sea and then came back again. The men looked at them for more than an hour and flung stones at them, but they would not move off. The large ones seemed to be lying on their faces; their upper parts were like those of human beings, and black or dark coloured, with very long hair hanging around them; their lower parts were of a bluish colour, and terminating in a fin, like fish. The sea would sometimes wash over them and then leave them dry again. Their movements seemed to be slow. The hair of these mermaids extended to a distance of 9 to 10 feet.

6 July 1827

[In the next issue of *The West Briton* it was reported that those who had seen the mermaids wished to correct the above report, in that the colour of the bodies of these creatures was "exactly like that of a Christian" while they were possessed of short arms, resembling fins.]

A STRANGE MODE OF WORSHIP

On Sunday last a congregation of Ranters, consisting of about one

A rustic scene in Penryn

Fishing boats in Mousehole harbour

hundred and twenty persons, assembled at Falmouth, in a large loft over a stable, where they have for some time held their meetings. In the course of the service, the fervour of the devotees was so strongly excited, that, as is frequently the case, they commenced jumping, in imitation of the description of David's dancing before the ark, &c. Having continued this exercise, in which both sexes join, for some time, the beams suddenly gave way, and the minister and his dancing congregation, were suddenly precipitated into the stable beneath them. Screams and cries for assistance speedily succeeded to the joyous exclamations and violent gestures of the late zealous actors in the strange mode of worship already described. The uproar was great and continued for some time . . . 20 July 1827

[The name "Ranters" was given to the Bryanites or Bible Christians (see p. 168) on account of their peculiar mode of worship, which was after the manner of Primitive Methodists. Both groups were offshoots of Wesleyan Methodism, the latter being of northern origin (see p. 168), while the Bryanites were founded in Cornwall by William Bryant of Luxulyan.]

A CAPITAL OFFENCE

Henry Randell was indicted for breaking into the dwelling-house of John Scantlebury, and stealing two cotton shirts. From the statement of the prosecutor and his wife, it appeared that they live at Landrake, in this county, that on the 26th of July last, between one and two o'clock in the afternoon, they left their home, having locked the outer door; that on their return, about half-past two, they found that a pane of glass had been broken out of a window, and two shirts which lay on a table opposite, and which could be reached with a stick, were stolen. The prisoner who was seen near the house, about half-past one o'clock, was suspected, and being taken into custody by a constable, two shirts, which were identified by the prosecutor's wife as those she had lost, were found on him. The Chief Justice in summing up said, the case came under one of Mr. Peel's Acts, which came into operation, the 1st of July last, by which breaking into a dwelling-house and stealing to *any* amount, is a capital offence. Breaking a window and taking things out of the house with a stick, through the window, clearly came under the meaning of this Statute. Guilty—sentence of death recorded. 17 August 1827

A CAMP-MEETING ON EASTERN GREEN

A camp-meeting will be held between Penzance and Marazion, on the 16th of September, when the following ministers are expected to address the meeting; Messrs. Driffield—Garner—Stranger—Morris &c.—Service to commence at ten o'clock in the morning, and continue until five. Wm. Driffield, Primitive Methodist minister. 7 September 1827

[Primitive Methodism came to Cornwall from Staffordshire in 1825 and quickly gained many followers, some of them formerly Bryanites or Bible Christians (see below). Camp meetings of this kind were held in various parts of Cornwall, the most recent having been attended by several thousands on a common "within three miles of Truro, on the Redruth road."]

SCHOONER FOR SALE

For sale by private contract, the schooner *Susanna*, burthen per register about 77 tons, and carries full 100 tons. Shifts without ballast, and sails very fast; is well adapted for either the coasting or foreign trade; is well found in materials, and may be sent to sea immediate, being by lately returned from a voyage to Wales. Further particulars may be known, on application to John Pearce, if by letter post-paid, Mevagissey.

7 September 1827

THE SAILING OF THE 'ARGUS'

The French brig *Argus*, Lative, master, which some time since put into St. Ives in distress, after being repaired, was this week about to sail, when the tradesmen who had supplied the materials, &c. finding they were about to be deprived of what they considered as the only available security for their demands, became clamorous, and having obtained assistance, got into boats and boarded the vessel when under way, when after a scuffle they succeeded in bringing her back into port, where she was detained, until security was given for the payment of different claimants, which being done, she was allowed to depart. 21 September 1827

THE NOISY BRIANITES

For some weeks past the town of St. Columb has been disturbed by frequent assemblies of Brianites, in a room over the market-place. What with the ravings and shrieks of the preachers and their disciples within, and the shouts and laughter of the crowds without, the place has been a perfect Babel, and a complete stop has been put to the comfort and repose of the more rational inhabitants of the neighbourhood . . . To stop these proceedings, one of the proprietors of the market-house had the door locked, and stood on the outside to forbid the Brianites from entering it. They were, however, deaf to his remonstrances, and having assaulted and thrust him from the spot, broke open the door with an iron bar, and forcibly took possession of the place, and renewed their noises and riots to the terror of all the neighbours. 5 October 1827

WANTED, FOR SOUTH AMERICA

Wanted, by the Bolivar Mining Company, two able ball carpenters, who are fully qualified to erect water wheels, stamps, whims, capstans, shears, &c. to go out under an engagement for three years, to the company's copper mines, at Arao, near Puerto de Cabello, by the Leeward Islands packet, which will leave Falmouth, on the 10th of November next. Apply to Captain William Trebilcock, St. Day. No one need apply, who cannot produce satisfactory testimonials of his ability as a ball carpenter, and of his sobriety and honesty. 12 October 1827

SACRILEGIOUS THEFT

Whereas William Niness, (son of William Niness, the younger), *alias* Young Cross, of the borough of Penryn, in the county of Cornwall, brazier, stands charged with having broken into the parish church of St. Gluvias and Penryn, and sacrilegiously stolen therefrom five pieces of silver plate, and other articles, and has since absconded. We, the undersigned, do hereby offer a reward of ten guineas, to be paid to any person or persons who shall apprehend the said William Niness, and shall bring him before William Pender Roberts, Esq. one of his Majesty's Justices of the Peace for the said county of Cornwall, at Penryn aforesaid.

The said William Niness, is about 22 years of age, about 5 feet 6 inches high, rather stout made, has a heavy slouching walk, is of dark complexion, marked with the small-pox, black eyes with a downcast look, has an aquiline nose, and black hair; he generally wears an olive fustian short jacket and trowsers, has made one voyage to America, and has exhibited himself in this county and Devonshire on a mountebank stage. Any person after this notice discovered harbouring or concealing the said William Niness, will be prosecuted. Henry Rowe, churchwarden of St. Gluvias; Thomas Pearce, Thomas Rogers, churchwardens of Penryn.

19 October 1827

THE SCILLY PACKET IN PERIL

Last week, the Scilly packet, on returning to the islands from Penzance, experienced such violent weather, when off Lemorna, that she carried away the head of her mast; in consequence of which, the mainsail came down on the deck, and her situation became imminently perilous. Although there was a tremendous sea rolling, it was judged expedient to come to an anchor; and, as there happened to be some efficient passengers on board, besides the few hands that usually navigate the vessel, the damage was at length so far remedied, as to enable her to reach the place of her destination. She has since been fitted with a new mast, which has delayed the time of her departure. A steam-packet here, would be a great public convenience, and, probably, no unprofitable speculation to the owner.

9 November 1827

THREE ASSES AND A PONEY

The good folk at St. Agnes were not a little surprised, on Tuesday, at seeing a carriage heavily laden with the cylinder of a steam-engine; its bottom; cover; piston; piston-rod, &c. &c. for Wheal Charles mine, drawn by three asses and a poney; the latter leading. The weight of the articles was, apparently, far beyond what these animals could move.

7 December 1827

WOOLLEN MILLS NEAR MENHENIOT

To be sold by public auction, before the major part of the commissioners in a commission of bankrupt, against Mr. Richard Maynard, at the King's Arms, in the borough of Liskeard . . ., the following desirable property; Lot 1. All that building, consisting of three stories, in which a woollen manufactory has long been carried on, known by the name of Kelly's factory, containing in length one hundred and twenty feet, and in breadth fifty feet (more or less,) parcel of a tenement called Kelly's otherwise Trewint Marshes, within the parish of Menheniot, in the county of Cornwall. The above factory is well supplied with a powerful stream of water, is most advantageously situated for obtaining wool of the best quality, and distant only four miles from water carriage. These premises are held for the residue of a term of fifty years, of which twenty-five are now unexpired, subject to a ground rent of £5. 10s. Lot 2. The fee-simple and inheritance in possession of and in all that building, consisting of four stories, in which the woollen manufactory has also been long carried on, and known by the name of Hoyle's factory, together with a wash-house, drying loft over, kiln and dwellings for labourers belonging thereto, being respectively parcel of Hoyle's tenement, in the said parish of Menheniot. This factory is situated within one hundred yards from Kelly's factory and possesses every convenience necessary to the conducting of an extensive trade. Lot 3. Also the fee-simple and inheritance in possession, of and in all that tan-yard, with drying lofts, laborers' dwellings, and other premises, with the appurtenances thereto belonging, situate and adjoining Hoyle's factory.

4 January 1828

A RESCUE IN CARRICK ROADS

On Monday last, it blew a tremendous gale from the south-east, which continued without intermission during the whole of the day. About noon, the brig *Sarah*, of 150 tons burthen, Thomas Collingwood, master, from Newfoundland to Poole, with a cargo of fish, oil and lumber, sought shelter from the storm by running into Falmouth harbour . . . As the gale continued with unabated fury and the night was falling in, the lives of those on board were placed in jeopardy. At the suggestion of Capt. Sutton of H.M. packet *Stanmer*, the inhabitants of Flushing made a good light with furze and tar barrels on an adjacent hill, which was of great advantage; the masts of the brig were necessarily cut away, and a cable being conveyed on shore, the crew, with a gentleman and his two daughters, passengers, were got safely to land in an empty cask which was slung and traversed on the cable. 11 January 1828

A METHODIST SEAN COMPANY

To be sold by auction at Mevagissey, on Monday the 4th of February next, the stop and tuck seans, three boats, and the whole of the materials, belonging to the Methodist concern. 18 January 1828

MINERAL RICHES IN GWENNAP

From the parish of Gwennap alone, the copper ores sold in the last seven years amount to one million nine hundred and twenty thousand pounds. In the last year (1827) the amount was upwards of three hundred and seven thousand pounds, besides what was received for tin, fluor-spar, &c. and which may be estimated at fifty thousand pounds more.

1 February 1828

A BARGAIN AND SALE

John Cook, a day labourer, lately appeared at a petty sessions held at Five-lanes, on a summons obtained by the overseers of the parish of Tintagel, to shew cause why he did not maintain his wife and children. On being asked what he had to say in explanation of his conduct, he very deliberately made the following statement. His wife and he having lived very unhappily together, and having no children, he resolved to sell her, which he did, about sixteen years since, in the public market at Camelford, to a person who bid half-a-crown for her. Since that time she had lived with her purchaser, by whom she has had seven children; but having lately declined in health, she was compelled to apply to the parish officers for relief, and they called on Cook, who told his story, and readily agreed to appear before the magistrates. Their worships not being disposed to sanction the aforesaid bargain and sale, Cook was in a fair way of being saddled with his wife and her offsprings, when a difficulty as to the place of his settlement being discovered, the final decision was postponed to a future day, when he will, probably, be compelled to pay a reasonable sum to the parish for the support of the woman and her children, or visit the tread-mill. 8 February 1828

CUTTING RICH

A correspondent observes, that having seen a paragraph in the West

Briton, some weeks since, stating that a miner named Peters had unexpectedly made his appearance at Redruth, and had paid off some debts he had formerly contracted there, whilst nobody could tell how he got the money—lest anything prejudicial to the man's character should be surmised from the remark, he is induced to state, that Peters obtained nearly £1000, in a few months, by working at tribute on a silver lode, in the Great St. Vincent lead and silver mine, near Callington.

15 February 1828

[In January Peters had been reported as reappearing in Redruth after an absence of seventeen years, with ample money to pay off a considerable number of long standing debts.]

THE PILCHARD FISHERY

Number of seans employed, 186; not employed 130,—total number of seans, 316. Number of drift boats 368. Number of men employed on board drift boats, 1599. Number of men employed at sea on seans, 2672. Number of persons on shore, to whom the fishery affords direct employment, 6350. Total number of persons employed in the fishery, 10,521. Cost of seans, boats, &c. used in the fishery, £209,840. Cost of drift boats and nets, £61,400. Cost of cellars and other establishments on shore, for carrying on the fishery, £169,975. Total capital invested directly in the pilchard fishery, £441,215.

It may be proper to observe that in addition to the number of persons employed in the catching and curing of pilchards, the fishery furnishes employment to numerous others, and to nearly the whole population of particular places, in proportion to the success which attends it, in the building and repairing of sean boats and small vessels, the manufacture of netting, cordage and canvass, the making of casks, and in a variety of other branches connected therewith; and that on the raw materials required for such purposes, as well as on the malt and spirituous liquors consumed by the fishermen, a considerable sum is paid to Government in the shape of duties.

7 March 1828

[At this time the government was considering withdrawing the protection this trade had enjoyed in the form of a bounty of six shillings per hogshead.]

RINGING IN CROWAN

On Monday the 12th of May, the following prizes will be rung for, on the bells of the parish of Crowan: 1. Six gold-laced hats; 2. Six white hats; 3. Six silver-lace hat-bands. Each set of ringers to bring an umpire; and all questions to be decided by the majority of umpires; but should they not agree, three others will be chosen by the parishioners of Crowan, whose decision shall be final. The ringing to commence at nine o'clock in the morning. 14 March 1828

DRESSED AS SAILORS

On Wednesday afternoon, as a poor woman named Mary Thomas, who resides at Helston, was proceeding from St. Austell to Truro, on her way home, she was overtaken by three fellows dressed as sailors, with blue jackets, canvas trowsers, and straw hats, lackered over with blacking or tar. One of the fellows made her an insulting proposal, which she indignantly rejected, when he snatched at a handkerchief she twisted round her hand, and in the corner of which she had tied up five shillings for safety. After a struggle, he got the handkerchief, and finding the money, the fellows made off towards Truro. 11 April 1828

HOMEWARD BOUND

A poor sailor named Michell, travelling on foot from London to Falmouth, his native place, had got as far as Liskeard last week, when, overcome by want of food, exhaustion and fatigue, he suddenly dropped down and expired. 25 April 1828

AN ADROIT MANOEUVRE

Last week the Mayor of Truro ordered the constables to inspect the weights and measures used in the markets, and the different shops, and to weigh the butter offered for sale in the market. Out of the whole quantity weighed, but about 15 lbs. were found deficient, which being seized, were given to the poor. A woman named Brown practised an adroit manoeuvre on the constables; she had a piece of butter which weighed about an ounce and a half, and which she contrived to stick to the bottom of each half-pound of butter, as she handed it from her basket in order to be weighed, but which she dexterously removed when it was handed back, and stuck on the next half-pound she delivered to the weighers. By this means all her butter was made weight. Unfortunately for her, the trick was observed by a thrifty housewife who watched the process, and communicated the result to the constables . . . The weights and measures used in trade, throughout the town were also inspected. There are in Truro, seventy-one grocers; fourteen drapers; twenty-five inns and public-houses; six retail breweries, five coal and four lime-yards, in all of which the weights and measures were examined and found to be perfectly correct. 9 May 1828

A RIDE TO BODMIN GAOL

A hawker named John Morris was committed to Bodmin gaol, on

Saturday, by H. M. Grylls, Esq. mayor of Helston, charged with picking the pocket of Mr. William Jose, a farmer, of his pocket-book, containing several local bank-notes, whilst standing amongst a crowd in the market place. As the person who conveys prisoners from Helston to Truro, on their way to Bodmin, was returning from placing Morris in safety, he overtook two women who were proceeding to Helston, to attend the fair on Monday, as venders of gingerbread; and having bargained with him for a ride, they got into a car he was driving. On the road, the party stopped at a public-house to get some beer, when the girl who was serving them discovered on one of the women, a pelisse which had been stolen from her at Penryn fair, on the 12th of the present month. The possessor of the stolen property was taken into custody, and being unable to give a satisfactory account of the way in which she came by it, she was treated with a ride to Bodmin gaol the next day. 30 May 1828

DESTITUTE GERMAN EMIGRANTS

A meeting will be held at Falmouth this day (Friday) in order to consider of the best means of affording present relief and effecting the removal of the unfortunate Germans who were some time since landed there from a vessel in which they had embarked for the Brazils. They now refuse to proceed in the vessel, which has been repaired, under the idea that on arriving in Brazil, they will be sold to pay their passage money, &c. They sleep in stables, &c. around the town, and are in a state of great destitution. 6 June 1828

[The Dutch galliot, *Helena Maria*, had been towed into Falmouth, a wreck, by one of the packets early in January. On board were 350 impoverished Germans, bound for Rio de Janeiro, who were permitted to land while repairs, paid for by the Brazilian government, were made to the vessel. The emigrants were penniless and £75 was immediately given for their use by the local Society for the Relief of Distressed Foreigners, but by June they were becoming somewhat of an embarrassment to the town of Falmouth, although they were hardworking, honest and uncomplaining. They sailed for Brazil in December.]

PICK-POCKETS AT PENZANCE FAIR

The pick-pockets were in attendance and did a good deal of business in their particular line. One farmer was disburthened of £26, in a very masterly manner; another was relieved of the charge of £18, and several others were eased of smaller sums. One of these dexterous practitioners was secured, we believe in the very act of exercising his calling, and after having given some explanation to his worship, the Mayor, was accomodated with lodgings in the town prison. The gaoler, who is a very worthy man, having given him his breakfast the next morning, returned to his house, leaving unlocked the door of the cell, which opened into a court surrounded by high walls; supposing that, as he locked the door of the court, there was no danger of escape. In this, however, he was mistaken; the fellow felt desirous of changing his quarters, and by placing the iron bed-stead belonging to his cell against the wall, contrived to make his exit without the ceremony of taking leave. There were two other persons also in confinement, in the place, but they declared they knew nothing of the purpose of their companion until he had carried it into full effect. No trace of the fugitive has been discovered. 13 June 1828

LIZARD FISHERY ESTABLISHMENT

For sale by public auction, at the Star Inn, in the borough of Helston, on Friday the 18th day of July instant, by three o'clock in the afternoon, the Lizard Fishery Establishment, consisting of two stop seans, and one tuck ditto, with boats and every other materials requisite for carrying on the said concern. The whole will be found in very complete order, and ready for sea without any supply whatever. A capstan house and slip are attached to the concern, which gives it the command of the valuable stem [the strip of coastal water allocated to any particular sean] of Tilcoben. 11 July 1828

THE BISHOP IN TRURO

On Friday, the Lord Bishop of this Diocese, confirmed nearly 900 children at St. Mary's Church, Truro, from that and the adjoining parishes. On Saturday morning, his Lordship consecrated the chapel of St. John, in Lemon-street, with the usual ceremonies. Prayers were read by the Rev. J. D. Coleridge, vicar of Kenwyn, to whose indefatigable exertions, the erection of the chapel is chiefly owing; it is principally intended for the accomodation of the poor, of that part of the parish immediately connected with Truro, and contains 800 free sittings. 1 August 1828

AN ASSOCIATION FOR FIRE-FIGHTING

We take this opportunity [report of a serious fire in the bark lofts of the Chyandour tannery—see also p. 156] to recommend the inhabitants of other towns in the county, the adoption of a system which has been for some time so successful at Penzance. Many of the respectable inhabitants have formed themselves into an association, as volunteers, to attend on all occasions of fire. The engines have been placed at their disposal, and they have a committee of ten persons, who select in rotation, one of their body as managing director. They defray the expenses of all the people employed at the fire, calling on the parties afterwards, for repayment. These arrangements prevent confusion, and the beneficial effects of them were evident on the present occasion. 8 August 1828

DIVERSIONS AT PORTREATH

At Portreath, on Monday the 18th of August instant, there will be boat-racing, jingling, pack-jumping, pole-climbing, running for a gold-laced hat, ribbons, &c. &c. And a variety of other amusements, calculated to produce a novelty never before observed in Cornwall. The boat-racing will be confined to boats belonging to Portreath, and of which there will be two classes. 1st class—The fishing boats exclusively of Portreath. 2nd ditto—The boats belonging to the several vessels on that day at Portreath . . . Every boat on entering to run, to pay two shillings and six-pence. The boats to start from the Horse-Rock, on the signal of a cannon being fired from the light-house, and to sail around the rocks called the "Man and his Man", off St. Agnes Point, and return to the western point of the Horse Rock. This part of the amusement will be subject to certain rules and regulations, and under the entire management of Mr. Stephen Knight. The other amusements will be conducted by a committee of gentlemen selected from the list of subscribers. Booths will be erected on the hill, near the light-house, where refreshments may be had, and a full view of the boat-races seen throughout. N.B. There will be a pigeon shooting-match in the course of the afternoon. 15 August 1828

IMPRESSED IN RIO

The fine Brazilian frigate, *Izabel*, lately in Falmouth harbour, is manned by a crew composed of natives of almost every maritime state in the old and new World. She has on board about 60 English seamen, most of whom, it is said, were impressed from on board Brazilian merchant ships, at Rio . . . About one o'clock on Tuesday last, an alarm was given that five of the English sailors had got through one of the ports and had seized on a boat which had conveyed a party [of visitors to the *Izabel*], in which they were seen pulling with their utmost force, for the shore. Immediately all was bustle, but before one of the ship's boats could be launched and manned, the adventurous tars were nearly half a mile from the vessel. A smart chase immediately commenced. In the Brazilian boat were 16 seamen and a party of marines, and they so far gained on the fugitives, as to be within about 200 yards of them, when jumping into the water, which reached about to the middle, they ran from the beach up the hill at the foot of which Falmouth is built, and made off across the country. This being observed on board the frigate, the officer in command thought it best to hail the pursuers and direct them to return, as a chase through the country might be attended with serious consequences to the foreigners. 22 August 1828

A MEMORIAL TO WESLEY

Within a mile of Penzance is a large rock, standing unconnected with any other mass of stone, and which was formerly situated nearly in the centre of a common, but which by late agricultural improvements, has been converted into fertile meadows. On this rock, upwards of eighty years since, the celebrated John Wesley frequently took his stand, in order to address the multitudes that thronged to hear him from the surrounding country, when he was prevented from preaching in the town of Penzance. William Pengelly, Esq. of Trannack, having lately returned to Cornwall after an absence of several years, has in order to commemorate his respect for the memory of the venerable founder of Methodism, caused a marble tablet to be let into the rock, with the following inscription: "On this rock, the Rev. John Wesley, and others preached the Gospel of Christ, from the years 1742 to 1760. W. Pengelly, 1825."

22 August 1828

PENPOLL LEAD SMELTING WORKS

To be sold by public auction . . . all those newly-erected capital lead smelting works, situate at Penpoll, in the parish of Feock, in which Mr. John Swan lately carried on the business of a lead smelter; comprising two calcining furnaces, two flowing furnaces, three refining furnaces, and one reviving furnace, with all the necessary working tools, test rings, moulds, &c. and a stock of bone ashes. These premises are in complete repair, and in every respect fit for immediate use, and are calculated for smelting 180 tons of lead a month. Also, all that substantial newly erected and extensive quay, adjoining to the said lead works, called Lemon quay, with the ore hutches, at the back thereof. And also the counting-house, and other buildings erected near to the said quay and smelting works. The quay has a very long frontage towards Penpoll creek and may be approached by vessels of 160 tons burthen or upwards, and is well adapted for carrying on the coal or timber trade with mines upon a large scale, the Redruth rail-way coming to the quay . . . 29 August 1828

CAMELFORD V. ST. COLUMB

Sir, as a member of the Camelford Cricket Club, I cannot pass over in silence the mis-statement that appeared in your paper of last week; imputing meanness, &c. to our club by refusing to play with the St. Columb Cricket Club for a higher stake than a shilling dinner. The fact is, since we received the challenge from the St. Columb club, we have played three matches, with three different *respectable* clubs, and won each match. In consequence of our success, the St. Columb cricketers were afraid of sharing the same fate, and to get off from the challenge they sent us, they acted with the *greatest duplicity*, and would come to no fair terms at all. We actually offered to play with them for from five to twenty sovereigns (at their option) and if they will now play with us for that sum (the game to be according to Lambert's Guide) we will meet them at their own door to decide the bet. A member of the Camelford Cricket Club.

12 September 1828

MOGGY'S FAIR AT PERRANWELL

The above fair has been usually held on the 27th of September; but this year, that day falling on Saturday, it has been thought necessary to postpone the fair until the Monday following, the 29th inst. in order to avoid it interfering with different markets. Perranwell being centrally situated with reference to different towns, and a populous neighbourhood, and the fair having heretofore been well supplied with cattle, &c. there is every reason to suppose it will this year be well attended. The innkeepers of the place are determined to use every exertion in their power to accomodate those who may attend, and hope to meet with due encouragement from the public. Dinner on the table, at the different inns, at two o'clock precisely. 26 September 1828

RELEASED FROM SLAVERY

By the French brig *Le Mereure*, Cabaret master, which arrived at Penzance on Monday, from Brest, nine Maltese came passengers, having been released from slavery at Tunis, and conveyed by a French frigate to Brest, and from thence forwarded by the British consul at the latter port, to England, as British subjects. 3 October 1828

WIFE WANTED

A tradesman, aged 42 years, of the first respectability, in a certain town in Cornwall, whereof he is a native, and now carrying on a long-established trade, which is most respectable, the advertiser is a remarkably temperate, sober, steady man, who would study domestic comfort, and is in every way qualified to render the marriage state desirable. Any middle aged, agreeable lady, who can command £1000, who feels desirous of meeting with a sociable, tender and kind companion, will find this advertisement worthy of notice. Not any part of the above sum is wanted in trade, that being entirely independent. The advertiser having a great taste for building, the money would be laid out in that way, and the wife to have the sole property settled on her for life. The advertiser will have a personal interview anywhere in the county. Honour and the greatest secrecy may be depended on. As a security against mere curiosity, letters, post-paid, with real name and address, will meet with most respectful attention. Direct to A.B. to be left at the Post-office, Falmouth until called for.

3 October 1828

INFERIOR BRITISH BRANDY

Last week, a man named John Curgenven met with some officers of the Customs at Truro, and offered to sell them smuggled tobacco and French brandy, part of a cargo which he said he had landed. He produced three quarts in two jars and a bladder, as samples, for which he asked 24s. per gallon, and said he could supply them with any quantity. Upon this they took him into custody, and on searching his person, found upon him a small measure and a funnel; he was kept in charge until the following morning, and taken before the Collector, who examined him and also the spirits seized, and found that the French brandy, for which he had asked 24s. per gallon, was British brandy of a very inferior quality, which he had purchased at one of the taps in Truro, the same day, at 3s. 3d. per quart; in this manner the lovers of that precious article are nine times out of ten duped.

10 October 1828

[Curgenven was incautious in approaching strangers thus, although virtually everyone in Cornwall, directly or indirectly, was associated with smuggling, and approved of it. In fact, while it was illegal to land contraband, to sell smuggled goods was not.]

VERY FALSE PRETENCES

Aaron Smith was charged with obtaining from Sarah Nancollis, by false pretences, five shillings, a pair of shoes, and a watch. Sarah Nancollis lives in Egloshayle, she has been twice married; her first husband was called Moses Simmons, and by him she had two children called Moses and Aaron. Moses is in London and Aaron went to India about eight years since, as a soldier. On the 17th of last month she went to Bodmin, and was informed that her son Aaron had been looking for her. She went to the New Inn, and after a short time the defendant came in; he called her his dear mother, shook hands with her and kissed her. She said he was greatly altered since he left; when he left he was marked with the small-pox, and had a large scar in his forehead; he had now light hair and was much shorter. The defendant said that in foreign countries the marks of small-pox came out, and that it was the effects of the climate, that changed the colour of his hair and made him shorter. On hearing this explanation she was satisfied and believed he was really her son. After a little while the defendant said he wanted a pair of shoes, which she bought for him—he then asked for some money, and she gave him half-a-crown. They went home together, and had some supper; the defendant then went upstairs, and asked for his watch, which was given him by her daughter; he then asked for a clean shirt . . . 24 October 1828

A YOUNG SHEPHERD

On Friday evening as two boys, the one aged eleven, and the other nine years, were driving some sheep from Newlyn towards Chacewater, the youngest became exhausted and was left by his companion on the common, where he perished from the inclemency of the weather.

21 November 1828

OF DARK COMPLEXION

Absconded from his family, chargeable to the borough of Bodmin, Edmund Lane, wheelwright, aged about 48 years, black coarse hair, dark complexion, about five feet six inches high, and usually washes his face about once a month. Whoever will apprehend the same, and lodge him in either of his Majesty's gaols, shall receive forty shillings reward and all reasonable expenses, by applying to the Overseers of the said borough.

28 November 1828

NEAR CONSTANTINE CHURCH TOWN

Whereas it has been represented to the commissioners of his Majesty's Customs, that in the night of the 19th November, instant, a large party of men (armed with pistols, bludgeons, and knives) in the act of conveying smuggled goods from the coast, were intercepted by two officers of the Customs near Constantine church town, in the parish of Constantine, in the county of Cornwall; and that the said officers seized from the said persons several horses laden with spirits, which had been run on shore without payment of duties; and that after the said officers had so seized the horses and goods, the smugglers with force and violence rescued the same from them, at the same time feloniously assaulting and ill-treating the said officers, so that the life of one of them is despaired of. The said Commissioners are hereby pleased to offer a reward of £300 to any person or persons who shall discover or cause to be discovered any one or more of the persons concerned in the said outrage so that he or they may be apprehended and dealt with according to law, to be paid by the Collector of his Majesty's Customs at the port of Falmouth, in the said county of Cornwall, upon conviction. 5 December 1828

GENTLE AND QUITE HARMLESS

Escaped, from the Cornwall Lunatic Asylum, about seven o'clock in the evening of the 21st of January, 1829, James Parsons, a criminal lunatic, from the parish of Modbury, in Devon, tried at Exeter, last

Spring Assizes, for horse stealing. He is about 5 feet 6 inches high, dark hair and eyes, small features, and darkish complexion; his manners gentle, and quite harmless. He is very artful, having before escaped from Exeter goal. He had firmly rivetted on his ancle, a flat ring, with the words 'Bodmin Lunatic Asylum' engraved on it. Supposed to have had £2 in silver, in half-crowns and one crown, and a silver hunting watch, stolen from one of the keepers. Whoever apprehends him will be paid all reasonable expenses, and receive the usual reward. 23 January 1829

[Parsons had previously escaped from Bodmin gaol, having first stolen £5 from a keeper. He scaled the wall, visited a public-house, and returned to gaol of his own accord. His earlier escape from Exeter was made by placing a dressed dummy in his bed; on his recapture he was chained to a post, but expertly picked the lock with a piece of wire torn from a saucepan. Some of his contrivances for escape were described as "too clever for publication", and presumably the flat ring, "6½ inches across the outside and 3½ in internal diameter . . . case hardened and secured with four counter sunk rivets on his right ancle", was considered irremoveable and an effective deterrent to his travelling very far.]

SHEEPSTEALERS DROWN AT KYNANCE

For several years, the district of Meneage and the neighbourhood of Helston have been infested by a gang of depradators of desperate character, who conducted their system of plunder so adroitly and contrived so to intimidate the inhabitants by apprehension of their vengeance, that though there is scarcely a farmer within some miles who had not been robbed, in one way or another, by them, still they were allowed to go at large; it being well understood that they had extraordinary means of concealment. On the night of Wednesday last, four very fine rams . . . were stolen from the farm of Mr. Silvester, about half a mile from Helston. The gang were naturally first thought of . . . In the house of Jose, 82 lbs of mutton, cut up and salted, were found, some of it being concealed in a bed, and there was little doubt of its being part of the largest sheep stolen. At the house of Hocking, who is a butcher, two legs of mutton, and some sheeps' skins, from which the wool had been plucked off, were discovered. Jose and Hocking were apprehended and sent to Helston, when the latter gave such hints as induced a party to set off early on Tuesday morning with intent to apprehend Stephen Jose—brother of the prisoner James Jose—and William Harris . . . A hue and cry was raised, and the party proceeded to search the cliffs and caves on the shore . . . Soon after, Jose and Harris were seen at a distance near Kynance Cove. Chace was instantly given, when these desperate characters, finding their retreat cut off, made towards the sea, into which they desperately plunged, notwithstanding the warning of one of the pursuers who was nearly up with them. They continued to float for about 20 minutes, when they sank and were both drowned. 20 February 1829

COTTAGE ORNÉ AT DEVORAN

To let on lease, for seven or fourteen years, with immediate possession, a comfortable residence, with proper farming offices, and 36 acres of excellent arable and pasture land, well fenced and lately in the possession of Mr. Samuel Hugo. The above premises are situated on the line of the new Falmouth turnpike road immediately above the new port and quays at Devoran, on the Redruth rail road, and very convenient for a person engaged in mining or mercantile pursuits; or it may be converted, at a trifling expense, into a complete cottage orné, for a small genteel family, commanding beautiful and picturesque views over Carclew Park and Perran and Restronguet Creeks. 6 March 1829

ELOPED FROM HER HOME

Whereas, Amelia Bray, a young lady of 19 years of age, about 5 feet 3 inches in height, feminine appearance, rather prominent features, hath eloped from her home with a young man named Isaac Coombe, 5 feet 11 inches high, dark complexion. Whosoever will apprehend the said fugitive, and restore her to her friends, at Helset, Lesnewth, near Camelford, shall be entitled to a handsome reward. 27 March 1829

STEALING A PONEY

Cornwall Assizes, John Parkyn, aged 24, was found guilty of stealing a poney, belonging to Jacob Grigg, off a common, in the parish of St. Dennis, on the 9th of September last. The prisoner took the poney from the common and moved it about from place to place, evidently not knowing what to do with it, until the 19th of the same month, when he was taken into custody, and in consequence of what he stated, the poney was found near Newlyn. Sentence of death recorded. 27 March 1829

INCONVENIENCES AND INTERRUPTIONS

Great confusion being occasioned in the principal thoroughfares at Truro, in consequence of not attending to the understood regulation of keeping to the *right* on passing, as is the case in London and other places, the Mayor has published a notice on the subject, earnestly recommending that persons walking should uniformly incline to the right on meeting with others, by which means the inconveniences and interruptions now experienced will be generally avoided. He also desires that the young men and labourers of the town may not assemble in parties at the corners of the streets, and on the bridges, as they generally do at present, by which

The town and harbour of Falmouth from Pendennis Castle

The church and harbour, Fowey

the way is frequently obstructed, to the great annoyance of respectable femalès. The constables are ordered to keep the streets free from interruption. 27 March 1829

A BATTLE AT CHACEWATER

The inhabitants of Chacewater were grievously annoyed on the evening of Good-friday. When returning from public worship they found two drunken men who had been turned out of the Brittannia Inn fighting in the street. A mob was quickly collected and the spectators taking different sides, a general battle ensued. It is high time that effective means were taken to preserve tranquillity in this village. 24 April 1829

GEORGIAN APPETITES

On the 23rd instant a party of farmers having met at the King's Arms Inn, St. Columb; after enjoying a cheerful glass, some of the party proposed that 2 lbs of beef steaks should be provided for each person present, and he who took most time in dispatching his portion should pay for the whole. One of the company who had already dined, offered to eat 3½ lbs, with bread, &c. in half an hour, for a wager. The bet was speedily made; the steaks were procured, and when they were half dressed, the glutton set to, and actually cleared the whole, with two penny loaves, a pint of beer and a glass of brandy, in 29 minutes, after which he danced a hornpipe, to the astonishment of the spectators. 1 May 1829

A FORGERY AT FOWEY

An advertisement in another part of our paper offers a reward of £500, for the discovery of the person who committed a forgery of a novel description on the Commissioner of Customs for the sum of £1,973, which was paid without suspicion. The order purported to be drawn to cover the deficiency of cash in the hands of the Collector of the port of Fowey, to meet the demands upon the revenue there. 1 May 1829

PAY DAY ON THE MINES

It was also much to be wished [on account of the prevalence of drunkenness] that the agents and pursers of mines, instead of paying several of the men together—to make up a round sum—and sending them to divide the money amongst themselves, at the public house, would give each man his respective share, at the mine account-house . . . There would be considerable difficulty in doing this, especially at the moment, when in consequence of the diminution of the one-pound notes in circulation, there was such a scarcity of change. 1 May 1829

IN WHEAL VOR

Two miners, named Arthur and Vaside, met their death in Wheal Vor mine, on Saturday last, under the following melancholy circumstances. Whilst at work in one of the levels of the mine, at a considerable depth, Arthur had his leg broken by one of those accidents so frequent among the adventurous class of men to which he belonged, and in consequence his fellow workmen prepared to get him taken to the surface, in the easiest way possible. They prepared a kibble (bucket) which was suspended by a 9-inch [circumference] capstan rope, and in this they placed the sufferer. Vaside stood in the kibble to support him, but scarcely had the kibble with the two individuals in it, been cast off from the level and became suspended over the shaft which is of great depth, when the rope broke, and the two unfortunate men were precipitated to the bottom of the shaft, in presence of their agonized companions, who on reaching the spot, found them quite dead. Each of the sufferers has left a widow and four children.

29 May 1829

BATHING AT THE PUBLIC QUAYS

Whereas the young men and boys of the town [of Truro] make a frequent practice of bathing at the public quays and in the open rivers, to the great annoyance of the decent inhabitants, this is to give notice, that bathing, in such public places, is a misdemeanor, and that all such persons as shall be found hereafter offending, will be liable to be indicted, and in the mean while to find sureties for their good behaviour. J. W. Chilcott, Mayor.

29 May 1829

SEIZED OFF CAWSAND

On Saturday evening last, about eight o'clock, Mr. Foot, of the preventive waterguard, at Cawsand, captured a sprit sail boat, called the *Five Sisters*, belonging to Cawsand, with 98 tubs of foreign brandy and geneva on board, together with three men and a boy. The boat was first discovered by one of the preventive men on the look out from the hill, and conceiving her to be suspicious, he informed Mr. F. of the circumstance, when the latter accompanied by four men well armed took one of the pilot boats from the bay, and proceeded towards the boat in the offing. The smugglers did not suspect the persons in the pilot boat of any design on them until they were close to them; but on perceiving who the intended visitants were, they immediately crowded all sail, to effect their escape. This they were likely to effect when the preventive men shewed their colours and commenced firing musketry at the smugglers. The seventh shot fired cut away the sprit-sail halliards, when the main-sail fell, and the pursuers came alongside and secured the boat with its cargo and crew.

10 July 1829

A RELIC OF PAGANISM

Sir, Many of your readers and myself have, with regret, read in the columns of your paper the details of a sport which every one must allow to be a relic of paganism; and the revival of which, after it had become almost obsolete, forms a very humiliating contrast to the general progress of the community in religious and intellectual improvement. The part which the civic chief of a neighbouring town is reported to have recently taken in rewarding and eulogising wrestlers will not, it is hoped, find many imitations. I had designed to submit to your readers an extended view of the evils of wrestling matches. That intention, however, has given place to the publication of a small pamphlet on the subject, which will be extensively distributed prior to the wrestling match of next week . . . P.S. The following is respectfully submitted for the consideration of your readers:—Why do you not go to the wrestling! For eight good reasons. Because I should get no good there. Because I can employ my time better. Because it is throwing my money away. Because I wish not to be seen in bad company. Because I would not encourage idleness, folly and vice. Because I should set a bad example. Because God has forbidden it. "Abstain from *all* appearance of evil."—1st Thess. v. 22 . . . Because I must soon die. I remain yours, &c. Philanthropos. 24 July 1829

DRUNK AT THE PORTH

On the 17th instant, William Ennor was found dead on the cliffs between Lower St. Columb Porth and New-quay. The deceased had been shipping [china] clay on board a vessel at the porth, and on returning along the road which lies near the cliff, it is supposed, he fell over, being rather intoxicated. Accidental death. 24 July 1829

HARVEST BEER

On Thursday the 23rd instant, Mr. Jethro Harris, a farmer of St. Just, went to the house of a neighbour to brew his harvest beer, his own apparatus not being in order. Having completed the operation, he poured the liquor, boiling hot, into casks, which he had put into a cart, and in which he was about to take it to his own house. Three of his children, boys, were with him, and were allowed to ride on the cart. When they had gone some distance, the pin which confined the fore part of the cart fell out, and Mr. Harris supported it behind, hoping to be able thus to reach home, where he could get assistance. Unfortunately, on ascending a short hill, the weight of the contents of the cart became too much for his strength, when it was upset and the contents, with the children, were precipitated into the road. One of the boys was severely bruised and was so dreadfully scalded by the hot liquor which poured from the bung hole of one of the casks, on his head and body, that he expired in a few hours; another was so dreadfully bruised that his life is still considered in danger; the third escaped with, comparatively, little injury; Mr. Harris was also severely scalded in his efforts to rescue the children. 31 July 1829

FOX OINTMENT

Power's alopecian or fox ointment. The alopecian complaint, or falling off of the hair, is thus designated by the proprietor or inventor of this infallible remedy, on the ring-worm in the human species so nearly resembling a complaint in foxes, which occasions their hair to fall off in the same manner. 31 July 1829

A BUILDER'S APPRENTICE

Ran off, from his master, John Blake, builder, of Wadebridge, Richard Brewer, his apprentice, about 19 years of age, five feet six inches high, full face, and rather fair complexion; flat nose, grey eyes, dark coloured hair, generally much frizled; no beard or whiskers; has lost the top part of the thumb on the left hand. Carried off his working dress, a fustian coat, light-coloured waistcoat, corduroy trowsers, and pink striped neckcloth. Also his Sunday's dress, blue coat, light-coloured waistcoat, drab trowsers, yellow and red silk neck-cloths. Whoever harbours or employs the said Richard Brewer, after this notice, will be prosecuted as the law directs.

14 August 1829

THE HARVESTS OF SCILLY

The harvest has been commenced on the different islands. Appearances warrant the expectation of an abundant crop of all kinds of grain. Considerable quantities of potatoes have lately been exported hence to Gibraltar and the Mediterranean; besides smaller quantities to Plymouth, Bristol, and other places. Great numbers of that fine little fish, the scad, have been caught almost every night, for two or three weeks past, by fishermen and others from the several islands, at the Cove, St. Agnes. These fish, salted in, form the chief winter-provision of the poor. The deep-sea fishery has not been very successful. 14 August 1829

THE UNDER-TURNKEY

Cornwall Assizes. Daw v. the Executors of Chapple. This was an action brought by the plaintiff, Roger Daw, against the executors of the late governor of the county gaol, at Bodmin, to recover a sum alleged to be due to him for wages. It appeared that previous to the death of Mr. Chapple, a manufactory of coarse cloth was carried on at the prison, for the purpose of finding employment for the prisoners. This had been superintended by a person named Clemence, who was paid 12 shillings a week, as wages. In June, 1824, the plaintiff, who had been a respectable clothier, but who was then in very indigent circumstances, was engaged to succeed Clemence, and he superintended the manufacture up to the death of Mr. Chapple. To that period he had been paid five shillings a week, and the present action was brought to recover the difference between the sum paid and 12 shillings a week, the rate of wages paid to Clemence, his predecessor . . . On the cross-examination [of two witnesses] they admitted that, in addition to superintending the weaving, Clemence acted as an under-turnkey, and that the plaintiff was upwards of seventy years of age. 28 August 1829

[Daw did not recover the money, the defence arguing that five shillings a week was adequate, he having been taken on at the age of 76 largely on the grounds of humanity.]

HIGH LIFE IN CORNWALL

Mr. J. Dawson, professor of dancing and fencing, has the honour to announce his return from London; at the same time begs most respectfully to say, that he has profited by the instruction and experience of the most able professors. Mr. J. D. has acquired all the new and fashionable dances, the celebrated gallopades, Spanish dances, &c. &c. He has also entered into treaty with M. Geroux, Ballot Master of the Italian Opera, who is engaged to supply the earliest intimation of every change in the fashionable assemblies. Mr. J. D. therefore hopes to merit a portion of public patronage. 11 September 1829

FROM THE LAND OF SQUAB PIE

The postponement of the Cornish mine cause occasioned some loss, or rather prevention of some gains, of the tradespeople of Bridgewater, and particularly to the innkeepers at whose houses the witnesses were stationed. At one of these inns one party actually drank, in the night of Tuesday only, the profligate quantity of three hundred and seventy grogs, and fifty bottles of wine. On the ensuing morning, each man on his departure provided himself with a "pocket pistol", containing half a pint of brandy. The captain of a mine from the land of Squab Pie, as part of his breakfast on the road, picked clean the bones of a cold duck, and a few hours after nearly demolished two hot roasted ones! This gastronomical performer, no doubt, acquiesces in the quaint opinion avowed by a predecessor in that line of distinction, who said that "a goose was a foolish bird, being rather too much for one, and too little for two." 11 September 1829

[Eighty Cornishmen were in Bridgwater for the Assizes, as witnesses in the important and lengthy mining case, Rowe v. Brenton, before the Nisi Prius Courts of the Western Circuit.]

TWO AMAZONS IN KENWYN

Jane and Mary Ann Waters, sisters, were committed by the Mayor of Truro, to Bodmin gaol, for assaulting the master of the poor-house belonging to the parish of Kenwyn. It appears that these amazons were taken into the poor-house as paupers, and as is the custom there when girls of doubtful character are received into it, the governor ordered their hair to be cut short. To this they resolutely refused to submit, and, in resisting the operation of the shears on their locks, assaulted the master and a female attendant, threatened the life of the mistress, and filled the whole establishment with confusion and alarm. In the end, they were shorn and delivered over to the discipline of the house of correction in the county, as the only place in which they could be safely trusted.

11 September 1829

HURRICANE AT PADSTOW

The severe gale of wind, which was felt along our coasts on Thursday the 11th instant, was experienced with particular severity at Padstow and its neighbourhood, where the tempest raged with greater violence than has been remembered on any similar occurrence, for many years. In the morning the wind varied from S.E. to N.E. but about noon it suddenly flew round to N.N.W. and blew a complete hurricane, which, we regret to say, produced the most disasterous consequences to several vessels that were unhappily exposed to its fury. The *Hector*, of Sunderland, Ormond, master, with a cargo of iron, from Cardiff for Ipswich, was driven on shore near Pentire-glaze; the crew are safe and it is expected she will be got off; the *Francis*, of Torquay, Hunt, master, in ballast, in attempting to enter Padstow harbour, was upset, and all on board perished. The *Atlas*, of Fowey, Scantlebury, master, laden with coals, was driven on shore near Portquin, and went to pieces; the crew with great difficulty saved their lives; the *Sprightly*, of Padstow, Richards, master, with a cargo of coals, went on shore to the westwards of Bude; the crew are saved; the *Mary*, of Plymouth, Guswald, master, laden with coals, went on shore near Padstow, but was got off the next tide, though with considerable damage . . . Since the storm twenty-five vessels which were exposed to its fury, have happily arrived, many of them with loss of sails, spars, bulwarks, &c. and some of them leaky.

18 September 1829

A CONJUROR CALLED JOHNNY HOOPER

A poor man named John Rowe, who resides at Tremoor, in the parish of Lanivet, and who is far advanced in life, had by industry and economy scraped together twenty pounds, which he converted into sovereigns and put in a box, the key of which he always kept in his possession. On Sunday last he went to add something to his store, and on counting over his treasure, he observed that the pieces were not all alike. This led to a scrutiny, when he discovered that 16 of the sovereigns had been abstracted, and fourteen farthings, a shilling and a button without a shank, all covered with leaf gold, put in their stead. The poor man is in the greatest distress at being thus deprived of the savings of a long life; he suspects a particular individual of the theft, but in place of instituting an enquiry through a magistrate, he has resolved to apply to a conjuror called "Johnny Hooper", to ascertain if his suspicions are well founded, in the hope that some part of the money may be restored through the influence of the "cunning man". 25 September 1829

ON THE LATEST YORKSHIRE PLAN

To be sold by auction . . . all that factory or building [at Bissack, near Ladock], about 36 feet in width and 46 feet in length, and three stories high, together with or without the worsted machinery therein, consisting of 4 spinning frames, of 72 spindles each, and a twisting machine, of 60 spindles, on the latest improved Yorkshire plan, with a water wheel of 24 feet in diameter, and three feet wide. 2 October 1829

THE COFFIN BRIGS

On Monday last, the committee for the distributing the money collected for the relief of the unfortunate widows and children of the seamen and petty officers, of the crews of the packet-brigs *Hearty*, *Redpole*, and *Ariel* met at the vestry-room of the Wesleyan chapel, at Falmouth, to divide amongst the claimants the sum of £55—being £50 contributed by the Mexican Mining Company for that benevolent purpose, and £5 collected by the committee since the last distribution. 30 October 1829

[The three vessels were small sloops of war introduced into the packet service after its take-over from the Post Office by the Admiralty in 1823. These 10-gun brigs, deep waisted and low decked, unlike the original Falmouth-built packets, proved entirely unseaworthy and many returned from voyage without their guns, never jettisoned unless a vessel was in great distress. By 1834 eight of these coffin brigs, as they became called, had foundered, six of them on the packet service. They were lost without trace, together with their passengers, crews, bullion and important commercial mails.]

GLASSON, THE FERRET

A female gypsey, of rather youthful appearance, has been telling the fortunes of the spinsters, widows, &c. of Padstow and its neighbourhood, for the last fortnight. On one occasion she boasted that she had obtained fourteen shillings the preceding day. Under various pretences, she obtained from several of her dupes, trinkets and articles of wearing apparel, which she was to return on Monday last with valuable additions; it is unnecessary to add, that she failed to keep her appointments, to the no small chagrin of the expectants. She dresses in a gaudy style, and is accompanied by a fellow of low stature, called Glasson, a native of Truro, nicknamed, the Ferret.

13 November 1829

[A week later the fortuneteller was busy on the tread-mill, having assaulted a person at Port Isaac.]

HEAVY GALES OFF LAND'S END

The Scilly packet-boat, which should have arrived at Penzance on Tuesday se'nnight, did not reach that place until Saturday last; the delay was caused by the prevalence of heavy gales from the eastward. A great number of woodcocks shot at Scilly, were brought by the packet for sale at Penzance.

4 December 1829

ATTACKED BY A RAT

Last week, during the dead of night, a family in the parish of St. Stephens were alarmed by cries of murder! uttered by a woman named Trethewey, who was one of the inmates. A light was speedily procured, and on proceeding to the bed of the poor woman, a large rat was seen to jump from it, and make its escape; the woman was found to be covered in blood, which flowed from her right shoulder which was dreadfully lacerated, and from a severe wound on her cheek. She stated, that she was awaked by feeling her shoulder torn by the teeth of the rat, the terror and anguish arising from the attack caused her to scream and endeavour to free herself from the assailant, when the rat fixed its teeth in her cheek where it held until the approach of the persons who had been roused by the cries of the sufferer, with a light, induced it to seek its safety by flight. The poor woman is still ill of the fright and of the wounds she received, the marks of which will probably remain through life.

11 December 1829

A FOX HUNT IN FALMOUTH TOWN

On Friday, the Four-borough hounds met at Mainporth, near Falmouth, and after a short time, found a fine fox which broke cover in high style and ran to Pennance, but finding the earths stopped there, he crossed the country through the grounds of Capt. Bull, near the Swanpool, thence down the Bowling-green fields, at the back of Killegrew-street, Falmouth, the inhabitants of which found their houses, which are built at the base of a hill, assailed by the dogs, who clambered on the roofs from the rear, and from one of which a hound leaped into the street, without being much hurt, whilst about sixty sportsmen on horseback drew up in front. After some search reynard again broke ground and finding himself nearly surrounded, he made for the upper church-yard, on the top of the hill, thence he leaped into a mason's yard, where he was taken by some boys, without resistance. 18 December 1829

SCHIEDAM HOLLANDS GENEVA

At less than half the price of imported Hollands, and at the highest strength allowed. Rosevear and Sloggatt beg to inform their friends and the public, that they have received a further supply of this unrivalled spirit, being the same wholesome, unadulterated article produced in Holland, (liable to a duty on importation of 22s. 6d. per gallon) and held in such deserved estimation on the Continent, as well as the rest of Europe, Asia, and America, and now introduced to the public, at a British duty, by sanction of Government, in order to extirpate smuggling.
1 January 1830

AN EXCEPTIONAL WINTER

The frost has again set in with increased severity, accompanied by partial and light falls of snow; the degree of cold exceeds what has been remembered by the oldest persons, in this county; on Wednesday and yesterday the thermometer at Truro was as low as 22 degrees of Fahrenheit, being about the point at which strong wine freezes, and 10 degrees below our ordinary winter temperature . . . The poor at Launceston receive a weekly supply of coals and potatoes from a fund subscribed by the inhabitants; this week 250 pairs of stockings were distributed amongst the children of the Sunday school belonging to the established church at the place. 5 February 1830

CONTRABAND IN A ST. JUST MINE

The men on the preventive service at St. Just, near the Land's End, aided by a party from the *Dove* revenue cutter, last week seized 173 tubs of spirits and 20 tubs of tobacco, which had been landed from a cutter, and hidden in a shaft of a mine at that place. During the search, one of the preventive men named White, fell from a plank into a shaft of the mine and was killed on the spot. The deceased was a native of St. Just, and led the party to the place where the seizure was effected.
19 February 1830

ONE SIDE OF A STORY

A poor man named Alsop, living at St. Austell, with a wife and nine children, and who has not been able to obtain work sufficient to provide the means of existence, whilst conveying some coals in a wheel-barrow, for hire, fell through exhaustion, and shortly expired. The unfortunate family were found in the most destitute condition, and it was clearly proved that the unfortunate man had actually died of starvation!!

12 March 1830

THE OTHER SIDE

Sir . . . Alsop lived on the Downs, a mile and a half from St. Austell, and was employed in Pembroke mine. Three weeks before his seizure, he received six gallons of potatoes, a bushel of Newport coals and 2s. 6d. in money from the Charitable Fund at St. Austell, having just before received a blanket from a lady; in the same week his three children, who are employed with the mines, brought in forty shillings, with which part of the rent was paid, and the rest was kept for the family. In the week following, he sold his sieve at Lanescot mine, for which he had no further use, for four shillings and sixpence, and the Saturday before his death he brought in six shillings and two-pence halfpenny, and the next day he received two shillings more from the Charitable Fund. On the following Tuesday he went with an *empty* wheelbarrow to bring home half a bushel of coals for his own use, and on the way had a seizure and died. There was money due to him from Pembroke mine, and if he had been in great distress, he might have received twenty shillings in advance. He had a plot of ground for growing potatoes, and the right of cutting turf on the Downs . . . We are, sir, your obedient and humble servants, J. Wheeler, John Andrew, Churchwardens of St. Austell. 19 March 1830

[From a letter replying to the implication that the overseers of the poor in St. Austell had allowed a man to die of malnutrition.]

FISH FOR LONDON AND BRISTOL

During the past week the boats engaged in the mackarel fishery at Penzance have been more than ordinarily successful. Several boats' crews sold their fish for the London and Bristol markets, for which they immediately proceeded with a favourable wind. 26 March 1830

SMUGGLING NEAR PORTREATH

On Monday morning, 48 tubs of brandy and 16 tubs of gin, were lodged in the St. Ives custom-house stores, by the coast guard stationed at Portreath. The spirits were captured the preceding night together with a boat . . . It appears the boat came from a small sloop rigged vessel which was seen on Sunday hovering off the coast, and the persons on board were in the act of landing the cargo within Hell Bay, about 3 miles west of

Portreath, and which is bounded by terrific cliffs, termed Hell's Mouth. Mr. Mortly, the officer of the Portreath preventive guard, with three of his men descended these cliffs at the imminent hazard of their lives, as a single false step would have precipitated them down the precipice, which is about 50 fathoms in height, and at the foot of it they came upon the smugglers, when the boat, her cargo and two of the crew were secured. It appears the smugglers had resolved on making a desperate resistance, as two of the preventive guard who had been at Hayle, and were proceeding to join Mr. Mortly and his party, were encountered near the summit of the cliffs by eight smugglers, who were armed. Shots were exchanged and the preventive men were overpowered, one of them named Rice, having received a ball in the thigh. Rice lies ill at Gwithian, to which place he was carried, and is under the care of Mr. Angove, surgeon, of Hayle, by whom the ball has been extracted. 2 April 1830

PODDLING AT LUXILLION

Cornwall Assizes. Joseph Thomas Austen, Esq. v. John Manley, Thomas Spargo, and James Spargoe. The prisoners were indicted for having, on the 27th of February, last, unlawfully, maliciously, and feloniously pulled down a certain waterway belonging to Lanescot, Fowey Consolidated, Wheal Hope and Wheal Union mines, situated in the parish of Tywardreath, the property of the prosecutor and others, with the intent to hinder and delay the working of the said mines . . . About seven years since, Mr. Austen, the prosecutor, had, at very great expense, cut a watercourse about three miles in length, from a place called Grediow Moor, in the parish of Luxillion, to the mines mentioned in the indictment. The water conveyed by this means, to these mines, had been applied to work the very expensive and powerful machinery by which these concerns were carried on. The prisoners had formerly worked at Lanescot mine; the two Spargoes under-ground, and Manley above ground. About two years since an order was given, that all able-bodied men belonging to the mine should work under ground, leaving the work at surface, or as it was termed "grass work", to men who were disabled and could not work below surface. Manley, who is an able-bodied man, refused to comply with this order, and was discharged in consequence. Some time after he with the two other prisoners and a man called Harper commenced streaming the moor for tin . . . On the morning of the day mentioned in the indictment, the prisoners cut down the wear at the head of the watercourse, in two places, each about 15 feet in width, thereby turning nearly the whole of the water, equal to that of 10 mill-streams, out of the water-course, to run to waste on the moor. There were previously about 2 mill-streams of water to spare, running over the wear, and which was more than double the quantity that was required for streaming the moor, but the prisoners did not even make any pretence of using the water which they allowed to run to waste, until some men were sent up from the mines to make up the breaches. Soon after they had done so and left the place, the prisoners returned and broke down the wear, turning the water to waste, as before. It appeared that the little work the prisoners and their party had done on the moor did not indicate any intention on their parts of carrying on a regular and *bona fide* stream work. (one of the witnesses subsequently termed what they were doing, as "poddling".) 2 April 1830

THE NEW FIRST AND LAST HOUSE IN ENGLAND

To be let . . . a newly-erected dwelling house, with a large and commodious stable (capable of receiving 12 horses) adjoining, situate on the Land's-End of England . . . The chief object in erecting the dwelling-house and premises was to afford accomodation to the great number of persons who so constantly visit this spot, there having been no house for the reception of parties or their horses within a mile and a quarter of Land's End, till the erection of the present house and its premises. It is presumed that this circumstance will render it highly desirable not only to the taker, but to the public, who will thus be relieved from the necessity of leaving their horses and carriages at Sennen, and walking for upwards of a mile from thence to the Land's End, while at the same time every accomodation will be afforded to them of taking their refreshments at the real first and last house in England. 9 April 1830

BREAD FOR THE NEWLYN FISHERMEN

We regret to learn, that great distress prevails amongst the fishermen at Newlyn, in consequence of the failure of the mackarel fishery, in Mount's Bay. The families of these industrious and hardy fishermen are often nearly destitute of food, and had not the parish vestry consented to give each fisherman a shilling, on the Monday morning, to provide bread for the sea trips, the poor fellows would be wholly unable to pursue their hazardous occupation. 23 April 1830

LIME KILN LATELY ERECTED

The public are respectfully informed, that the lime kiln lately erected in Kiln Lane, adjoining the rail-road, near St. Austell Bridge, [the Pentewan railway, which terminated in St. Austell], will be opened some time in the ensuing month of May, when there will be a constant supply of lime. N.B. A good lime-burner wanted immediately. 23 April 1830

[Dozens of lime kilns were formerly to be seen along the coasts of Cornwall, burning limestone for manuring the generally acid soils of the county. The rock was brought from Devon and South Wales, chiefly during the calm months of summer, and discharged with safety on the shores of numerous creeks and the beaches of sandy coves. Furze was originally used to burn the lime, later Welsh coals (see pp. 134 and 215)].

CORNWALL QUARTER SESSIONS: I

James Olmud was found guilty of stealing a pair of worsted stockings, belonging to Thomas Bryant, which were drying on a hedge, on the 30th of last month, and which the prisoner put on, having taken off his old ones, which he left by the hedge. When taken into custody, he had the prosecutor's stockings on, and fell on his knees and begged for mercy. To be imprisoned for twelve months, at hard labour. Jane Tinner was found guilty of stealing a sheet and several articles of bedding, and wearing apparel belonging to William Rowe, near Madron church-town, which were placed to dry near the prosecutor's house, on the 27th of March last, and which were found in possession of the prisoner. To be imprisoned for three months at hard labour. 23 April 1830

CORNWALL QUARTER SESSIONS: II

The following are the sentences passed on the prisoners convicted yesterday; we shall give a report of the trials in our next publication. John James for stealing a watch, &c. seven years transportation. Samuel Harris, for stealing a hen from James White, three months hard labour and whipped. William Robins, for robbing his mistress, Eliz. Goodman, fourteen years transportation. William Sim, for robbing his master, Walter Cock, of Falmouth, fourteen years transportation. 23 April 1830

CORNWALL QUARTER SESSIONS: III

Issacher Binney, a boy 15 years of age, was convicted, chiefly on the evidence of a companion of his named John Sims, a boy 11 years of age, of stealing 2 lbs of candles, from a box belonging to Stephen Michell, a miner, in the changing house of Poldice mine, on the night of the 10th March last. It appeared that on the night mentioned, these two youngsters were prowling about the mine for plunder, and the prisoner finding an opportunity, went into the changing-house, got his hand between the lid and body of Michell's box, which did not close, and took out the candles. To be transported for fourteen years. 23 April 1830

[Binney was an old offender and served his sentence overseas, not in the prison hulks at Plymouth.]

UP A CLUB-POLE AT FOWEY

A man named May, having drunk more liquor than he ought, contrived to ascend a club-pole, 40 feet in height, which stands in front of the Ship Inn, at Fowey, on Sunday the 16th instant, during the time of Divine Service. Having perched himself on the top, he remained for some time bowing, &c. and at length quietly descended, when he was taken into custody and committed to the town prison, in which an iron bar was opportunely left to aid him in making his escape, which he accordingly effected by breaking through the wall. 28 May 1830

ON THE PENTEWAN RAILWAY

It begins at St. Austell bridge, and goes on through "St. Austell moor" chiefly on an inclined plane, to its termination on Pentewan pier. Considerable traffic is daily conveyed over the road which is in itself of admirable construction; but what renders it extraordinary is this, that four wagons linked together with about fifteen tons of china clay on them, are put in motion at the depot at St. Austell by two men gently impelling them, they then move forward, their speed gradually increasing, and when they arrive at the lime-kiln lately erected, a distance of two or three hundred yards, they proceed with the celerity of a mail coach. Sometimes twenty persons are seen riding on them at once. They continue thus to proceed for upwards of two miles, the man who has charge of them having to put his horse to a gallop in order to keep up with them. Having arrived at level ground, the speed of the extraordinary vehicles gradually diminishes until at length they stop, when the conductor attaches his horse to the foremost carriage, and they are thus drawn to Pentewan wharf where a greater quantity of china-clay is shipped for Liverpool, Scotland, &c. than from any other port in England.

11 June 1830

IN LITTLE LONDON

A person who parades the streets playing on a bag-pipe, evidently disguised, and wearing green spectacles, is now making the tour of this county. He was at Truro last week, and has been since at Falmouth. He walks quietly and very deliberately along, playing his pipes, though not in a very loud strain, and makes no application, but accepts any money, not exceeding six pence from an individual, that may be offered him. If a shilling be tendered, he declines accepting it. Part of the money he collected here, he gave for the use of the poor, he is about 50 years of age, is nearly 6 feet in height, and is by no means corpulent. 18 June 1830

[The following week "The Piper", then in Penzance, wrote to *The West Briton* to the effect that he had always accepted any sum offered to him, and that on his return to Bodmin he was again spending time in Little London (Truro) to collect for the Royal Infirmary.]

PRAZE FAIR

The Earl Marshal of England having announced that the interment of his late and most gracious Majesty King George the Fourth, will take place on Thursday, the 15th day of July instant, this is to give notice, that the said [St. Swithian's] fair will be held on Monday the 19th instant, instead of Thursday the 15th. 9 July 1830

WITH A WOODEN ENGINE-HOUSE

To be sold by private contract, at New-quay, Lower St. Columb, a steam engine, cylinder 22 inches diameter, of the best construction, and equal to new, with the wooden engine-house in which it stands. It may be shipped or removed at a trifling expense. For further particulars, apply to Mr. James Sims, Engineer, Chacewater; or to Mr. Joseph Lyle, Perranzabuloe. 16 July 1830

ST. IVES SEANS

Owing to some misunderstanding between the sean-owners of St. Ives, the usual co-operation will not take place this year, so that all the seans are to be put to sea—the numbers is nearly 100. One-half have hitherto been found fully equal to the business of the fishery; but the present plan will give increased employment. 16 July 1830

MOURNING AT PADSTOW

About eleven o'clock at night [on the day of George IV's funeral], the principal tradesmen and other inhabitants formed a procession, and walked through the streets, preceded by a band of music, playing the dead march in Saul, and accompanied by twelve young men, bearing torches. 23 July 1830

PROCLAMATION OF WILLIAM IV

His Majesty King William the Fourth was proclaimed at Liskeard on Monday the 4th inst. The mayor, corporation and principal inhabitants assembled at the Guild-hall, and proceeded thence in procession, accompanied by a delightful band, composed of young gentlemen, inhabitants of that place, and with banners, &c. At the usual places, the proclamation was read by a herald, who was mounted on a fine spirited charger. At the conclusion of each reading, the band struck up the National Anthem.
23 July 1830

A WAGER FOR FIVE SOVEREIGNS

On Friday last, a wager for five sovereigns was decided between Mr.

Shear of Penryn, and Mr. Blamey of the same place, each backing his horse in harness, for eight miles on the Truro road and back again; the animal that performed the distance in the shortest time to be the winner. After a spirited contest, Mr. Shear's horse won the race by nearly five minutes, going over the ground—16 miles—in an hour and one minute.

17 September 1830

A PRACTITIONER IN MEDICINE

Nearly four years since, a man of about 45 years of age, a perfect stranger, of very common place and very eccentric appearance, came into the vicinity of Mevagissey, in this county, and taking up his abode in a very obscure lodging, set up as a practitioner in medicine. His grotesque appearance, his imperfect pronunciation of English, and his refusing to give his name, acquired for him soon among the multitude, the appellation of the French doctor . . . Although his mode of practice was barbarous, and his blunders every day palpable and mischievous, yet he retained his ascendancy over their minds, and proceeded in a career of practice that was surprising and lamentable. He now by degrees issued out from within the shell of his former mystery, spoke English very well, assumed an habitation and a name, proclaimed himself related to the Duke of Marlborough and the Royal family, and yclept himself Sydney Guelph Churchill . . .

In the month of April last, the doctor went to a village called Cairne, to extract a tooth for a person, when an old man about 87 years of age, accidentally meeting him, asked his opinion upon a small tumour he had upon his lower lip . . . At a time appointed, the operator came to his house [to remove the tumour] . . . a profuse bleeding took place, which after some continuance, excited the remonstrances of a bystander, and induced faintness in the aged patient, the operator now rather discomfited, sent out into the village for some cobler's wax as a styptic, which failing, still rich in resources, he next searched a neighbouring barn for cobwebs, but these also refusing their efficacy, the bleeding sunk the unhappy patient, and he was carried up stairs to bed in an exhausted state. The doctor now appalled at the failure of his means of suppressing the bleeding, rather abruptly took leave of the alarming scene, giving the patient's daughter, the balmy consolation, "that the blood would certainly stop, when the sun went down!!"

1 October 1830

SILVER ORE TO REPAIR THE ROADS

We are informed that a rich silver-lead lode has been discovered a few days since, in the lands of Mr. Key, and Mr. Hart Nickell, in the neighbourhood of Wadebridge; it is rather singular that a part of the lode composed of rich silver ores, was carried out to repair the roads, until Mr. Powning, of Wadebridge, in passing, observed it. This rich vein is now worked by Mr. Powning and a company of adventurers.

22 October 1830

DR. LAMB'S MEDICINE

To all persons afflicted with worms, indigestion, bilious and liver complaints, difficulty of breathing, and delicate constitutions, where strengthening medicines are required, a course of Dr. Lamb's medicines will be found more efficacious than anything hitherto offered to the public, as they require no restraint from business or change of diet, and so easy in its operation that children a month old, or a person a hundred years of age, may take it with the greatest safety. John Code, aged 35, manager of Screade Moor Clay works, in the parish of St. Austell, after taking a course of Lamb's Worm medicine, passed a tape worm 7 feet long, and has upwards of 200 joints; the symptoms which more or less affected him were as follows: pain and giddiness in the head, pain in the back and side, weakness between the stomach and the bowels, tightness across the chest, &c. &c . . . Walter Nancarrow, miner of Mount Charles, near St. Austell, after taking a course of Lamb's medicine, passed a tape worm 3 yards long and has upwards of 400 joints; further particulars may be had by applying to Moses Morrish, or to Mr. Lamb, where the worm may be seen . . . Isaac Thomas, miner, of Trevarian, in the parish of Breage, after taking a course of Lamb's worm medicines, passed a tape worm which measured 30 feet 9 inches long, and has 804 joints . . . Terms for children from 3s. to 5s. and persons from 18 and upwards, from 7s. to 14s.

22 October 1830

IN THE WORKHOUSE AT PENZANCE

It may be worthy of record that in the workhouse at Penzance, where there are only 47 paupers as inmates, the united ages of 20 of this number should amount to upwards of 1600 years, being an average of 80. Twelve of them are women and eight men. Many of these old folks are still able to assist in their own maintenance, one of them only is bedrid, and all are in full possession of their mental faculties. Of the 27 young paupers, 2 are idiots, and 8 are children under ten years of age. 19 November 1830

FOR SHIPMENT AT MEVAGISSEY

On Tuesday se'nnight, as some farmers were conveying a quantity of wheat to Mevagissey for shipment at that place, in order to its being sent to an eastern port, a number of persons, chiefly composed of women and boys, collected and expressed their displeasure at the measure. The persons employed in conveying the wheat, became irritated and resorted to blows, which were returned by the sturdy dealers in fish, with which the place abounds, and the husbands, brothers, &c. of the Amazons coming to their assistance, a general scuffle ensued, which ended in the ripping up of a number of the sacks, and the scattering of the wheat which they were unwilling their fellow countrymen should eat, about the streets.

26 November 1830

DIED OF COLD AND FATIGUE

On Sunday morning, a man named Merrifield, a lath render, residing at Falmouth, was found dead, at the end of the new prison. It came out in evidence, at an inquest held before James Cornish, Esq. coroner, that the unfortunate man had been at work at Ruan, and was returning home with a bag of tools, on Saturday night. Between nine and ten o'clock he was seen on the Terrace and asked a man to carry his bag, as he was benumbed with cold, but the fellow refused to do so. A boy afterwards carried it to the end of the prison, which was within a few yards of the man's house, but which it appears he was unable to reach; he sat on some stones belonging to the building, where he was seen by some persons who, supposing him to be intoxicated, passed on. He was it seems unable to make an alarm, and perished within hearing distance of his home in which were only two children, his wife having been some time dead. On his person were found 27 shillings in money. Verdict died of cold and fatigue.

3 December 1830

IN ANTICIPATION OF FOOD RIOTS

During the past week it has been currently reported at Falmouth, that Government have ordered a body of 300 soldiers to garrison Pendennis Castle, in which there are at present but about 30 men, the only military force in Cornwall. There are at Pendennis several thousand stand of arms in perfect order, &c.

3 December 1830

FISHERMEN'S TITHES

The fishermen of the parish of Paul, near Penzance, have been thrown into a state of agitation by the demands of the lessees of the fish tithe to which they are liable. The poor men have not been at all successful, and are many of them in want of bread for their children; and they declare they are wholly unable to pay the demand which they assert is exorbitant.

They were lately visited by a solicitor who came to enforce the propriety of compliance with the demand of the tithe-holders, but he was roughly handled, and was glad to escape with his clothes torn from his back. On Friday last, a bailiff came to Mousehole to serve writs relative to the tithe, when he was surrounded by the women; he pulled out a pistol to intimidate them, but it was soon taken from him and thrown into the sea, and almost all his clothes were torn off; he was glad to escape towards Newlyn, but here fresh disasters awaited him, as the women rose and belaboured him so severely that he was scarcely able to reach home. 31 December 1830

[The fishermen of Newlyn and Mousehole in the parish of Paul paid a certain sum in lieu of tithes, but the latter having recently been let, they were increased from 6s. to 60s. per boat, and then to £6. Fish tithes all fishermen by now regarded as outdated in any case, having arisen, in the words of *The West Briton*, as "a free-will offering made in the days of Catholic superstition, to purchase the prayers of the monks."]

NO LUDDITES IN CORNWALL

With respect to machinery, the labourers in this county are much too intelligent and bear too high a moral character to attempt to destroy one of the principal sources of our prosperity. They well know that the whole of the mining population of the county depend for support on the use of machinery . . . 7 January 1831

SHIRTS FOR THE TINNERS

Mr. Robarts [of Lanhydrock] . . . has given to thirty-nine stream-tinners, who work on Redmore, each a shirt made of blanketing, and which is so necessary an article for these poor fellows during the wet and cold weather, to which, in their labour, they are necessarily exposed.
7 January 1831

REFORM MEETING AT LAUNCESTON

The inhabitants of Launceston are about to hold a meeting for the purpose of petitioning Parliament in favour of parliamentary reform, and particularly the extension of the elective franchise in that borough, which contains upwards of 3,000 inhabitants, only *fourteen* of whom can be said to be represented, if a return of members uniformly nominated by a patron can be considered a representation of any party but the nominator. 14 January 1831

[The increasingly insistent demands for parliamentary reform during the 1820's reached a climax in 1830 with the death of its strong opponent, George IV, and the accession to the throne of the more liberal William IV. With the new reign, the Duke of Wellington, Tory Prime Minister, resigned and Lord Grey, leader of the Reform party, was requested to form a new government. Throughout the land reform meetings were then held and petitions sent to parliament, the Reform Bill finally being brought in in April 1831. It was narrowly defeated in the House of Commons, however, and Grey therefore resigned and dissolved Parliament, a turn of events keenly felt in Cornwall (see p. 219). There followed the most important and exciting of all elections in this country; the Tories were defeated, and the Act subsequently passed amid general rejoicing (see p. 220).]

BEER SHOPS AT SHORT-LANE-END

The farmers of the neighbourhood complain much of the depradations committed on them, since the establishment of two retail beer-shops at Short-lane-end [north of Truro], and which, we are informed, are kept open long after the time prescribed by the Act, frequently with music and dancing. We are assured that in one of them dancing, &c. was kept up, the week before the last, until four o'clock on the Sunday morning.

11 February 1831

[The legislation referred to was the Goulborn Act of 1830, which repealed the tax on beer and legalised its sale by the resident occupier of any house whose rates were duly paid and who provided himself with a licence costing only £2. By 1831, hundreds of disreputable beer shops had appeared in Cornwall, with widespread drunkenness and rowdiness as their inevitable concomitants.]

A LONG-ESTABLISHED TANNERY

To be sold . . . all those extensive and commodious premises, situate at East-street, in the town of Penzance, in which the tanning and bark business have been carried on with great profits by the late Messrs. Cunnacks, for nearly a century past. The premises are well supplied with water, and comprise a compting house, convenient warehouses, buildings, sheds, kilns, layers and every other requisite for the dressing and manufacture of 3,000 hides annually, and attached to the premises are four cottages, now let at about £12 per annum. Good and ample supplies of raw hides may be procured weekly from the extensive markets of Penzance, St. Ives, Camborne, and other adjacent places, and the sales of bark, at the fishing villages in the neighbourhood, have been to a very considerable extent.

11 February 1831

THE BLACK SHEEP OF EAST CRINNIS

A miner named Edward Remfry, of the parish of St. Blazey, was on Saturday last, placed on an ass, his legs being tied under the belly of the animal, and two pieces of paper, with "I am the black sheep of East Crinnis mine" inscribed on them in large characters, placed, one on his breast, the other on his back; and in this situation he was led from Tywardreath to St. Austell bridge, a distance of four miles, accompanied by more than five hundred miners. It appears that Remfry had subjected himself to this novel mode of punishment, by taking a pitch in East Crinnis mine, whilst he, at the same time, held one at Pembroke mine.

25 February 1831

MINERS ON THE MARCH

On Tuesday last, about eight o'clock, a party of 3,000 miners collected from the parishes of Breage, Gwennap, Crowan, Wendron, &c. passed through Helston in complete order, having selected eight men for their leaders, for the avowed purpose of preventing further shipments of corn at Helford. Near Mawgan, they were met by H. Grylls, Esq. on his way to Bosahan, who intreated them to return, but they would not. One of their leaders said, "If you, sir, will go with us, we will not do any mischief, but if you do not, perhaps we shall be unruly." Finding all his endeavours to induce them to return useless, Mr. Grylls and Mr. Black, accompanied them to Geer, where were deposited about 150 bushels of barley, which the proprietor promised should be sent to Helston market on Saturday.

They next proceeded to Treath, near Helford, and found only a small quantity; there, also, a promise was given, that it should not be shipped, but brought to market. From thence, they went to Gilling, where they found in Mr. Roskruge's cellars several hundred bushels of barley and wheat. Four of the leaders entered the cellars, and measured the depth, length and breadth of each pile of corn, and computed the quantity. Having been promised by the son of Mr. Roskruge, that all the barley should be sent to the market, they set out for their homes without committing any acts of violence . . . About five o'clock in the evening they entered Helston in perfect order. The peaceable demeanour of these men, who declared that their only object was to obtain an adequate supply of barley at the different markets, induced the inhabitants of Helston, generally, to supply them with bread, &c. for which they expressed themselves grateful. After partaking of the refreshment thus afforded, they returned peaceably to their homes.

25 February 1831

THE RIOT ACT AT ST. BLAZEY

The miners in the neighbourhood of St. Blazey have lately been forming combinations for the purpose of superseding, in a great measure, the authority of the agents, and the regulations of the mines. Early on Tuesday morning last, a great number of men collected at Fowey Consols and Lanescot mines, and attempted to seize two men who had refused to enter into any combination, and who from the threats of summary punishment being inflicted upon them, had been compelled to take refuge in the counting-house of these mines. The agents after waiting a considerable time for the dispersion of this assemblage, were obliged to appeal to the magistrates, who promptly repaired to the spot; and after entreating them, without effect, to disperse, they stated the necessity they should be under of reading the Riot Act, unless they separated, which they allowed them a quarter of an hour to do; and pointed out to them the consequences if they should fail to do so within one hour after reading the Act. On the expiration of the quarter of an hour, the crowd not dispersing, the proclamation was read to them, but without effect. On the expiration of the hour the magistrates present . . . ordered the constables to take seven of the rioters into custody; on their being put into chaises for conveyance to prison, a violent attempt to rescue the prisoners was made by several hundred persons present.

25 February 1831

[The following day the mob, whose grievance was the alleged low rates of pay at these mines, gathered again with the intention of freeing their comrades from the gaol. The High Sheriff promptly swore in over 30 special constables and the Royal Cornwall Militia was placed on guard about the prison. The miners marched to Bodmin where they were given food, and dispersed peaceably.]

THE COAL DUTY ABOLISHED

In consequence of the duty on coal having discontinued on Tuesday, the owners of cargoes belonging to the vessels discharging at the port of Falmouth and the coal-merchants at that place, gave notice by the public crier, that coal was to be sold at eight pence a bushel, being a reduction of two-pence on the former price.

4 March 1831

[For many years industrial interests in Cornwall had been petitioning Parliament for a reduction of the tax on sea-borne coal, without success. In a county where large quantities of fuel were required for steam pumping engines on the mines, its high price had adverse effects on industry, shipping and employment.]

TO QUEBEC, FROM MOPUS

The barque *Janus*, 308 tons register, John Richards, master, a regular trader to Quebec, will sail for that place about the 28th day of March next. This offers an excellent opportunity to persons wishing to settle in North America, as the *Janus* has always made good voyages, and will be fitted especially for the accomodation of emigrants. Passage money £3. Children at reduced prices. Apply to the captain on board, at Mopus, near Truro; or to Mr. Joseph Vivian, Roseworthy, near Camborne. Who is prepared to give information that may be of importance to settlers in reference to the terms and situation of Crown Lands, to be obtained at a low rate in Upper and Lower Canada. N.B. An early application is necessary. 4 March 1831

PIGEON POST TO FALMOUTH

Some gentlemen at Falmouth have trained a carrier pigeon, for the purpose of carrying there, every evening, the state of the poll during the county election. The bird has hitherto performed the journey in about two hours. The distance is 32 miles. 13 May 1831

CORNWALL COUNTY ELECTION

The highly interesting and most important contest for the representation of this county, commenced at Lostwithiel on Tuesday last, the 10th instant, About ten o'clock the High-Sheriff and a great number of gentlemen appeared on the hustings, near to which were erected a long range of booths, one being allotted for each of the nine hundreds [geographical subdivisions] in the county. There was a very full assemblage of freeholders; several thousand persons were present. 13 May 1831

THREE FUGITIVES

Escaped from Bodmin gaol, early this morning, the undermentioned prisoners, charged with felony, viz.: James Medland, a native of Launceston, aged 34 years, 5 feet 9½ inches high, dark eyes, brown hair, fresh complexion, and rather bald on the top of his head; he had on, when he escaped, a fustain shooting jacket and trowsers, and a low crowned hat, with a broad brim. Thomas Hore, of St. Austell, aged 27 years, 5 feet 6 inches high, gray eyes, brown hair, fresh complexion, has a scar on his right cheek, and also near the right eye; he had on, when he escaped, a fustain jacket, striped waistcoat and corded or fustain trowsers. John Burrows, of Bodmin, aged 45 years, 5 feet 8½ inches high, gray eyes, sandy hair, fresh complexion, has a scar on his forehead, is freckled and has sandy whiskers; he had on, when he escaped, a long blue frock coat, blue waistcoat and trowsers, and a glazed hat. The said John Burrows is well known in this county as a hawker, attending markets and fairs. Whoever will apprehend the said prisoners and lodge them in any of his Majesty's gaols, shall receive 5 pounds reward, for each person apprehended, on application to Mr. J. B. Everest, governor of the said gaol. 20 May 1831

INTO FALMOUTH, WINDBOUND

On Friday morning last, the *Wellington*, East Indiaman, from Madras, put into Falmouth, windbound. The passengers, upwards of forty in number, proceeded to town by land. A fine young female elephant; a tiger, and a variety of beautiful birds, were on board. The elephant was allowed to parade the deck, and appeared to be very docile; she suffered the sailors to mount her. The *Wellington* left the harbour on Sunday, for London.

3 June 1831

FOR A TRIFLING WAGER

In a public house at Truro, on Tuesday last, a man actually eat two eels and a plaice, undressed, for a trifling wager. The eels were alive at the time he commenced this brutal feat, and he devoured them, bones, &c. just as they were brought from the market. 3 June 1831

A VOTER AND HIS ASS

During the recent election at Lostwithiel, a freeholder, a thorough out-and-out reformer, shewed off in the following manner, and which excited a deal of amusement at the time. He came into the town mounted on an ass, gaily decorated with the colours of Pendarves and Lemon, and his ass's ears adorned with the colours of Vyvyan and Valletort. This strange appearance caused inquiry, to which the Cornishman replied, "My ass and myself have had a dispute relative to the merits of the different candidates and as we have been a long time acquainted, we were unwilling to come to blows, therefore we agreed that each should wear the colours agreeable to the vote he intended to give, and this is the reason why I am dressed in favour of Pendarves, and my ass's ears of that of Vyvyan."

10 June 1831

MILITARY PUNISHMENT IN 1831

Sir, It is under painful feelings that I call the public attention to the case of flogging, which took place at the Truro barracks a few days since. I by no means wish to exculpate the offender, or at all to extenuate his conduct. For disobeying orders, he undoubtedly deserved punishment; it is not punishment I object to, but the mode; his offence was desertion . . . for this offence the poor fellow was sentenced to receive 500 lashes. Although this is not considered excessive punishment, yet during the flogging, this poor man . . . fainted three times; the usual means of re-suscitation were resorted to, not for the alleviation of his sufferings, but that he might be fully alive to them, and I am told that notwithstanding his extreme state of exhaustion, 250 lashes were inflicted. From this the feelings of humanity must revolt; and this takes place near our own doors; and in England! Civitas. P.S. Since writing the above, I find another soldier—a veteran, who has seen 23 years of service—has received 300 lashes. The offence of this unfortunate man is understood to be, having gone, after hours, from the barrack to a public-house on the opposite side of the road, to get a glass of beer. For this he was sentenced to 400 lashes!! —but it was found impossible to inflict more than 300, without endangering his life. 10 June 1831

RELIEF FOR STARVING IRELAND

On Sunday last, in pursuance of a printed notice from the mayor and the borough of Truro, a meeting of the inhabitants of this town took place at the town-hall, in order to take into consideration the propriety of entering into a subscription for the relief of the inhabitants of the county of Mayo and other districts on the western coast of Ireland, who are suffering all the calamities of famine and consequent disease, from a failure of the potatoe crop there, the last season. Upwards of £40 was subscribed on the spot, and a committee was formed to apply at the houses of such of the inhabitants as were not present for their assistance, and to decide on the mode of applying the sum that might be obtained. 17 June 1831

[Similar meetings were held at Bodmin, Penzance and Falmouth, arrangements being made to ship a cargo of potatoes direct from Penzance to the west of Ireland. Collections were also made in churches and on various mines throughout the county.]

SEA EAGLES ON BURYAN CLIFFS

Two eagles having built their nest in Buryan cliffs, near the Land's End, some persons in the neighbourhood resolved to see what it contained. Accordingly they watched for the departure of the eagles in search of food, and a man was lowered on a rope from the edge of the cliff, when he got to the nest in which he found three eaglets, not fully fledged, but a good deal larger than a full-grown fowl. These he carried off in safety, and afterwards sold them for half-a-crown each. Fortunately for him, the old eagles, which are described as being larger than a goose, did not return whilst he was engaged in the plunder. 24 June 1831

A YOUNG SAILOR

Whereas, William Thomas, a seaman, and a native of Padstow, who resided at my house, the Daniell Arms Inn, Truro, for the last five weeks—being entertained by me from humane motives merely, he being destitute of money—left early on Tuesday morning, taking with him a percussion-lock gun, London made; a dog of the bull-terrier breed, white, with brindled spots, and answers to the name of Tiger; two pairs of shoes, and other articles, and has not since been heard of. The said William Thomas is about 5 feet 7 inches in height; sallow complexion, about 21 years of age, and wore a sailor's dress. Any person who shall give to me information of the said William Thomas, so that he may be taken into custody and brought to justice, or so as to enable me to recover the said dog or gun, shall be liberally rewarded. Any person detaining the said dog, or with whom the said gun may be found, after this public notice, will be prosecuted. William Sims.

24 June 1831

THE END OF THE UNREST

The depôt of the 73rd regiment for some time stationed in Truro, marched from thence for Falmouth, on Wednesday morning, in order to embark in one of the steam-vessels for Plymouth, whence they came into this county, in consequence of the disturbances at Lanescot mine, &c. a few months since. From the reports received by Government, it does not appear at all probable that their services will be required in Cornwall, where the utmost tranquillity prevails. A party of the regiment is stationed at Pendennis castle. Though many of the men were flogged during their stay here, we have not heard of acts of outrage committed by them.

1 July 1831

A CASE OF GLUTTONY

A correspondent assures us, that a person who lately attended a sale of *junk* (old rope) at one of the mines in this county, actually "laid in" the following quantity of viands, &c. at the dinner given to the persons who attended the sale: 4 lbs of beef and mutton; 6 large potatoes; one cabbage; ½ lb of bread; 5 glasses of porter; 2 glasses of brandy; 6 glasses of white wine; 5 glasses of port; 16 glasses of grog; and six plates of strawberries.

8 July 1831

DISINTERRED AND EXAMINED

The dead body of a young man, inclosed in a case, was picked up near Treyarnan Bay, near Padstow, and which was ordered by the coroner to be interred, on the cliff. But a report having been circulated that a vessel bound for Liverpool from the Baltic, having several ill on board, had thrown a body, inclosed in a case, overboard, in the Channel, the body was disinterred and examined, and those who had picked it up and who were about it, have been put under quarantine.

8 July 1831

[During 1830 Asiatic cholera had spread from the East Indies, through India, Persia and Russia, to Poland and the Baltic countries. With maritime connections all over the world, Cornwall was particularly vulnerable to the disease and an outbreak was feared almost daily, the first false alarm being given at Mevagissey early in July. Cholera reached England (Sunderland) in November.]

CORNISH WRESTLING IN LONDON

The annual grand wrestling match, according to the Cornish system, will take place in London [at the Eagle Tavern, City Road], on the 1st of next month. We are informed the subscriptions [for the prizes] are very liberal; and this being the case, no money will be paid for bringing men from the country; but as the charge for a passage by the steam-boats is very moderate, and there being no doubt that any able players who may be induced to visit the metropolis on this occasion will be liberally treated, in case of being unsuccessful, it is fully expected that some of our first rate Cornish players will be present; we are informed that Rodda and Rowe, of Crowan; Smith, of Camborne, and Moyle, of Wendron, mean to attend if possible. 22 July 1831

HORSE DEALING

Cornwall Summer Assizes. Nisi Prius. Reynolds v. Vincent. The plaintiff resides at Tregony, and last autumn, being in want of a horse, he went one day, in company with a person named Snell, a colt-breaker, in search of one. Shortly after setting out, they met the defendant mounted on a mare which the plantiff fancied; he asked if she was for sale, and after some chaffering, he purchased the animal for £10, and went to the defendant's house where the money was paid, and the parties were liberally supplied with home-brewed beer, &c. The plaintiff and the colt breaker then set out for Tregony together, on the mare, at full gallop. But soon after, it was found that the mare was pig-mouthed, old, and had a bad spavin. The defendant was applied to, but he refused to take the mare back, and the present action was brought. The jury after a consultation of several hours, found for the plaintiff—damages £3. 5 August 1831

THE ST. IVES BOATS OFF IRELAND

Several of the St. Ives drift-boats brought in from 6,000 to 10,000 fish each, yesterday morning. It is understood that the whole of the St. Ives boats are on their return from the herring fishery, on the Irish coast, where only those who went early have done well. On Tuesday night, as one of the boats—the *Agenora*, Berriman—was on her return from the Irish coast, she fell in with a vast shoal of pilchards, 20,000 of which fish she brought into St. Ives on Wednesday morning. 5 August 1831

THE THANKS OF THE EMPEROR

Messrs. G. C. and R. W Fox, and Co. have received authority from the Russian government to reward two poor fishermen, of Mevagissey, with fifty ducats (about £24) each, for their meritorious exertions in saving the crew of the Russian brig *St. Nicholas*, which was wrecked at Port Holland in December last, also to pay £1 each to fifty other persons, revenue officers, fishermen, &c. for their assistance, in saving part of the cargo and materials. The thanks of the Emperor are also to be given to the superior revenue officers and other individuals who assisted on the occasion.

5 August 1831

COALS, CHARCOAL AND BRIMSTONE

The schooner *Sophia*, Richards, master, from Neath for Padstow, with a cargo of coals, charcoal and brimstone, was discovered to be on fire about eleven o'clock on the night of Monday the 4th instant. After every exertion to extinguish the fire, which was occasioned by the igniting of the charcoal, some of which was put on board shortly after it was made, and before it was allowed to cool properly, the crew took to their boat, and reached Padstow.

12 August 1831

[The *Sophia* was towed into Padstow a mass of flames, scuttled opposite the town, and floated off on the next tide.]

SLOOP STRUCK BY LIGHTNING

The sloop *Friend's-good-will*, Dark, master, which had left Padstow harbour, on Tuesday, laden with malt and flour, for Swansea, was becalmed near Pentyre-point, when a storm burst. A black cloud rapidly covered the horizon, and discharged sheets of water, whilst the lightning split the mast of the sloop in splinters, set the sails on fire and would have destroyed the vessel had not the torrents of rain speedily extinguished the flames. The man at the helm was rendered senseless for a time, but he recovered, and the vessel was happily got into Padstow.

19 August 1831

TEN THOUSAND SCADS

On Tuesday evening, upwards of 10,000 fish called "scads" were taken by a foot sean near Marazion. These fish frequently come so near the shore as to enable persons to take them by hand. On Wednesday evening another shoal appeared, and a number of men, women and children went into the water to catch them, whilst numbers of persons stood on the sand to see them throw the fish on shore; and by this means a considerable quantity was obtained.

19 August 1831

FIRE ABOARD THE SCILLY PACKET

An accident, which threatened serious consequences, occurred on board the Scilly packet last week on her passage from Penzance to the Islands. A quantity of lime, which had been taken from the kiln before it was cool, suddenly burst out into a flame, which threatened to communi-

cate to every part of the vessel. The terror and confusion on board was very great, as there were seventeen passengers, beside the crew, whose only hope of escape (in case of extremity) must have been by means of a small boat not capable of carrying half that number of persons. Happily, the bags of lime were removed from the hold, in their burning state, and thrown into the sea, before any very considerable damage was done to the vessel.
26 August 1831

FISHING ON THE SABBATH

It is supposed that shoals of pilchards, sufficient to fill 20,000 hogsheads, passed through St. Ives Bay on Sunday, and sufficiently near the shore to be enclosed by the seans; no attempt, except in one instance, was made to secure any part of this vast glut of fish, in consequence of an agreement between the seaners, not to shoot their nets on the Sabbath. The men of one sean broke the contract, and secured about 500 hogsheads.
2 September 1831

A BENEFICENT LANDLORD

On Wednesday last, the annual fete of the Crowan Sunday-school, took place in the noble riding-house of Sir John St. Aubyn, Bart. at his seat, Clowance. The children, amounting to above 400, having assembled at the school-room, marched in regular order through the village, accompanied by above 20 teachers. From thence they proceeded to the riding-house, which had been prepared for the occasion with great taste; the walls were so concealed by large branches of trees, in full foliage, so as to give to this magnificent apartment—above 400 feet in length—the appearance of a large arbour . . . A more interesting spectacle can scarcely be conceived than that presented by the children while at their repast, if indeed it was not exceeded by their innocent gambols in the park, after they had retired from it. . . It is but just to add, that though absent, Sir John can scarcely be termed an absentee, so magnificent are his permanent benefactions, extending not only to individual families, but to the general education of every male child in the parish, and likewise to a munificent provision for professional attendance on all the sick of the lower classes within its boundaries; the result cannot but be gratifying to him; nearly 5,000 inhabitants, under great trials from the depressed state of the neighbouring mines, continue to present an appearance of good order, and of attention to their moral and religious duties, that is most edifying to those around them.
2 September 1831

REPEAL OF THE SALT TAX

About 80 hogsheads of very fine pilchards were taken at New-quay, on

Tuesday evening. They were all sold to the country people, the repeal of the salt-tax having enabled the poor to save fish at a cheap rate.

9 September 1831

[In 1822 the duty on foreign salt was increased from 3d. to 2s. a bushel, and that on pit or Liverpool salt (i.e. from Cheshire) reduced from 15s. to 2s. The latter was still too dear for many of the poor in Cornwall to use it for themselves, while for exported fish foreign salt had to be used, as pit salt turned pilchards a rusty colour, which was unacceptable abroad.]

HAYLE FOUNDRY

The inhabitants of this place celebrated the coronation of our beloved sovereign [William IV] and his royal consort in a manner becoming their long-established character for loyalty and public spirit. The day was ushered in by a royal salute from ships' guns; the ringing of the bells of the parish church, &c. At eight o'clock a signal gun was fired, and by arrangement, the whole of the vessels at the wharf displayed their flags, whilst on the different counting-houses, the lofty stacks of furnace chimnies and other parts of the extensive works, the national banners were unfurled, at the same moment. The effect of this display, when so many British standards were at once given to the breeze, was very striking; colours were also displayed on the other vessels in the harbour, on the different inns, &c. The firing of cannon was continued at intervals, throughout the day, and in the evening bonfires were lighted, and there was a brilliant display of fire-works. At seven o'clock, a large party sat down to an excellent dinner, at the White Hart, which was served up under the direction of Mrs. Trevithick [innkeeper, and wife of the engineer Richard Trevithick] in a style that did her great credit.

16 September 1831

CAUTION TO MARINERS

Although the ground within the pier or quay of Penzance has, after long exertion and great expense been cleared of all rocks, and is by that means a fine sand-bottomed harbour, capable of affording shelter for 200 vessels; notwithstanding a very useful part is now and has been for a considerable time past, occupied with several huge piles of lime stones, which have been thrown overboard at different times from different vessels, and which are scarcely covered at high water. It is therefore necessary for vessels entering the harbour, not to run to the northward of the pier more than 70 fathoms, least they run thereon, or to take a pilot. By attending to this they will avoid those lime stones so irreconcilable and so inconsistently left near the middle of the harbour. A few years ago a vessel ran on a pile of lime stones near the same spot, and was considerably damaged; the owner of the lime stones paid the expense of repairs, since which he has failed [gone bankrupt] and states the circumstance as being, in part, the cause of his failure, so that the claim for damage may be on a lime burner not worth a groat, instead of on a wealthy corporation, which allows a continuation of the obstruction. Wm. Harvey, merchant and ship-owner, Penzance. 7 October 1831

TREAD-MILL AT PENZANCE

Cornwall Quarter Sessions. James and Philip Thomas were convicted of having entered the brewery of Mr. John Luke and having stolen from thence a quantity of beer. James Thomas was sentenced to transportation for seven years and Philip Thomas to twelve months' imprisonment and hard labour at the tread-mill at Penzance. 28 October 1831

FEVER AT PORTSCATHO

It seems that a fish cellar has recently been erected in the upper part of the village, and which has been appropriated this season, for the first time, to the cure of pilchards; the draining of the exuviae from this cellar, has passed into the street, and part of it has sunk into the interstices of the small limestone with which the road has lately been paved, and there furnishes an offensive odour to all persons passing. The remainder of this draining runs over to the opposite and lower side of the road, where, in conjunction with other filth, it accumulates against a wall, part of it remaining stagnant, and the other part filtering through the ground underneath, down upon a spring which supplies a well, from which a majority of the inhabitants usually procure their water. The water has often of late been found by those using it, extremely unpleasant, and possessing a disagreeable taste as if fish had been boiled in it. That the draining from this cellar has been the cause . . . of the present attack of fever, follows as a necessary inference from these facts that, up to the period of the pilchards being deposited there, the whole village was in a state of the greatest healthiness, and that the disorder first shewed itself in the immediate vicinity of the cellar, and proceeded down each side of the street to the beach. 11 November 1831

PRECAUTIONS AGAINST EPIDEMICS

The following resolutions were adopted at the first meeting of the Bodmin Board of Health, on the 7th instant; that in pursuance of the Order of his Majesty's Council, already posted in the town, the borough and parish be divided into ten districts and inspectors attached to each. That it shall be the duty of the inspectors to examine all the houses, drains, sewers, courtyards, and other places within their district where any dung or filth, &c. are deposited; and require the inhabitants or owners to remove the same; and if the same shall not be cleansed or removed, within five days after such notice, that a report thereof be made to the Board, who will take all lawful means for enforcing their directions. That the mayor be requested to order the scavengers and surveyors of the turnpike and highways to clean all the streets, lanes, roads, &c., and fill in all catchpits, and remove all nuisances, which may be found upon, or near the same.

A Board of Health has been established at Launceston, and its members are taking very active measures to prevent the introduction of cholera into that town. Every house has been visited and the inhabitants requested to attend to the cleanliness of their habitations, particularly to their being white-washed. In order to remove all nuisances, a cart is daily provided to carry off the ashes and filth from the houses, and a supply of water to cleanse the streets of the town has been obtained.

18 November 1831

MORE PRECAUTIONS

It will be easy, in villages and small towns where there are no scavengers, for a group of cottagers to employ such of their children as are fit for the work, and have nothing better to do, to remove, in wheelbarrows or small carts, every morning, the accumulations of the preceding day. At Truro, it is intended to pay the poor a sufficient sum of money for each barrow full of manure brought to the scavengers' carts as they pass their doors.

25 November 1831

DROWNED IN DELABOLE QUARRY

On Friday last, an inquest was held on the body of James Davey, who was drowned about three weeks since, by falling into a pool in Delabole slate-quarry. The owner of the quarry refused to be at any expense in getting the body, and the fellow-workmen of the deceased were compelled to obtain pumps which they worked night and day until they succeeded in their object.

2 December 1831

EXPLOSION AT ST. TUDY

On the evening of Tuesday, the 27th ultimo, whilst Mr. Wright, a shopkeeper at St. Tudy, was weighing some gunpowder, from a barrel for a customer, a spark from the candle fell on some loose grains on the counter, which communicated to the barrel, when the whole instantly exploded and blew up the roof and walls of his house. Mr. Wright was so dreadfully scorched that his recovery is considered doubtful. His two children were most providentially saved by one of the girders falling across the bed in which they were, and protecting them.

6 January 1832

FOR BRITISH NORTH AMERICA

The *Alchymist,* Wills, master, is appointed to sail on the 25th of this month, for St. John's, New Brunswick. This very fast sailing vessel, of 500 tons burden, being fitted out on a superior scale for seaworthiness and comfort, is recommended to the choice of emigrants to British North America. Fare £3. Children and families at lower rates. Further information will be given by Foxes and Co., Perran Wharf; or by the master, on board, at Restronguet. 2 March 1832

THE MISER OF NEWLYN

Died on Friday, at Newlyn, (Penzance) John Richards, Esq. aged 67 years; he was for many years an extensive brewer at that place, and amassed a fortune amounting to more than £60,000; the principal part of which he has left to a illegitimate son. The deceased was never married, and was not very liberal to his neighbours, the poor fishermen of Newlyn, a large party of whom cheered as soon as the body was placed in the hearse in which it was conveyed to the place of interment. 23 March 1832

BULLION FROM SOUTH AMERICA

The manner in which bullion is generally stowed away in the packets from South America, is the best adapted to their capacity; and the Vice-Admiral is of the opinion that 18 tons (about 692,300 dollars) is the greatest weight of treasure a packet, whether a King's or a hired packet, may with safety convey across the Atlantic. It appearing that these packets often take out from Falmouth each ten tons of quicksilver [for the treatment of silver ores in Mexico], the Vice-Admiral thinks it too large a quantity, and that they should not take more than seven tons; considering that the vessels are quite full of provisions and stores on their sailing to last for their whole absence from England; while on their voyage home, however, their stock is but just enough for the passage. 30 March 1832

[From a report on the Falmouth packet establishment, by Vice-Admiral Sir Pulteney Malcolm.]

THE EXODUS BEGINS

The rage for emigration that now prevails in the north of this county is wholly unprecedented in Cornwall; in different parishes from 200 to 300 persons each, have either departed or are preparing to leave for

Canada or the United States. Last week a vessel named the *Spring-Flower*, sailed from Padstow, having on board 180 passengers, and another—the *Economist*—is now ready to sail with 200 more. The recent regulation of the Privy Council, requiring that a regular medical practitioner be engaged for the voyage, in every vessel taking more than 50 passengers, has caused some delay.

6 April 1832

THE FIRST AND LAST INN

The want of good accomodation for the visitors of this fascinating scenery, having been complained of, R. Botheras begs leave respectfully to state, that he has added to his inn—(the First and Last, Sennen Church-town,)—a large and extensive suite of rooms, every one of which commands a beautiful view of the sea. Also, that a good larder, superior wines and liquors of all descriptions, with well-aired beds, excellent stabling and coach-houses and every requisite accomodation, will always be found at his house.

13 April 1832

UPROAR IN LISKEARD CHURCH

An extraordinary and disgraceful scene occurred at Liskeard church on Easter-day, just at the commencement of the morning service. It seems that for some time past a dispute has existed among the singers. A vestry had resolved that no one should occupy the singing gallery except those whose names were on a list, furnished by the leader of the choir, and that the church-wardens should station themselves at the gallery stairs for the purpose of enforcing this order. Two young women who had at first been accepted and approved by the singing master were afterwards excluded from this list, in consequence of a family quarrel. These girls (there being no imputation on their character) refused to abide by the vestry decision. They accordingly came with several others to the church, on Sunday morning, accompanied, also, by some young men. Their demand to be admitted into the gallery was quietly refused, when forthwith a desperate struggle took place between the applicants and the churchwarden; the latter was roughly forced back, and the young women with their friends gained the gallery. Whilst this unhallowed proceeding was going on, the congregation, amounting to 1,000 persons, was thrown into violent consternation and uproar; some took part with the young women, others with the churchwarden, and a scene ensued which baffles description. Yells, hisses, shouts, and even cursing and swearing disturbed the quiet of the Sabbath and the church; the corporation left the church in a body, many females were carried out faint, &c. Order being at length restored, the clergyman, after quietly waiting a considerable time, commenced the service without further interruption.

27 April 1832

ASPARAGUS ISLAND, KYNANCE COVE

The Danish brig *Ospra*, Beck, master, with a cargo of sugar and coffee, from the Havannah for Hamburgh, worth £10,000, was wrecked on the Lizard, during a fog, at half-past one o'clock on Sunday morning last. The vessel struck the perpendicular rock of Asparagus Island, when the crew, with the exception of one man, who was drowned, got on the rocks whence they walked to the shore at day-light. The vessel and cargo have been lost. 11 May 1832

MITIGATED PUNISHMENT

On Saturday last, Charles Penrose, Benjamin Bright, and Henry Millet, against whom sentence of death was recorded for burglary at the late Assizes for this county, were removed from Bodmin prison to the *Captivity* hulk, at Devonport, in order to undergo the mitigated punishment (transportation for life) since awarded them. 11 May 1832

PARLIAMENTARY REFORM IN JEOPARDY

Soon after the news of the resignation of Earl Grey, &c. reached Redruth, on Friday last, a large black-flag was displayed over the town-clock, and a band paraded the streets, playing the dead-march. Yesterday, however, on the receipt of the gratifying intelligence that the Reform ministers were likely to be reinstated in office, the black flag was exchanged for a blue one, amidst the reiterated huzzas of the inhabitants.

18 May 1832

THE SAND HILLS OF PERRAN

For more than 70 years, the farmers within several miles of Perran-sands have been in the habit of resorting to these vast mounds for sand which they use as manure. The Dean and Chapter of Exeter have claimed these sand hills as their property, and have occasionally demanded payment from the carriers, in assertion of their claim; but these demands have been unattended to, and the carrying of sand has continued. Within a short time, however, the Rev. claimants have ordered a fence to be erected and a gate to be put up, near Wheal Budnick mine, so as to prevent the passage of carts to the sand hills. The farmers were resolved not to submit to the demand made on them, of three pence a cart load, for sand, and on Saturday a considerable number of persons assembled, with between 70 and 80 carts, &c. when they forced open the gate and loaded their carts, as they were used to do. Mr. Coleridge, land-surveyor, agent for the Dean and Chapter, under whose directions the fence and gate were erected, ordered the gate to be restored, which was done, and on Monday he attended with several constables, to prevent any further attempt to take sand by force. On that day, George Simmons Esq., of Trevella, came to the place, when finding between 200 and 300 men with upwards of 70 carts and waggons, he asked by what authority the gate was put up, and being told, by that of the Dean and Chapter of Exeter, he demanded that it should be opened in order that his servants might obtain sand, as they had done for many years, without payment of any kind. This being refused by the agent of the Dean and Chapter, the gate was speedily forced, and the hedge was, in a very short time, levelled, so as to make a free passage as heretofore . . . We presume the question will afford some employment for the Gentlemen of the long robe.

1 June 1832

ORE FROM THE MOUNT

We have been informed that several of the copper companies have recently sent a portion of their ores for shipment at St. Michael's Mount, which had been discontinued as a shipping place for several years, in favour of Hayle. The increasing difficulties of the port of Hayle, arising from the accumulation of sand on the bar, and an apprehension that from this cause the port will be scarcely accessable in winter, are alleged reasons for the change.

8 June 1832

[Neglect of the port of Hayle had occurred during a long dispute between two rival engineering companies, Harveys & Co.'s Hayle Foundry (see p. 214) and the Copperhouse Foundry, situated respectively at the western and eastern ends of the town.]

THE TRIUMPH OF REFORM

When the joyful intelligence that the Reform Act had received the Royal assent reached the village of Chacewater, the inhabitants resolved to celebrate the happy event by a fete. A public meeting was held at the market-place, when Friday last was fixed on for that purpose. On that day, flags were displayed from nearly every house in the principal street, many of them with suitable mottoes. A husting decorated with laurels, flags, &c. was erected in the centre of the village. About five o'clock in the evening a procession was formed at some distance from the village; two flags carried by persons on horseback led the way; on one was inscribed *Earl Grey*; on the other, *The People.* A number of the inhabitants followed two and two; then came the schoolmaster on horseback, bearing a flag, with the motto *The schoolmaster is abroad*; 400 children followed in regular order, then came two flags carried on horseback; then a band of music, which preceded a large flag inscribed, *The Duke of Sussex, the Poor Man's Friend*; a number of poor men and women, two and two, each wearing a sprig of laurel, followed; flags, inscribed to Lord J. Russell, Lord Althorp, Mr. Pendarves, and Sir Chas. Lemon were next followed by inhabitants, two and two, each bearing a card in his hat, with the motto *Earl Grey and his colleagues, the restorers of our rights.* Flags inscribed to *Mr. Peter, the Reformers of Cornwall,* &c. were also borne. The procession extended over half-a-mile; on reaching Chacewater, the poor persons composing it were seated on forms provided for them; the men were plentifully supplied with beer and cakes, and the women and children with tea, &c, the band playing "Rule Brittania", &c. At nine o'clock a general illumination took place; about ten o'clock there was a splendid display of fireworks, &c. several tar barrels were lighted up in the street. It is supposed that upwards of 3,000 persons were assembled on the occasion; no accident or disorder marred the festivities of the day. 22 June 1832

MIDSUMMER EXCURSION

On Monday morning next, the 25th inst., if the weather be favourable, *The Herald* will leave St. Ives at nine o'clock, on an excursion in the Channel, will call at Portreath at ten, thence proceeding eastward to the River Gannel; will then take a westerly course along the coast to Cape Cornwall, near the Land's End, returning to Portreath in the evening and thence back to St. Ives. Fares: Quarter deck and cabin 5s. od., Main deck 2s. 6d. An excellent band of music will attend the excursion.

22 June 1832

[The *Herald*, built at Greenock in 1831, was a paddle steamer, employed on the steam packet service from Hayle and St. Ives, alternately, to Bristol.]

ROCHE REJOICINGS

On Monday the passing of the Reform Bill was celebrated at Roche, in a manner that fully manifested the feelings of that parish and its neighbourhood on that great national measure. The morning was ushered in with the ringing of bells; by ten o'clock, upwards of 2,000 persons were assembled; arches were constructed, and flags with appropriate mottoes displayed; at twelve o'clock, a person on horseback in corporate costume, entered the throng, escorted by two men dressed as town sergeants, and read what he termed "the last dying speech of the boroughmongers". When he concluded he fell from his horse, with a groan, which was echoed by the surrounding multitude; afterwards the emblems of boroughmongery were formally buried, amidst the huzzas of the people. About 200 individuals dined at the different inns in the village; two fat bullocks and five sheep, purchased by subscription, were distributed amongst the poor, in portions suited to the number of their respective families; in the evening the females were regaled with tea. At night bonfires were lighted in several places. The festivities were throughout conducted with the utmost harmony.

20 July 1832

CHOLERA COMES CLOSER

On Monday, the schooner *Gage*, from Liverpool, arrived in Mount's Bay, when it being ascertained that the master, Mr. T. Everete, had died of the cholera during the voyage, the vessel was ordered to the quarantine pool, in Falmouth Harbour [St. Just Pool, on the Roseland coast]. As the body remained on board, the mate communicated his desire to bring it on shore for interment, but this was peremptorily refused.

27 July 1832

FALMOUTH MAKES PREPARATIONS

The Falmouth magistrates and Board of Health are taking active measures to meet the threatened danger arising from the appearance of the cholera in nearly all the ports from which vessels arrive coastwise; the lanes and alleys have been examined and nuisances removed; the streets are washed daily by means of fire-engines, and every other precaution that prudence suggests has been taken.

27 July 1832

A SEWER FOR LAUNCESTON

A Board of Health has been appointed at Launceston, and immediate steps are to be taken to compel persons to remove all nuisances, and thoroughly to drain the streets, &c. by the formation of a large common sewer. No case of cholera has yet been reported at Launceston, but the daily intercourse with Plymouth, [where the disease had a firm hold] by vans, waggons, &c. renders it imperative on the local authorities to adopt every proper precaution against the introduction of the disease.

3 August 1832

A SPLENDID BALLOON AND CAR

Mr. Graham, aeronaut to his Majesty (by special appointment), will make his 116th ascent with the magnificent silk balloon, (wind and weather permitting), from an enclosed and eligible piece of ground, near the gas works, Truro, on Tuesday next, August 14th, 1832, at three for four o'clock in the afternoon. The splendid balloon and car are the same with which Mr. G. had the honour to ascend in the presence of his Majesty from Windsor in September last, and also with which Mr. and Mrs. G. ascended by appointment of Government, from the Green Park, London, on the day of their Majesties' Coronation. It is the largest balloon in the kingdom, more than 100 feet in circumference, and is capable of carrying nearly 30,000 cubic feet of gas, and will conveniently carry up three persons four miles above the clouds. Mr. G. will commence the process of filling the balloon on Monday morning the 13th of August, to witness which, as well as the ascent on Tuesday 2s. each; children, half-price, mechanics, &c. 1s.; children half-price. 10 August 1832

AN ILL-FOUNDED PREJUDICE

Sir, An appeal having been made to the medical profession, in your paper of last week, for an opinion respecting the propriety of using fish at the present season, I beg leave to inform you that at a meeting of the Truro Board of Health, held this day, the question was duly considered, and it appeared to be the unanimous opinion that *fresh fish*, far from being injurious, is a very salutary, and to Cornishmen in particular, a very valuable article of food. Now that the prospect of a successful pilchard fishery is before us, I shall feel much pleasure if this communication should assist in removing a very ill-founded prejudice existing in the public mind against the use of *fresh fish*. I remain, yours, truly, E. J. Spry, Secretary to the Truro Board of Health. 24 August 1832

[The people were refusing to eat fish, or to salt it down, however fresh and wholesome, as they had persuaded themselves that to do so was to catch cholera.]

PUT IN THE STOCKS

On Sunday last, [at Chacewater] there were no less than three fights, and while the bell was tolling to summon us to the House of God, two drunk men were about to commence a row on the bridge. On observing a constable approaching one of them left, and the other was earnestly requested to leave, but refused to do so; after striking the constable and tearing his clothes, he was put in the stocks during the time the Divine Service was performing. Immediately after it was concluded he was released, but instead of going to his place of residence, he collected a great many boys and insulted those that passed. 31 August 1832

CURED WITHOUT A SURGEON

A man named Josiah Thomas was attacked with [a] terrible disease, at the 170 fathoms level, in the Consolidated Mines, on the night of the 28th inst. He was taken with violent vomiting and very severe pain in the lower part of the abdomen, after a short time cramp in his arms and legs came on, which appears, from the accounts published, to be the characteristics of a decided case of cholera. It was with much difficulty, by the assistance of three men, that he was brought to the surface; when he reached it, he appeared almost dead, being speechless and motionless. It being late in the night, and a surgeon not being near, one of the agents administered some rum to him, but which his stomach immediately rejected; at the suggestion of one of the men present, he was immersed up to the neck, with his head covered with flannel, in the hot-water cistern of Bowdon's [Bawden's] steam-engine; the heat of the mineral water being 112 degrees. After being kept there about a quarter of an hour, the cramp and pains completely left him, and all he complained of was weakness; he was then bound around the bowels with flannel, and was able to walk to his home, which is more than two miles from the mines. The man is now fast recovering, and is likely to resume his labours in a few days. Should any person wish any further information respecting this case, it may be had by applying to the agents, if by letter post paid. 31 August 1832

A DRAW-BRIDGE FOR HAYLE

Last week a communication was opened between the Cornish Copper Company's south and north quays, at Hayle, over a beautiful cast-iron draw-bridge. The bridge, which was manufactured at the company's foundry, is 10 feet wide and 65 feet long, and is sufficiently long for sustaining any weight that may be necessary to pass over it. Shipping will derive great advantage from the use of this bridge, as vessels will not in future be required to come above the flood-gates, either to discharge or take in their cargoes. The wharf on the north quay is the best sheltered and most convenient one in the harbour; the water is deeper there than at any former quay. On Thursday last 28 tons of ores belonging to Mines Royal Company, were carried over the bridge in eight waggons, on the front of the foremost of which one of the company's agents took his station displaying an appropriate flag. 7 September 1832

THE RISE OF HALSETOWN

At the Halsetown Fair on Tuesday se'nnight, and which was previously advertised in this paper, there was a large supply and sale of cattle and horses . . . This being the first establishment of the fair, under the auspices of the gentleman by whom the town was founded, the novelty of the occasion attracted thither an immense concourse of all ranks, and many of them from a great distance. Mrs. Hodge of the hotel, with her accustomed liberality and judicious management, provided an excellent ordinary [meal, at a fixed price and time] in her new room, with liquors of a superiority consistent with her own good fame, and at which upwards of fifty gentlemen and respectable farmers, with perfect convenience to themselves, dined together at one table (the room being of a capacity amply sufficient for the accomodation at dinner of more than double that number) the worthy founder presiding. In the evening there was a splendid display of fireworks in an adjoining field. 21 September 1832

[Halsetown had recently been built by James Halse, of nearby St. Ives, to house some of the labour force of his neighbouring mines. Occupancy of each house, moreover, gave the miners the franchise, and with the help of their votes Halse was returned to Parliament as the member for St. Ives.]

NEWLYN AND MOUSEHOLE

On the breaking out of the cholera at Newlyn, the inhabitants of Mousehole established a quarantine, prohibiting all communication with the infected place, and keeping watch to prevent persons coming from Newlyn passing through. The people of Newlyn were naturally displeased at this interdict, and resolved on retaliation as soon as the disease had ceased amongst them. This having so far taken place that the Mousehole people no longer objected to allow the passing of persons from Newlyn, the inhabitants of the latter place prohibited any of the Mousehole folk from entering their town. This prohibition was attempted to be put into force on Thursday last, when some persons from Mousehole were attacked in the streets of Newlyn and were compelled to fly, in consequence of being assailed by missiles of different kinds. 5 October 1832

[Newlyn was one of the places most seriously affected in Cornwall, the disease having been introduced by a fisherman of the village, who distributed some old clothes brought back from Ireland, where the disease was raging. So many died in Newlyn, that the parish churchyard at Paul became filed, and a meadow adjoining was given as an additional burial ground by James Halse, Lord of the Manor. It would appear that the precautions taken in Cornwall some twelve months earlier to rid towns and villages of those insanitary conditions in which cholera thrives had not been followed in Newlyn, which in *The West Briton* of 14 September was described as "a very narrow street between [the cottages] and the edge of the precipice. Down this precipice the filth from the houses, fish offal, &c. flows, but instead of being allowed to flow into the sea, which washes the cliff, it is intercepted in its descent and received into open pits, from which such an effluvium arises that it is a matter of surprise how the inhabitants can continue to live in the midst of it."]

TO SECURE THE COMFORT OF A HUSBAND

A clergyman, somewhat advanced in years, who having lately resigned a rich living, now resides near his old abode, is desirous a second time of entering the connubial state. Of ample fortune and amiable manners, he devotes his life to the pursuit of learning and the practice of piety. To a person possessed of such qualifications every offer cannot be acceptable. The lady must unite to the utmost natural refinement of mind, an education at once cultivated in literature, and in those arts which are necessary to secure the comfort of a husband, and to qualify for the superintendence of a small economically managed family. The lady must not be much above or below the middle age; nor must her fortune be under £100 per annum. Long retirement from the world has compelled the advertiser to have recourse to this somewhat unusual mode of obtaining the highest human felicity. Those ladies to whom this advertisement may reveal the author's name, are requested to address him (by post-paid letters) in proper person. Others are begged to direct their letters (post-paid) to X.Y.Z., Mrs. George's, Stationer, St. Columb. N.B. The advertiser's honor is pledged for the observance of the strictest secrecy, with respect to every communication. 2 November 1832

DIRECT FROM LABRADOR

Just arrived, and now landing, ex schooner *Messenger*, direct from Labrador, about 60 tons of very superior first quality dry cod fish, for sale, on reasonable terms. Apply to Jas. Bastian, merchant. Who has also for sale, about 10,000 Stourbridge fire brick, well worthy the attention of tin and lead smelters. Quay, Truro. 7 December 1832

PRIME BEEF FOR CHRISTMAS

The poor at St. Austell, will, for the third time, be regaled with prime beef, at the market-house, on the Christmas-eve, by J. Sawle G. Sawle, Esq. Two prime oxen, costing £46, have been purchased by Mr. Sawle for that purpose. Too much praise cannot be given to the worthy donor for this, his third donation to the poor of St. Austell. 14 December 1832

FILLING IN A MINE

Cornwall Quarter Sessions. James Phebe, James Trembath, James Toon, Richard Chellew, John Uren, and John Nance, the younger, were indicted for having feloniously filled the shaft of a mine belonging to L. C. Daubuz, Esq. with rubbish, in order to hinder the working of the said mine. From the evidence, it appeared that in 1803, Mr. Daubuz commenced working a tin-stream called Wheal Bob stream, in the parish of Ludgvan, and on the estate of the Marquis of Cleveland, who received the dues on the tin raised from it. Some time since, the Marquis granted a set of a mine to be called Wheal Darlington, and in which set Wheal Bob stream is included. The adventurers and Mr. Daubuz not being able to come to an agreement respecting the claims of the latter to the stream, on the 12th of November last the prisoners came on the stream-work, where three or four men were at work; they ordered them to desist and said they were sent by Captain Treweek, to fill up the shaft of the stream-work. This they commenced doing, and having filled the air-shaft, they proceeded to throw rubbish into that in which the men were, who got into a drift [level, or gallery] but who were endangered by the throwing in of the rubbish. The prisoners finding the men would not leave the shaft, desisted before the air was quite excluded. Several tons of rubbish were thrown in.

4 January 1833

MINE SHAFTS IN GWENNAP

Two miners, named George Saunders and Thomas Hichens, who worked at the United Mines, in Gwennap, were drinking at the Miner's Arms inn, near these mines, on [Saturday] evening; they were rather tipsy, but not what is termed drunk, and left the inn to go to St. Day, on their way home, about half-past seven o'clock. They were walking arm in arm when they left, but as they did not reach home an inquiry was made for them. After a search their bodies were found at the bottom of an open shaft, about 25 fathoms in depth, and which is about 11 fathoms from the road and quite level with the surface of the ground around it. As the night was very dark, there is no doubt that they missed their way and fell in. Saunders has left a widow and eight children; Hitchens, who was about 23 years of age, was also married but had no child. The dangerous state of old mine-shafts which abound in the parish of Gwennap demands the attention of those whose duty it is to see that such dangerous nuisances are rendered secure, especially in a densely populated neighbourhood.

18 January 1833

TWENTY-FOUR TRAMPERS

We learn that the magistrates of Penzance have found employment for some of the vagrants that infest our county; twenty-four of these trampers were committed last week to the town tread-mill for a month's hard labour. A similar mode of treatment in the other towns of the county would speedily rid us from these visitants.

18 January 1833

RINGING THE BELLS BACKWARDS

On Wednesday last, whilst Mr. Pendarves [see p. 153] and his lady stopped to change horses at Launceston, the ringers at that place, always on the look out, got an intimation of the circumstance; struck up, a merry peal, and in the mean time sent some of their party for the fee. They, however, met a reception they did not anticipate, for the Hon. Gentleman after telling them he was aware of the treatment the Reformers had got from them at the late election, and that he regarded the insults offered to them as offered to himself, sent them away empty. The gentry in question were by no means convinced of the justice of this mode of reasoning, and to show their dissatisfaction at it, and at the loss of their expected treat, they immediately commenced ringing the bells backwards.

1 February 1833

AFTER THE REFORM BILL

We learn that S. T. Spry, Esq. M.P. for Bodmin, has generously given £200 to be expended in the purchase of blankets and shoes, which are to be distributed to the poor within the boundaries of the new borough, and who shall each produce a ticket from an elector who voted for Mr. Spry.

8 February 1833

[In the boroughs which had not been disfranchised, the Great Reform Bill gave the right to vote to the occupant of any building of an annual value of £10 or more. The working class generally were still not enfranchised therefore, while the bribery of electors, this time the "ten pound householders" as they were called, still continued.]

SALTASH FLOATING BRIDGE

It will be seen by an advertisement in another part of our paper, that this bridge, which is worked by steam, has commenced plying across the Tamar, thus affording a safe and expeditious communication between Cornwall and Devonshire. The bridge is composed of a float, 50 feet in length and 30 in breadth; it is open at both ends; in the centre are two engines, each of six-horse power, and which are boxed over, so as to be concealed externally. These engines work two wheels, over which pass two chains, that are fastened at each side of the river, and which traverse through the engine-room. Carriages are run on the bridge without detaching the horses, and there is full accomodation for foot passengers—the passage is effected in five minutes. Commodious landing places have been formed on each side of the river. 8 February 1833

FOUNDERED OFF ZENNOR

On Saturday night, the schooner *Union*, from Truro for Wales, with copper ore, foundered off Zennor, about two leagues west of St. Ives, in consequence of having sprung a leak. The crew, four in number, got into a small boat, which they were forced to allow to drive before the wind and sea. After being for 17 hours exposed to the greatest perils, they made the shore at St. Agnes, and by the assistance of a number of persons assembled there, they were enabled to land safely. 15 February 1833

NANSWYDEN GARDENS AND NURSERY

John Coombs has for sale, 40,000 once-transplanted pineaster fir, from 6 to 9 inches high, at 18s. per thousand. 40,000 transplanted Scotch fir, from 5 to 9 inches high, at 15s. per thousand. 100,000 one-year's pine-asters, at 5s. per thousand. 12,000 oak, from 1½ to 2 feet high, at 30s. per thousand. Nanswyden. 15 February 1833

[The fine mansion of Nanswhyden near Newquay was built in 1740 by the wealthy Richard Hoblyn, who also had beautiful gardens and plantations laid out there. These latter were maintained after the house was gutted by fire in 1803.]

RIOTOUS FUNERALS

We are desired to state, that a paragraph which appeared in the *Falmouth Packet* of last week, headed "Marazion", &c. is extremely incorrect and defective; and the public are requested to suspend their judgement till the termination of the legal proceedings against the parties who are charged with having riotously and tumultuously assembled, &c. and aided and abetted in the unprecedented violation of decency and decorum, which subsequently took place in the church-yard of St. Hilary. It is true that the vicar of the parish has a decided objection to Sunday funerals, if they can possibly be avoided, in consequence of the increased drunkenness and disorder, to which the collecting of such large bodies of persons in such a densely peopled neighbourhood, is calculated to give rise. Under circumstances of urgent expediency, he has occasionally waved these objections, but in the case under consideration, the interment of the body of John Carter, *who died on the previous Monday*, no such necessity was or could have been pleaded; on the contrary, his nearest connexions had, on the preceding afternoon, signified, through the sexton, their consent that the burial should be solemnized on the following Monday at four o'clock. Of their subsequent and arbitrary determination to inter the body on the Sunday afternoon, no intimation reached the vicar before eleven o'clock the same day. 8 March 1833

SHOP SIGNS OF COPPER

A rather novel species of depradation was last week committed at this place [Truro], a large globe copper-gilt tea-kettle, used as a sign over the door of Mr. John Cock, brazier, Boscawen-street, and an oval tea-kettle, of a like description, used for a similar purpose by Mr. John Williams, brazier, St. Nicholas-street, were carried off during the night. A reward of £5 has been offered for the discovery of the offenders. Persons using such articles as signs, should have them made of a material less valuable than copper. The above mentioned kettles have been found hanging from a lamp, this morning. 8 March 1833

WANDERED BEYOND HIS KNOWLEDGE

Whereas, James Symons, of the parish of Crowan, being of weak intellects, is supposed to have missed his road, in following his father to work, at a mine, on Monday the 25th of last month, and to have wandered beyond his knowledge. Since which time he has not been heard of but once, when he was found at Mawgan, and was put back to Michell, by a parish officer, who, it is believed, supposed he would find his way home; but his friends have not since that time—about the 4th instant—heard any intelligence of him. The said James Symons, is about 26 years of age; 5 feet 4 inches in height; slight made; dark hair and reddish whiskers; and had on a blue-striped shirt; blue and white neckkerchief; blue jacket, fustian waistcoat and trousers; blue and white socks; high shoes, and an old hat. He is of reserved habits; talks to himself, and is capable of telling his name and the place of his residence. Whoever may meet the person above described, are requested to restore him to his afflicted parents, for which a handsome reward will be given. 22 March 1833

A RUNAWAY SON

If the young man who left his parents, at St. Wenn, on the night of Thursday the 21st inst., will return home, he will be kindly received, and relieve the feelings of his relatives, who are almost distracted at his absence. The above young man is about 23 years of age, 5 feet 4 inches in height, florid complexion, and brown hair, with whiskers of the same colour extending under the chin. He was dressed when he left home in a fustian short coat, cut back over the thighs, fustian waistcoat and corduroy trowsers, and wore a black striped neckherchief round his neck. Whoever will give such information as will enable his parents to have communication with him, shall receive the above reward [£5]. 29 March 1833

PRISON INTO HOSPITAL

The Vice Warden [of the Stannaries] said he wished to notice some remarks that had appeared in some of the county papers, on the case of three persons who had been committed to the Stannary prison at Lostwithiel, for contempt of that court . . . It had been represented to the Duchy Board, that these persons had been confined in a wretched place where no sort of accomodation existed. This, however, was not the fact, for the prison had been fitted up as a cholera hospital.

19 April 1833

A GATED ROAD TO PADSTOW

Having to travel from Newquay to Padstow—a distance of eleven miles—I had *sixteen* gates to open, and nearly forfeited my life in endeavouring to open the first. While I had hold of the latch, an ass which was on the road before me, set up such a braying that my horse started, and ere I could loose my hold on the gate, I was thrown; and had my arm seriously injured; so much so, that I fear I shall have cause to recollect the accident through life. In my subsequent progress, I had to dismount fifteen times to open gates, as from the injury received I was unable to do so when on horseback. On the road I overtook a farmer's wife, the mother of nine children, riding to market with a basket of butter and eggs; as she was unable to open the gates, I had to assist her; she complained of being obliged to travel to market at the risk of her life, on such miserable roads. I next observed a traveller in a gig, which was drawn by a spirited horse; he ran very serious risks in opening the gates, whilst all along the road, fishmongers' diseased horses, asses and cattle, were turned loose to depasture, and were kept from straying by the aforesaid gates.

3 May 1833

DRUNK, AND DROWNED

On Friday as a young man named Butters was floating on a balk of timber on the Liskeard canal, being rather intoxicated, he fell into the water and was drowned. 7 June 1833

WAGES SEVEN POUNDS

Wanted as laundress, a strong active woman, not less than 5 feet 6 inches high. Wages seven pounds a year, with an annual increase, if merited. Personal applications to be made at the Lunatic Asylum, Bodmin.

21 June 1833

CHARLESTOWN SEA WATER BATHS

Charlestown, St. Austell. The warm and cold sea water baths, will be opened on Monday next the first of July. The benefits derived by invalids, in general, from the use of warm sea water baths, are well-known at the present day; but, to those suffering under cutaneous, pulmonary, and rheumatic complaints, it is impossible to eulogize their efficacy too highly.

28 June 1833

FOUR HATS FROM AN OTTER

A large otter was killed at Perranzabuloe, on the night of Tuesday the 18th instant; on the Thursday following, the fur was used by Mr. Oke, hatter, of Truro, in making four hats, which hats, on Sunday last, were worn by four persons residing in four different parishes. 28 June 1833

THEFT OF MOLTEN TIN

Cornwall Quarter Sessions. Samuel Jennings (16), Joseph Symons (16), and John Symons (18), were indicted for stealing a quantity of smelted tin, the property of Henry Harvey and others, from Wheal Vor Consolidated Mines, in the parish of Breage. It appeared from the evidence that the prisoners—Jennings and Joseph Symons—John Symons being blind—got into the smelting-house on the above mines while the workmen were absent, and conveyed the tin from the furnace, while in a liquid state, to some moulds they had prepared near the door; and that they managed to escape with their booty before the men returned. 5 July 1833

BODMIN MEAT MARKET

An Act of Parliament was obtained some time since for the erection of a new market-house [at Bodmin]. Whether all the money designed for accomplishing this work was laid out in procuring this Act is best known to the parties concerned, but one thing is certain—that the spot of ground on which it was intended to erect it, was sold a short time since, although it had been purchased for that express purpose. It is very probable that by far the greater part of the inhabitants of this county are not aware, that the market-house in Bodmin is the Assize-hall; here the corn market is regularly held, while all the other commodities are vended in the open air; even the butchers are obliged to stand in the open street, and the shambles, to the no small annoyance and disadvantage of those tradesmen who do not belong to the select few, are placed immediately before the windows. During the summer season there is the advantage of having the meat partly dressed before it is bought, and, in wet weather, the poor butcher has the comfort of a good soaking. A greater nuisance than Bodmin meat market never was indicted. 12 July 1833

ONE HUNDRED PIECES

On Wednesday evening a lad about 15 years of age, called Jas. Oliver, who worked at the Consolidated Mines, in Gwennap, fell from the ladder on which he was ascending to the surface, to a depth of 200 fathoms [1200 feet], and was literally dashed to atoms. The pieces of his body when collected amounted to at least one hundred. 12 July 1833

A CROWD AT THE COUNTY 'DROP'

In consequence of a report that an order for the execution of Pascoe and Jenkin—the young men convicted of a rape at the late Bodmin Assizes—on Wednesday last, great numbers of people repaired to Bodmin from all parts of the surrounding country. So early as eight o'clock in the morning a crowd was collected in the vicinity of the gaol, which continued rapidly to increase until noon, when it became fully known that no order for the execution of the unfortunate men had been received, and the multi-

tude, the majority of which was composed of females, began to disperse.
23 August 1833

KILLED BY A WATER WHEEL

An inquest was held on Tuesday last, on the body of Wm. James, a boy of about 10 years of age, son of a miner who lives at Wheal Raven Comb, in the parish of Redruth, and who came by his death in the following manner. The parents of the deceased live in the neighbourhood of West Wheal Tolgus mine, in the parish of Illogan; a large water wheel belonging to that mine had not been used for some days, but in order to prevent its being injured by the sun, a small stream of water was allowed to run over it, so as to cause it to revolve slowly, and at intervals. The deceased with some other children were at play near the place on last Sunday evening; during a cessation of its motion, he went to look into the pit in which the lower part of the wheel worked; it commenced a revolution while he was so engaged, and a crank attached to the centre struck him severely on the back . . .
23 August 1833

MIDNIGHT HEARSES AND BONFIRES

Sir . . . As there is a probability that the blue Asiatic cholera may again spread over our land, I would impress upon all my countrymen the necessity of getting rid of their midnight hearses, separate burials, consuming bonfires, and all these adventitious horrors which they threw around the dead in 1832—all of them useless, unless they wish to make more melancholy the atmosphere over which the gloom of pestilence is already thrown—and in place thereof, of endeavouring to dissipate the sorrow of the survivors, and by rational amusements, to throw a sunshine around us. Many a victim has been added to the cholera pile, because their friends have fled in terror from their sides, and they have felt themselves deserted in the hour of extreme trial . . . I remain, sir, your ever respectful servant, Robert Hunt.
23 August 1833

[Cholera had reappeared in Southwark and was soon to manifest itself in Falmouth. During the previous epidemic, many cases had in fact been suffering not from cholera but from a relatively minor complaint. This was British or summer cholera, an illness caused by unclean food or tainted water, whereas Asiatic cholera, which turned the body blue, passed directly from person to person, or from anything which had been in contact with the diseased. The two had certain symptoms in common—cramps, vomiting and diarrhoea—and similarly occurred principally among the dirty poor. The latter were usually incapable of distinguishing the terrible disease, in its early stages, from the summer malady (see p. 223) and, as a result, many who might have recovered were, from fear and ignorance, left to die.]

STILL WANDERING

The friends of James Symons, at Praze, in the parish of Crowan, whose absence from home was stated in an advertisement in this paper, on the 22nd of March last, have received information that the poor lunatic was seen in the neighbourhood of Liskeard, about a month since. As he is not capable of inquiring his way, it is earnestly requested, by his distressed father, that he may be detained by any person who may meet with him, and information be sent, by post, to Mr. John Symons, Praze, Crowan, who will immediately proceed to take him home, and who will pay all reasonable expenses incurred.

6 September 1833

THE DARK STREETS OF LAUNCESTON

A correspondent informs us that the streets of Launceston are so much out of repair and the funds of the corporation, on whom the duty of repairing them devolves, are so low, that the surgeons of the place begin to keep a sharp look out for broken bones. Should the intention of lighting the town with gas be carried into effect, it will tend to allay the apprehensions of the friends of those who may have to go out of doors after night fall, during the winter.

20 September 1833

IN THE ECCLESIASTICAL COURT

I, the undersigned, Joseph Branwell Sutherland, the younger, of the town of Penzance, butcher, having on Monday last, most unjustifiably and improperly uttered reports defamatory to the character of Mr. James Permewan, of the parish of St. Buryan, farmer, and proceedings being about to be instituted against me in the Ecclesiastical Court for the slander, do hereby declare that the same reports were utterly unfounded and untrue, and that I feel great regret for having acted so improperly. I thank Mr. Permewan for his kindly consenting to forego those proceedings, on my making this public apology, and I promise never to be guilty of the like conduct again. Witness my hand this 12th day of September, 1833. Joseph Branwell Sutherland, jun. Witness, John Ceely.

27 September 1833

'BOROUGH JUGGLING'

On Tuesday last, the Corporation Commissioners sat at Lostwithiel, and entered into an inquiry relative to the corporation of that town. During the last 13 years the regular expenditure of the corporation was about £447 a year, and the income, about £180; but no debt had been incurred, as the noble Recorder and late patron always made up the deficiency. There were also extra charges in that time, amounting to about

£2000, which were also paid by his Lordship. Among the charges were the following: annual dinner for 24 corporators, £90.0.0; two new cloaks for the town sergeants, £25.7.9; newspapers for the corporators, £25.3.11. There is a property belonging to the town which on the death of an old person will be worth some hundreds of pounds annually; had it not been for this investigation, it might have been appropriated to the service of the corporate body at the annual dinner; happily the enquiry has thrown *light* on the subject. 27 September 1833

[A Royal Commission had recently been set up to make public enquiry into the existing state of corporations in England and Wales and investigations in Cornwall into the affairs of the boroughs were currently being made. Without exception at Looe, Lostwithiel, Bodmin, Launceston, Liskeard, Camelford, Tintagel-Bossiney and elsewhere, enquiries revealed widespread mismanagement and misappropriation of corporation funds, unconstitutional influences at work, and irregularities in the "election" of corporators. At St. Ives, for instance, seven of the twelve members of the corporation were related or connected by marriage; at Truro, the corporators elected themselves, and were only half the number required by the town charter. Penzance, Helston and Penryn emerged relatively unscathed from the inquisition.]

PILFERING AT HOLMBUSH

Nathan Sowden, a miner of St. Austell, and his wife, were on Tuesday last committed to the county gaol, on the charge of having stolen several articles of clothing, which were left at night to bleach on the garden hedges of some persons residing at Holmbush, near Charlestown.

4 October 1833

TO SUPPLEMENT THE SCAVENGERS

Sir, In answer to your enquiry—"What is the Truro Board of Health about?"—I am desired to inform you, for the satisfaction of the inhabitants, that its agents have been unceasingly engaged for the last twelve months, in cleaning such parts of the town as cannot be entered by the scavengers employed by the Commissioners of Paving and Lighting; that they have, in that period, collected more than £150 worth of manure, and thus they have so effectually prevented any considerable accumulations of it in the courts and backlets, that the farmer and gardeners who used formerly to buy it in small parcels, are now obliged to purchase of the Board. Two sluices have been erected, which have completely succeeded in cleaning out the channel of the Kenwyn River and the mouths of the numerous drains opening into it. Assistance has been afforded from the funds of the Board for building new, and repairing old, sewers; and necessaries have been built in some of the densely populated courts which were before destitute of them. Brushes for whitewashing, and hand-barrows for carrying manure to the carts are lent to any poor persons who may apply to the surveyor, George Hall, for them. In conclusion, I think I may refer with some satisfaction to the very clean state of our streets and courts, and ask what has the Truro Board of Health left undone? Your's respectfully, E. J. Spry, Secretary to the Truro Board of Health.

11 October 1833

TWO BOGUS FRENCHMEN

In the course of the last week two men calling themselves Frenchmen, and who spoke the English language imperfectly, came to a village west of Penzance, and called on a person there, stating that they had a quantity of teas at the quay at Penzance, which they wanted cash to get through the customs; they requested the gentleman to lend them £7, for which they would leave as security a gold watch, and a bundle of shawls, and promised that on the following morning he should have what quantity of tea he liked. The men produced some samples of teas, at less prices than the gentleman could procure them, and in hope of making a good profit by the concern, he lent them the money. On the following morning he posted into Penzance to meet his friends, but they were not to be found; he thought still that he had a prize in hand, and repaired with it to a goldsmith there, by whom he was informed the watch was brass-lackered, and the shawls proved to be of as little value; the whole not being worth more than 30s. One of the men is five feet five inches high, with large dark whiskers, and wears a blue frock coat; the other is about five feet nine inches in height, is dressed in black, and winks very much when talking.

18 October 1833

THE FIDDLER'S STAYS

Last week, an old blind woman named Ann Beales died of the cholera at Falmouth. When she was taken ill she manifested great anxiety about her stays, and in the progress of her illness, when it became highly probable she could not recover, she stated that in the stays she had concealed several Bank of England notes, and that she had hidden money in different parts of the room which she described. At her death, her relatives examined the stays, &c. when the statement of the old woman was found to be correct—rumour states that several hundred pounds were found, but the exact amount is not known. The deceased got her living by playing the fiddle at public-houses for the amusement of sailors, &c. and it is understood the money she has left was acquired in this way during the late war.

25 October 1833

WRECKED IN A CAVE

The Swedish sloop *Neptunus*, of Wisby, Malmen, master, laden with salt, during a strong gale at S.E. on Saturday last, came on shore near Porthleven, and ran up into a cavern, carrying away her top-mast against the roof, and her bowsprit against a projecting rock; her stern being at least a hundred feet within the entrance, which is not more than twenty-five to thirty feet wide. 1 November 1833

DESERTERS FROM THE 73RD

Two men were taken up at Bodmin by a recruiting sergeant at present stationed there, on a charge of being deserters from the 73rd regiment. On examination it was found that each of the men had recently lost a finger, the wounds being quite fresh; they say they were discharged about a fortnight since, in consequence of being thus mutilated, but the fingers have evidently been amputated since that time. It is believed they disabled themselves, after they had deserted, in order to avoid again serving.
29 November 1833

FUGITIVES FROM THE LAW

Escaped from the gaol at Bodmin, this morning, the 5th of December, 1833, four prisoners, viz.—John Walters, aged 41, 5 feet 6½ inches high, grey eyes, brown hair, sallow complexion, marked with ink on the left wrist and back of the left hand with a W and a heart; he is a native of Truro, and escaped in the county shirt only. Edward May, aged 32, 5 feet 9½ inches high, grey eyes, sandy hair, fresh complexion, bald on the top of the head, and sandy whiskers; he is a native of Plymouth and escaped in a county shirt and a blue flannel shirt only. Samuel Langley, aged 27, 5 feet 2½ inches high, grey eyes, brown hair, pale complexion, with a large mole between the shoulders; he is a native of Winkfield, in Berkshire, and escaped in the county shirt only. Thomas Jeffers, aged 27, 5 feet 7 inches high, grey eyes, dark hair, dark complexion, marked with ink on the left arm with a ship, an anchor and a sloop, and on the right arm with a sloop; mark of a wound on the right side of the face; he is a native of Bristol, and escaped in the county shirt only. A reward of five pounds will be paid on the apprehension of either of the above men, on being safely lodged in any of his Majesty's gaols. 6 December 1833

[Clad only in their nightshirts—day clothes were taken from prisoners each evening—and an old waistcoat each had acquired, Langley and Jeffers were recaptured in a straw-shed near Liskeard a week later. They had posed as escaped smugglers to beg for food, and were suffering badly from exposure.]

A LIKELY STORY

Cornwall Epiphany Sessions. Joseph Martin, 17, committed by William Warren, Esq. Mayor of Truro, December 10, for stealing a silver watch belonging to Mr. Lewis Truscott, of St. Nicholas'-street, Truro . . . The prisoner being asked by the chairman, if he wished to ask the witness [who had claimed seeing Truscott remove the watch] any questions, asked him, if he did not, at the time, observe a cow in the street, in pursuit of a dog. Witness, I did not. Prisoner, why the cow pushed his horns through the glass and lifted the watch on his horn, through the glass, into the gutter in the street, and I picked it up, and cut away . . . The prisoner said, in his defence, that he thought he ought not to be punished for what the cow did. The Court. What did the cow do? Prisoner, Why stole the watch from the window, and threw it in the gutter. Guilty. The prisoner is an old offender.

3 January 1834

COPPER WEALTH FROM TRESAVEAN

Tresavean mine continues to be as rich as at any previous time. At a meeting of the adventurers on Tuesday last, the 28th instant, a division of 100 guineas on each one-96th share was declared; this dividend was made notwithstanding the temporary depression of the standard, owing to the great quantity of ore detained at our ports by the tempestuous weather which has so long prevailed, and which has so greatly embarrassed the general trade of the country.

31 January 1834

A TREMENDOUS EXPLOSION

About twelve o'clock on the night of Saturday last, the boiler of the south-engine, at Great St. George mine, in the parish of St. Agnes [close to Perranporth] burst with a tremendous explosion, carrying away the roof; throwing down the walls of the engine-house, and scattering the materials about in every direction. Some idea may be formed of the force with which the condensed steam acted, by the fact, that parts of the boiler weighing upwards of a ton were thrown nearly a quarter of a mile from the spot; lighter materials were driven to a greater distance. The engine man, named James Phillips, who was on duty at the time, was killed, being found buried beneath a part of the wall. Happily from the time at which the accident happened, no other life was lost . . . Phillips was last seen about ten o'clock at night, when he proceeded from a neighbouring public-house to the mine; it is believed he was not sober . . .

28 February 1824

A GLUTTON

On Saturday last a young man of the parish of Cubert, named Henry

Scobell, undertook for a trifling wager, to swallow *thirty three eggs* in five minutes. To the surprise of the persons present he accomplished the feat without evidencing any inconvenience; he immediately offered to swallow *fifty more*, if they were provided for him, but no person was found to furnish the additional repast. 18 April 1834

DISTRESS ON THE OFF-ISLANDS

It is much to be regretted that the kelp manufactured at Scilly has fallen into such disrepute among the merchants, that no market can be obtained for it at any rate. The consequence is, that much distress exists amongst many of the poor on the off-islands, who have neither bread to eat, nor seed to put in their patches of land. 18 April 1834

TRANSFERRED TO THE CONVICT HULKS

On Monday the following prisoners were transmitted from Bodmin prison to the convict hulks at Portsmouth, pursuant to their sentences at the late Assizes and Quarter Sessions. John Calloway, for highway robbery; Henry Budge and John Rawling, for housebreaking, and James Uren, for burglary, to be transported for life. Jas. Edmunds and John Foster, for stealing from the person; William Gregory, for stealing wheat, and Charles Blight for cruelly wounding a sheep, to be transported for 14 years, Samuel Christophers, for burglary, and Hannibal Rowe, for stealing money, to be transported for 7 years. 16 May 1834

DEODAND, ONE SHILLING

Inquest held before Jos. Hosken James, Esq. on the body of Richard Thomas, a carrier, in the employ of Mr. John Hocking, of Kea, near Truro, who came by his death under the following circumstances. In the middle of the night of Friday last the deceased was sent with a waggon and four horses to carry a quantity of arsenic from Wheal Vor, tin mine, in Breage, to Perranarworthal. About two o'clock on Saturday afternoon he arrived at Tresavean mine, in Gwennap, on his return home after having completed what he was sent about, when having fallen asleep as he sat on the shafts of the waggon, he fell off, and the two near wheals passed over his body, by which he was so severely injured that he died on Monday morning. The deceased has left a widow and five children. Verdict, accidental death, deodand [forfeit to the Crown for alms, &c., on that which caused the death] on the waggon and horses, *one shilling*.

16 May 1834

TRURO CARPET MANUFACTORY

J. C. Williams and Co. has the pleasure to inform the nobility and gentry of Cornwall, that their new and splendid patterns of Brussels and velvet pile carpets, are ready for inspection, the quality of which needs no comment. Hearth rugs made to match. P.S. This establishment presents to their friends and patrons, the advantage of their carpets ordered, being made in breadth to suit each room, therebeing no waste in cutting to pattern. N.B. J. C. W. and Co. being importers of Turkey carpets, beg to submit their list of nearly 300 carpets, of all sizes, and at very *moderate* prices.

30 May 1834

DOING PENANCE AT REDRUTH

Yesterday, being Trinity Sunday, a Mrs. Brown "of our town" did *penance* in the church at *this place*, for calling Mrs. Michell a *naughty woman.* The church was beset by a concourse of persons long before the hour of the service, and at least 5,000 individuals witnessed this highly ridiculous piece of mummery; of these, as a matter of course, four-fifths were females. Mrs. Brown, in a *white* dress, came to the church in a post-chaise about midday, entering it in the midst of the sermon. The scene directly became completely bear-garden. Mrs. Michell occupied the clergyman's desk, where she looked more like the *penitent* than the injured party. Mrs. Brown was put into the desk usually occupied by the clerk, and was a regular good "flare-up", decorated with a smart bonnet, flowers and ribbons, green parasol, and a very long black veil, which being carefully tossed on one side, enabled her to shew a good set of teeth and distribute around her smiles to her admiring friends who, it is said, had promised to burn poor Mrs. M. in effigy. The purpose, however, was prevented by the interference of Mr. Stephen Davey, a deputy-lieutenant of the county, who called the parish constables to his assistance, and caused the effigy which had been prepared to be destroyed. No theatrical queen could have gone through the part assigned her with more effect than Mrs. Brown did. As soon as the sermon was completed, the clergyman left the pulpit, and the clerk gave out the 120th psalm, new version . . . adopted as expressing the feelings of the injured party. Then the following form was read by the clergyman and repeated by the *penitent*: "I, Jane Brown, do hereby acknowledge and confess that I did utter and speak several reproachful, scandalous and defamatory words of you Elizabeth Michell, and that I have defamed and abused you, for which I am exceedingly sorry, and ask your pardon, and promise not to be guilty of the like offence in future." When this was done, Mrs. Brown thanked the auditory for the honor of their attendance, and then said, in an undertone: "I'll go through the same form next Sunday, for a pint of toddy, if you Mother Michell will stand tip." . . . It is understood that the law expenses are rather serious . . . Mrs. Brown will have to pay them—if she can—by sentence of the Ecclesiastical Court.

6 June 1834

ST. ANTHONY LIGHTHOUSE

On Wednesday last, the ceremony of laying the first stone of the new light-house, about to be erected at the entrance to Falmouth harbour, took place. At eight o'clock in the morning, the *Astrea* frigate and the different packets in the harbour and the roads exhibited a splendid display of colours of all nations . . . About ten o'clock the *Active* cutter led the van, and was followed by a gallant array of yachts, boats, &c. conveying the members of the Falmouth Masonic Lodge; the corporate body of the town; the committee for erecting the lighthouse, and numbers of the fair sex, who adorned and enlivened the scene . . . A marquee was erected for the accommodation of the Masonic brethren, &c. in which they assembled, and whence they proceeded in procession to the spot fixed on, where the stone was prepared . . . Several coins inclosed in a bottle were then placed in a cavity of the stone prepared to receive them, which being secured by a piece of copper, the stone was placed in the spot proposed to receive it, amidst the firing of guns from the *Active* cutter, and the enlivening tones of the band which attended, and played "Rule Brittannia". The Brethren then retired in order to the tent, where they partook of a pic-nic repast, which they enjoyed, notwithstanding the beating of the rain and the increasing force of the wind; the band playing at intervals, national airs. After about two hours thus spent, the party embarked in the *Active* cutter and returned safely to Falmouth; but some of the parties were not so fortunate, for whilst Capt. Miller, of the *Active*, kindly accomodated all he could on board his vessel, several were compelled to remain at St. Mawes during the night. There were not less than two thousand persons present on the occasion. 6 June 1834

A NEW WOOL MARKET

Notice is hereby given, that a wool market will be held on Wednesday the 30th instant, at Pearce's Hotel, Truro, where upwards of 60,000 pounds weight of wool will be offered for sale, in the yolk. [i.e. unwashed].

25 July 1834

A CORRECTION

In the advertisement inserted in our third page last week, of a light grey colt, supposed to be stolen from a field near Sithney-Trough, it was stated that the further foot behind is "turned out", —it should have been, is turned *in*. 10 October 1834

DEATH AT BIZZOE

An inquest was held before Hosken James, Esq. coroner, on Monday last, on the body of Joseph Wolf, a boy eleven years of age; who on the preceding Saturday night, when proceeding to his home, at Bizzoe [Bissoe lead] smelting works, with a companion of his own age, missed the direct way to the door of his house, the night being very dark, and walked into a pit filled with water into which the smelters throw the hot metal, and which lies by the path. The water at the time was nearly at boiling heat, and the deceased was so dreadfully scalded that he died the next morning. Verdict, accidental death.

10 October 1834

DIED, A SAVER OF LIVES

Died at Tuckingmill, near Camborne, on Thurday the 2d. instant, after a protracted illness from paralysis, Mr. William Bickford, aged 60 years, formerly of Truro, and patentee of the celebrated safety-fuse, for preventing accidents in the blasting of rocks in mines, &c.

10 October 1834

DRESSED IN RAT SKINS

An ingenious individual of Liskeard, named Trethake, has for some time past been exhibiting himself to families in that town and neighbourhood, in a dress composed from top to toe of rat's skins, which he has been collecting for 3½ years. The dress was made entirely by himself, and consists of hat, neck-kerchief, coat, waistcoat, trousers, tippet, gaiters and shoes . . . The number of rats whose skins he has thus appropriated is 670, and when he is full dressed, he appears for all the world like one of the Esquimaux described in the account of Capt. Lyon's voyage; it should be mentioned that the tippet or boa (but not round like that worn by ladies) is composed of the pieces of skin immediately around the tails, and is a very curious part of the dress, containing about 600 tails and those none of the shortest.

31 October 1834

EVADING THE TURNPIKE TOLLS

At a petty sessions held yesterday at the town-hall, before Edward Collins, J. E. Vivian, and Edmund Turner, Esqrs. Their worships gave their decision on a complaint made at the last petty sessions, by the lessee of the Chapel-hill turnpike-gate, near this town [Truro], against a small farmer, who having purchased a quantity of town dung, proceded to convey it away in a cart, and after bringing the load up the steep hill leading to the turnpike-gate, deposited it at a short distance, returning immediately for another load which he deposited with the former one; in this way he took several loads through the gate, on the same day, and for one toll; removing them to his ground, a distance of about four miles, at his leisure. This the lessee of the toll considered an evasion, and he summoned the farmer to answer a complaint preferred against him before the magistrates. The magistrates took time to consider the case, and this day announced their decision to be, that in the present case, a single toll was sufficient, dismissing the complaint. 7 November 1834

A NEGLIGENT MOTHER

On Friday last, a child between two and three years of age, belonging to a shoemaker named Peters, who resides in this town [Truro], caught its clothes on fire, during the absence of its mother; one of its little brothers endeavoured by blowing to extinguish the fire, and one of the elder children perceiving that it increased the flames, tore the clothes off the little sufferer, who expired on Monday morning. The same infant about six months since, drank a cup of poison its mother had prepared for cleaning bonnets, but was soon restored by the application of proper antidotes. 7 November 1834

THE LAST OF AN OLD BUFF

Some weeks since, the body of a man was found in a field in the parish of Lanivet, having on a soldier's jacket and trowsers; but being in an advanced state of decomposition, the features could not be discerned; in his hat, which was at a distance from him, was found a discharge from the 3rd regiment of foot, or Old Buffs, in India, in December last; from this paper it appeared that his name was Pascoe, and it has been ascertained that he was a native of this town; and that after serving 27 years in the army, he was put on shore in this country with 26 shillings to enable him to reach home; on his way to this place, he perished, as before stated.
21 November 1834

ST. MARY'S, SCILLY

H.M. steamer *African*, from Lisbon for Falmouth, put in here yesterday for twenty tons of coals, being nearly destitute of fuel. The *Golden Grove*, Capt. Brown, with female convicts, sailed from here yesterday, for Australia, a surgeon having joined her that morning. 28 November 1834

[The plight of the steam packet *African* was not unusual. At least two other steam packets, also working out of Falmouth but to Mediterranean ports, had run completely out of fuel several years earlier, one off Scilly and the other near Brest. To reach these positions of relative safety spars, bulkheads, cabin partitions, and every spare piece of cable and rope had been burned.]

A MENDICANT AND HIS GUIDE

William Stockwell, a lad about 13 years of age, employed in leading about a blind beggar-man, has been committed to the county gaol, by John Borlase, Esq. for having on the 19th instant, stolen a silver watch from the house of William Kitto, in the parish of Breage, where the mendicant went to solicit alms, and the boy, seeing the watch hanging at the dresser, took an opportunity of carrying it off. 28 November 1834

'DAFFY DILLY' AND THE PILCHARDS

A man named Stephens of St. Columb, generally known by the designation of "Daffy Dilly", whilst last week at Newquay, undertook to eat for a wager fifty two fried pilchards, which feat he accomplished in the space of an hour, to the astonishment of a large assemblage of persons. He afterwards offered to wage that he would in the same space of time eat a moderate size leg of mutton, which proposal no one however seemed inclined to accept. 5 December 1834

BURGLARY AT TREVENSON

The late burglary at Trevenson, for which a reward of fifty pounds has been offered to any one who will discover and convict the offenders. The following is a description of Richard Pope, son of Richard Pope, of Illogan, the notorious young rogue who tendered one of the gold [mourning] rings stolen from Trevenson office to Mr. Rolling, of St. Austell, for sale, and who no doubt, in connexion with others, perpetrated the burglary in question. Pope is about 17 years of age, small of stature, regular features, black eyes, hair rather dark, marked a little with the small pox, complexion rather pale, hangs down his head, so as seldom to look any one in the face, has a trick of shrugging his shoulders, twisting his nose and mouth, and throwing his head rather sharply about, wears his hat close down over his brow which he frequently knits, thereby lifting his hat a little, and walks as if in a deep study, or as if looking for anything on the road. When last seen, he had on a baragan jacket, dark waistcoat, and duck trowsers; but is supposed to have had a new suit since then. He has friends residing at Helston, Mawgan, Crowan, St. Ervan, St. Columb, Padstow, Lanehead, and Newton Abbot, in Devonshire, some of which places he has been known to haunt. 26 December 1834

INDULGENCE IN ARDENT SPIRITS

Died suddenly, at St. Ives, on Wednesday evening, Nancy Humphries, aged 54 . . . she was noted for many years, as supplying the parishes surrounding that place with fish, and has been known to travel more than 20 miles in a day, carrying upwards of one cwt. of fish on her head, her passion for ardent spirits was extreme, and its indulgence is supposed hastened her death. 26 December 1834

INDEX